We Pursue Our Magic

We Pursue Our Magic
A Spiritual History of Black Feminism

Marina Magloire

The University of North Carolina Press CHAPEL HILL

This book was published with the assistance of the Authors Fund of the University of North Carolina Press.

© 2023 Marina Magloire
All rights reserved
Set in Merope Basic by Westchester Publishing Services
Manufactured in the United States of America

Library of Congress Cataloging-in-Publication Data
Names: Magloire, Marina, author.
Title: We pursue our magic : a spiritual history of Black feminism / Marina Magloire.
Description: Chapel Hill : The University of North Carolina Press, 2023. | Includes bibliographical references and index.
Identifiers: LCCN 2023008285 | ISBN 9781469674889 (cloth ; alk. paper) | ISBN 9781469674896 (paperback ; alk. paper) | ISBN 9781469674902 (ebook)
Subjects: LCSH: African American feminists—United States—History—20th century. | Feminist spirituality—United States—History—20th century. | African American women artists—History and criticism. | African American women authors—History and criticism.
Classification: LCC HQ1420 .M34 2023 | DDC 305.42089/96073—dc23/eng/20230403
LC record available at https://lccn.loc.gov/2023008285

Cover illustration by Nadia Wolff.

Contents

Acknowledgments vii

Introduction 1

CHAPTER ONE
An Ethics of Discomfort 14
Katherine Dunham's Vodou Belonging

CHAPTER TWO
Girls' Talk 40
Revolutionary Destinies in Hansberry and Simone

CHAPTER THREE
Uneasy Blackness 69
Warrior Goddesses in the Age of Black Power

CHAPTER FOUR
Weird Sisters 100
Spiritual Bridges to the Third World

CHAPTER FIVE
Looking for Marie 126
Hoodoo Histories and the Making of a Black Feminist Genealogy

Conclusion 154
Notes on a Community Deferred

Notes 161
Bibliography 185
Index 197

Acknowledgments

I am a notoriously solitary writer. Everyone who knows me has seen me dodge writing groups, decline help, and evade workshops—all to sit alone in the dark, swilling grit and expecting a pearl. Despite my best efforts, many people have slipped into my solitude, and changed the shape of my work with their voices, ideas, and curiosity. This pearl is yours.

The seeds of this project were planted in Durham, where Priscilla Wald and Aarthi Vadde were incredibly kind and patient dissertation cochairs. Gregson Davis was a bastion of calm and wisdom in tumultuous years, a constant reminder of the pleasure to be found in intellectual pursuit. Nathaniel Mackey gifted me with a litany for survival, formative texts on the Harlem Renaissance and Vodou theology that are the bedrock of my scholarship even now. I leaned especially on the guidance of Laurent Dubois, whose friendship, collegiality, and thirst for knowledge continue to sustain me. I thank Fred Moten for seeping into my brain a bit by osmosis through his operatic monologues in class. Laura Wagner and Claire Payton were late-breaking but much-appreciated friends at the end of my time in Durham, pushing me Sankofa-esque into a future informed by my Haitian ancestry. And of course my grad school friendships continue to be the source of growth and joy in my scholarship and in my personal life: Brenna Casey, Kita Douglas, Jessica Hines, and Carolyn Laubender. Over the years, I have been very lucky to have so many conversations with these four across a range of fields—our ability to share across differences is, to me, the platonic ideal of intellectual life.

In Boston, this project was molded by conversations with Paul Edwards, Jonathan Square, Ernie Mitchell, Todne Thomas, Durba Mitra, and Marena Lin. My students at this time—especially Mace Johnson, Sally Chen, Liat Rubin, and Isa Flores-Jones—were valued interlocutors whose perspectives shaped my own views and scholarship. I would also like to thank Lauren Kaminsky and the good people of the program in History and Literature at Harvard for facilitating such a unique and rigorous intellectual environment between students and lecturers.

I was blessed to receive ample institutional support for this project, beginning with a generous dissertation completion fellowship from the American Council of Learned Societies. The University of Miami's Center for the

Humanities also provided a lively intellectual community and two much-needed course releases at a crucial stage near the end of my final draft of this project. I would like to thank all of the archivists and librarians who facilitated my visits to archives across the country, including Southern Illinois University at Carbondale, the University of Florida, the Manuscripts, Archive, and Rare Book Library at Emory, and Spelman College. Special thanks to Holly Smith for modeling and an enacting a Black feminist, community-centered approach to archives. Another, crucial form of scholarly support came from Hurston the Horizon NEH Summer Seminar in 2021, organized by Maryemma Graham, Ayesha Hardison, and Kevin Quashie. This was a short but potent experience that forced me to engage in the difficult but generative work of community building—ironically, in the service of a historical figure who had her own struggles with community.

Speaking of short but potent experiences (and difficult but generative work), the lessons of the Haitian Summer Institute in 2015 are still with me. Nicolas "Tiko" André, the most gifted pedagogue I have ever known, facilitated the most holistic and effective learning environment I have ever experienced. "Se kouto sèlman ki konnen kè yanm," and those knife-edged times helped me know myself and my place in history. Through moments of turmoil and moments of joy, I was grateful for the friendship of Didier Sylvain and Ryan Joyce and the bond we established by speaking in our newly minted Creole.

Ryan became one of the key players in my New Orleans social world, and I am so happy that our bond was fated to continue in other Creolized spaces. New Orleans is a space that deserves a thank you in itself for the years of pure joy, growth, and surrealism it offered me. The people who made New Orleans what it was for me were Mama Jen and Mama Vera of Community Book Center, Don Edwards, Omar Casimire, Al Jackson, Ali and all the folks at Flora, and Annie and Leon Phoenix.

I thought I would never find any place as intellectually and artistically inspiring as New Orleans, but Miami proved me wrong. Tim Watson and Kate Ramsey were incredibly kind to me in my rocky Miami beginnings, and I continue to feel their unconditional support in tangible ways. Chantel Acevedo, Brenna Munro, Gema Perez Sanchez, Pam Hammons, Lindsay Thomas, and Jessica Rosenberg also supported my transition to Miami, socially and professionally. My squad, Suja Sawafta and Cae Joseph-Masséna, were crucial in providing mutual support and commiseration at the beginning of our careers, all while being very hot and glamorous. (Eziaku Nwokocha is a late but welcome addition.) Shout-out to the undergrads who took multiple classes with me, especially Luz Estrella Cruz—it was a privilege to watch you grow over the years. I also had the privilege to serve on graduate committees that have pushed and inspired me during my years in Miami: thank you, Julia Mollenthiel, Set-Byul Moon, Rachel Northrop, Tarika Sankar, Jovanté Anderson, and Gabrielle Jean-Louis. I finished and wrote parts of this book in the loving environment of Paradis Books and Bread—many thanks to Bianca Sanon, Brian Wright, and Audrey Wright for carving out this loophole of possibility in a bleak political landscape. Thanks to Nancy St. Leger for a spiritual education through dance. And lastly, Miami is not Miami without my beloved comrades: Bobuq Sayed, Zaina Alsous, and Helen Peña. You have taught me what solidarity and being in community truly mean, and with you building the Third World feels irresistible.

This project would not be without the timely rescue by Black women mentors at several crossroads moments. Marlene Daut and Tiphanie Yanique offered crucial career advice that changed my material conditions for the better. Kinitra Brooks, whose rigorous and generous feedback impelled me to get over my exhaustion and to make the final draft of this book its best self. Alexis De Veaux and Sokari Ekine, who adopted me in New Orleans and showed me that I, too, deserved that good Black queer life that is their gift to themselves and the world. And Donette Francis, who believed in me from the very start, who ferociously defended my time, and whose tough love is always in the service of abundance. In a book about the barriers and rough edges of community, I do not take these connections for granted.

I must also thank the editors and staff at UNC Press for shepherding this book through to its final form. Especially Dylan White, whose faith and guidance made this project better than I could ever have imagined, and Lucas Church, for picking up where he left off. I am honored that Nadia Wolff's interpretation of my words—a braid of Black women, climbing toward the sun—graces the cover of this book, and so perfectly captures the real and aspirational elements of the community I have tried to portray.

Finally, I want to thank my parents, my brother and sister, my niece, my aunts and uncles, my cousins, and my grandparents for creating the conditions of possibility for this book. I may not have shared with you what this book is about, but you created it by taking me to Powell's Bookstore to trade in used books as a kid, sharing Martinican legends, letting me stay in a Parisian garret during the last stages of my dissertation, and making me explain structural racism on the way to the mall. All that is in here, and much more. To all the ancestors who are in this book—known and unknown, familial and chosen—ayibobo!

We Pursue Our Magic

Introduction

To consider Zora Neale Hurston's time in Haiti is to observe a crack in Hurston's sanctified legacy. Haiti was incredibly generative for Hurston's artistic development. She famously wrote *Their Eyes Were Watching God* in seven weeks while researching in Haiti, and the text is replete with the influence of Haitian culture and religion, but Hurston's contribution to Haitian life and politics is more ambiguous.[1] Unlike her sympathetic account of New Orleans hoodoo in her 1935 ethnography *Mules and Men*, Hurston's account of Haitian culture in *Tell My Horse* (1938) is famously riddled with contradictions and apparent moments of cultural chauvinism.[2] Arriving just two years after the end of the brutal U.S. military occupation of Haiti, Hurston plays devil's advocate with Haitians who critique U.S. intervention in Haiti, and she consistently emphasizes the poverty of post-occupation Haiti. She goes so far as to write that for many Haitians, "their era of prosperity had left with the Marines" and implies that the 1937 massacre of Haitians by Dominicans might not have occurred if America had still commanded the Haitian military.[3]

Various scholars have attributed Hurston's reluctance to critique U.S. imperialism to censorship and the demands of the white publishing industry, citing differences between the original manuscript of her autobiography, *Dust Tracks on a Road*, and its published version.[4] The original manuscript of *Dust Tracks on a Road* includes a chapter called "Seeing the World as It Is," which contains some of her most strident critiques of the U.S. as a country that "consider[s] machine gun bullets good laxatives for heathens who get constipated with toxic ideas of a country of their own."[5] However, though Hurston voiced criticism of U.S. imperialism in an oblique sense, she never spoke out directly against the United States' war crimes in Haiti or named specific moments of U.S. intervention in the essay. If Hurston disapproved of the U.S. occupation of Haiti, it is deeply buried.[6]

In *Tell My Horse*, Hurston argues that "the N.A.A.C.P. [National Association for the Advancement of Colored People], The Nation and certain other organizations had a great deal more to do with the withdrawal of the Marines than . . . they are given credit for."[7] Here, she is alluding to the writing of her friend and fellow Black Floridian James Weldon Johnson, who reported on the U.S. occupation for *The Nation* and the NAACP's magazine *The Crisis* in 1920. Unlike Hurston, there is no ambiguity in Johnson's stance on U.S. intervention in Haiti. Johnson takes great pains to document the financial, legal, and military facets of U.S. violence against Haitians, as well as the dignity of the Haitian working classes—the same people for whom, in Hurston's possibly tongue-in-cheek phrasing, "freedom from slavery only looked like a big watermelon cutting and fish-fry to the irresponsible blacks, those people who have no memory of yesterday and no suspicion of tomorrow."[8] Unequivocally, Johnson writes, "The United States has failed in Haiti. It should get out as well and as quickly as it can and restore to the Haitian people their independence and sovereignty. The colored people of the United States should be interested in seeing that this is done, for Haiti is the one best chance that the Negro has in the world to prove that he is capable of the highest self-government."[9] Though Hurston's allusion to Johnson's writing perhaps implies her agreement with its content, it is troubling (to say the least) that she attributes the withdrawal of U.S. troops to the saviorism of benevolent Americans rather than the sustained resistance of the Haitian people. In fact, Hurston takes pains to villainize the Cacos, a group of Haitian militants who resisted the U.S. occupation, on multiple occasions by representing them as machete-wielding bandits who wantonly slaughtered and kidnapped their own people.[10]

Whether Hurston could not or would not critique the U.S. occupation of Haiti, her resulting stance cannot be entirely excused as irony or dismissed as conservatism. Unlike her complex renderings of the inner lives and sociality of Black Americans in the rural South, Hurston's inscrutable representation of Haitian culture provides little insight into the interiority of Haitian people. Hurston, it seems, was not wholly unaware of the limits of her representation of people suffering under the boot of U.S. imperialism, as she ends her anti-imperialist interlude in "Seeing the World as It Is" with a self-reflective turn:

> I have sat in judgment upon the ways of others, and in the voiceless quiet of the night I have also called myself to judgment. I cannot have the joy of knowing that I found always a shining mirror of my soul on those occasions. I have given myself more harrowing pain than anyone else can ever have been capable of giving me. No one else can inflict the hurt of faith unkept. I have had the corroding insight at times, of recognizing that I am a bundle of sham and tinsel, honest metal and sincerity that cannot be untangled. My dross has given my other parts great sorrow.[11]

Hurston's writing on Haiti is, perhaps, an example of "faith unkept." This interlude may have been the closest she could come to an autoethnographic interrogation of her own shortcomings in the field. Hurston's Haitian fieldwork was marked by crises of authority where funders and mentors questioned everything from her ability to speak Creole to her deservingness of funding.[12] Unlike Johnson and other Black male American intellectuals who spoke out against the U.S. occupation of Haiti, Hurston was a Black woman constrained by white publishing trends.[13] There was little room for Hurston to admit mistakes, incomprehension, or anti-American sentiment if her text was to be published as an authoritative account of Haitian Vodou. And when Hurston left Haiti in 1937 after a year of fieldwork and a debilitating "violent gastric disturbance," her limited financial means and career path never again led back to Haiti.[14] I like to believe that her inability to delve more deeply into Haitian life and culture was a fact that, on some level, gave her pause. It is telling that Hurston's barbed maxim, used to this day—"my skin-folks but not my kinfolks"—was written during her fieldwork in Haiti.[15] Skin-folk are not always so easily understood.

We Pursue Our Magic is a spiritual genealogy of the way these contradictions run through the heart of Black American feminism.[16] Its origin story is the pioneering ethnographic work of Zora Neale Hurston and Katherine Dunham in the 1930s, given that these two women were some of the first Americans to articulate the hopes and dreams of global Black feminist unity through an engagement with Afro-Caribbean spirituality. In the interwar period, Black American intellectuals like Hurston and Dunham rendered African and Caribbean culture through "eloquent readings [that] were at times nostalgic, but they were always the result of a change in perspective, the developments of a modern view, which was the result of purposeful travel."[17] It is no accident that this period of expanded travel for American women of all classes and professions led to some of the most cherished protofeminist texts of African American letters, including Zora Neale Hurston's *Their Eyes Were Watching God* (1937) and Nella Larsen's *Quicksand* and *Passing* (1928 and 1929), as well as the protofeminist blues music of Bessie Smith and Ma Rainey. Black feminism has, from its seedlings, been activated by travel and its productive tensions. As Angela Davis notes in her seminal study of women's blues of the era, "for people of African descent who were emerging from a long history of enslavement and oppression during the late nineteenth and early twentieth century, sexuality and travel provided the most tangible evidence of freedom."[18] But what happens when this freedom to travel, both literally and symbolically, unveils the ways in which certain varieties of Black feminism can be "predicated on a U.S.-centric and exceptionalist worldview"?[19] From the research and writings of well-traveled Black women of the interwar period to the birth of titular Black American feminism in the 1970s, enmeshed as it was with Third World women's movements, Black feminism has always trafficked in all the necessary missteps on the road toward transnational connection. Essentialisms, misunderstandings, and tensions abounded as Black American women strove for global liberation.

The failures of connection between women of the diaspora have by no means been resolved today by new ethnographic methods or by an increased sensitivity to global power dynamics, as today's Black anthropologists have noted. As Lyndon K. Gill, conducting fieldwork in Tobago in the early 2000s, notes on Black American desires for transnational connection, "This individualistic idealism is most naïve and most American, but subtle in its seduction of even those most skeptical of American exceptionalism. These are the hard revelations that bring the disillusioned among us cheek to cheek with the disturbing imprint of the United States upon us, especially when we've managed to leave it behind. It can never be left behind."[20] Similarly, in her ethnography of African American women's tourism in Jamaica, Bianca C. Williams argues that although Black American women's tourism "served as strategies for critiquing and responding to the ageist, racist, and sexist discourses that marginalize them within the United States," ultimately "Jamaicans they interacted with often reminded them that while they may all be 'Black,' American blackness was drastically different and made the travelers more privileged."[21] The past century of Black anthropology shows a history of Black Americans coming to the painful realization that people across the diaspora do not have a simple relationship to one another, and to imply that they do—even if it is for liberatory purposes—is to engage in the very oversimplifications by which white supremacists have denied us our humanity for centuries. Black women, too, can be hapless tourists. Black women, too, can inconvenience local people, be sloppy, sleep with their informants, hold troubling political beliefs, tear each other down. As both Hurston and Dunham did during their Haitian fieldwork.

This work's title, *We Pursue Our Magic*, comes from Audre Lorde's essay "Poetry Is Not a Luxury," in which she identifies poetry as the way "we pursue our magic and make it realized."[22] To me, Black feminism is a kind of poetry that must constantly conjure a relationality said to be innate but which actually requires active pursuit. Lorde's formulation reveals the work of living a Black feminist life in the face of the generational, linguistic, and cultural fracturing that defines diaspora. Lorde's notion of a pursuit depicts magic as an interior journey, not a physical one that can be accessed by returning to a fictive African space prior to conflict, alienation, and oppression. To theorize this, I focus on Black American women's quest for meaning within African diaspora religions. Drawing from the religion of Haitian Vodou, which "accepts conflict as an inevitable, in fact essential, ingredient of life," *We Pursue Our Magic* dwells in the impossibilities of diasporic community even as it attempts to build it.[23] Like the Vodou religion, Black American feminism builds an intergenerational community between living Black women and their ancestors, despite a sometimes lacunar archive. Making extensive use of archival research, I also cultivate a reading practice that argues that complexity is ancestor work. Drawing on the collected archives of Lucille Clifton, Katherine Dunham, Alice Walker, Audre Lorde, Toni Cade Bambara, Lorraine Hansberry, and Zora Neale Hurston, I argue that these archives offer unprecedented glimpses into the emotional landscape of Black women whose perspectives are often flattened by triumphal histories, and that to consider them in all their contradictions and complexities should be part of any Black feminist praxis.

Throughout this work, Vodou often functions as a template for diasporic identity formation rather than as a linear Haitian influence on Black American feminism. In its original context, Haitian Vodou crystallized in the eighteenth century as a direct response to slavery and colonialism in the French colony of Saint-Domingue. The spirits born out of these conditions of enslavement (the *lwa*, as they are known in Haitian Creole) are often traceable to analogous spirits in Nigeria, Benin, and the Congo but have developed distinct characteristics tailored to life in the Americas. Some, like the spirits Ezili and Agwe, are ostensibly mixed-race spirits who appear to be native to Haiti. In the crucible of colonial Saint-Domingue, nascent Haitian Vodou incorporated elements of every religious and magical tradition practiced by the uneasy mixture of people in the colony: the spirits and rituals of West and Central African enslaved people (which included African practices of Islam and Christianity), Catholicism, European folk magic and occultism, and the practices of the island's indigenous people. Today, Vodou incorporates cell phones, Barbie dolls, and white practitioners just as easily as it hearkens back to the Haitian Revolution and to Africa. Many ethnographies have noted that Vodou's remarkable elasticity has allowed it to survive through the centuries, and the ease with which this worldview confounds notions of racial or spiritual purity while still remaining rooted in its history and origins. It is with this same ease and elasticity that I wish to reflect the seemingly muddled and alienated experiences of Black women across the diaspora as strength rather than inauthenticity.

Like Jennifer Nash in *Black Feminism Reimagined: After Intersectionality* (2018) and Kevin Quashie in *The Sovereignty of Quiet: Beyond Resistance in Black Culture* (2012), who complicate the commonly held positive valences of terms like "intersectionality" and "resistance," respectively, I also seek to complicate the notion that African diasporic religions are always a means of accessing a self-realization that has been denied to us by slavery. Like Brent Hayes Edwards's concept of *décalage* in *The Practice of Diaspora: Literature, Translation, and the Rise of Black Internationalism* (2003), *We Pursue Our Magic* uses rigorous historical analysis to theorize the "haunting gap or discrepancy" that lies at the core of Black American women's engagement with African diaspora religions.[24] It demonstrates that a careful attention to Black women's archival and published work reveals the fact that even some of our most venerated Black feminist forebears did not seek to resolve contradictions in their transnational, transcultural, and transhistorical relationships with other women. Rather, they lived in these contradictions, sometimes painfully, but with intention. And to valorize only their achievements without also considering their shortcomings is to willfully refuse the gift of their hard-won lessons. In this, I take to heart Jennifer Nash's language of "love politics" and "intimacy" even while formulating what "black womanhood means when we inhabit it in the context of US global supremacy."[25] Like Nash, my cataloguing of some of the bad effects of Black feminism's most venerated ancestors is not a "call-out" of the ways they sought one another's hands in the dark, but an act of loving attention to the lessons they contribute to the ongoing journey of Black feminism. In the words of Audre Lorde, as written in the refrain of her devastating poem "Between Ourselves": I do not believe / our wants have made all our lies / holy."[26] I do not believe, either, that our desire for diasporic connection should allow us to indulge in the lies of unnuanced narratives, oversimplifications, and essentialisms. This is not an indictment of Black Americans' deep and long-term struggle for union with and through African spiritualties. This is a celebration of its complexity. This is a book about the endless recalibrations that keep Black thought nimble, flexible, and rigorous. Because Black spirituality, like freedom, is a constant struggle.

Our Lies, Our Wants: Feminist Geographies of Vodou

In the Americas, there is no more exalted and sough-after example of a Black genealogy of resistance than the nation of Haiti, and its continued existence in spite of international sanctions and internal strife. As Jeremy Glick argues in his study of texts inspired by the Haitian Revolution, literary imaginings of Haiti can serve as "blueprints, theaters of battle that prepare its participants for that other Pan-African, proletarian battle—the battle to come."[27] The proliferation of texts written by non-Haitian authors on the subject of the Haitian Revolution attests to its incredible tidal pull upon the diasporic imaginary, and to the desire of diasporic authors to write themselves into this narrative. Members of the African diaspora have long enlisted Haiti into their anti-colonial rhetoric under the presumption that there is a grand cosmic "we"—a Pan-African community—waiting for the same liberation that Haiti has achieved first. For many, Haiti serves not just as an example but as an inheritance. There have been a number of recent monographs published in literary studies that recognize the importance of Haitian revolutionary thought in the works of artists and intellectuals outside of Haiti, such as Omise'eke Natasha Tinsley's *Ezili's Mirrors: Imagining Black Queer Genders* (2018), Kameelah Martin's *Envisioning Black Feminist Voodoo Aesthetics: African Spirituality in American Cinema* (2016), and Jeremy Glick's *The Black Radical Tragic: Performance, Aesthetics, and the Unfinished Haitian Revolution* (2016).

My work follows in the footsteps of these important texts by considering the culture and religion of Haiti as a wellspring of inspiration for non-Haitians. It is important to note that with the exception of Katherine Dunham, none of the women in this study served the spirits of Haitian Vodou, though some, like Luisah Teish, serve the orishas.[28] *We Pursue Our Magic* is the first academic text to center the uncomfortable fact that Black feminist conversations about Haitian spirituality often take place without the input of Haitian women. Though it is beyond the scope of this project to consider the vast and rich tradition of Haitian women writers' engagements with Vodou theology and imagery—including the works of folklorist Suzanne Comhaire-Sylvain, novelist Marie Vieux Chauvet, and singer Mimerose Beaubrun—it is important to note that the American contemporaries of these Haitian thinkers seldom engaged their work.[29] In this way, Black American women can participate in what Gina Athena Ulysse calls "Vodou as Idea," in which Haitian Vodou can become a polyphonic meditation on diaspora without acknowledgment of its Haitian provenance and the fact that "there are still laws and there is a *regleman* (ritual order) that is essential to its function regardless of location."[30] My work is also the first text to consider Black American women's engagements with Afro-diasporic spirituality more generally as rife with conflict, trauma, and confusion. In this, my project runs parallel to Saidiya Hartman's devastating disambiguation of the hopes of reaccessing a precolonial past in *Lose Your Mother* (2008). Hartman's time in Ghana "shattered any illusions of unanimity of sentiment in the black world and exposed the fragility and precariousness of the grand collective *we* that had yet to be actualized."[31]

Haitian Vodou carries connotations of liberation and resistance that even nonpractitioners link to a collective Black identity. There is a lively discourse, both popular and academic, that attributes the practices of Haitian resistance to the revolutionary nature of Haitian religious practice. Undeniably, Haitian Vodou is a religious practice with a long history of resistance to racism and imperialism. While scholars disagree on the extent to which Vodou played a role in the Haitian Revolution, it has come to play a powerful role in the mythological apparatus of Haitian historiography.[32] Most historical accounts reference the August 1791 meeting at Bois-Caïman, where various members of the Haitian Revolution met to make a pact to end slavery. While there is some debate as to whether this gathering was in fact a Vodou ceremony, officiated by a putative *houngan* (Vodou priest) called Boukman and a *mambo* (Vodou priestess) named Cécile Fatiman, the existing written archival sources from the time period agree that a gathering incorporating elements of Haitian Vodou, including the sacrifice of a pig, occurred.[33] As historian Laurent Dubois notes in his study of the Haitian Revolution, the ceremony's mythological presence in Haitian postrevolutionary discourse is largely metonymic: "The invocations of the mysterious ceremony at Bois-Caïman serves as shorthand for the complex and varied presence of religion in the planning and execution of the insurrection."[34]

Viewing Vodou as a key export of Haitian revolutionary iconography can help to counter a largely masculinist diasporic fetishization of the Haitian Revolution as it has been taken up by non-Haitian intellectuals.[35] Haitian religion has inspired a rich scholarly tradition by and about women in Vodou, ranging from now-classic ethnographies by Katherine Dunham, Zora Neale Hurston, Maya Deren, and Karen McCarthy Brown to Haitian singer Mimerose Beaubrun's ethnographic memoir *Nan dòmi*. Vodou provides a useful rubric for Black feminist praxis because of both the stature of female spirits within its cosmology and the availability of women's leadership positions at its highest ranks. As Karen McCarthy Brown argues in her seminal ethnography of Vodou practice, *Mama Lola: A Vodou Priestess in Brooklyn*, "The adaptability of Vodou over time, and its responsiveness to other cultures and religions; the fact that it has no canon, creed, or pope; the multiplicity of its spirits; and the intimate detail in which those spirits reflect the lives of the faithful—all those characteristics make women's lives visible within Vodou in ways they are not in other religious traditions, including those of the African homeland. This visibility can give women a way of working realistically and creatively with the forces that define and confine them."[36] Brown positions Vodou as a religion that allows its woman practitioners unparalleled social and spiritual power. This is the kernel of truth that Black American women seek to access through Vodou feminism: that in the social and historical reality of the Haitian *mambo* that serves as the basis of the diasporic mythology of the "voodoo queen," she is a figure with real power. She is charged with communicating with ancestors and spirits and with mobilizing a community of living worshippers. In keeping with these tasks, the lens of Vodou feminism helps us to understand how Black women relate to history, community, and political obligation.

In the United States, however, Black women's relationship to the trope of the voodoo queen has always been uncomfortable. In popular cultural representations dating at least as far back as the nineteenth century, the stock character of the voodoo queen is represented in some moments as powerful, authoritative, and alluring, as is the character of Palmyre in George Washington Cable's 1880 novel *The Grandissimes*; and at other times oversexed, frenzied, and vengeful, as is the titular character of the 1974 blaxploitation film *Abby*, who is possessed by an "African" sex demon. This stereotype stands in ambivalent relation to Black women's engagements with Afro-diasporic magic and religion. In her comprehensive study of the trope of Black women priestess figures in American film, Martin establishes a dichotomy between stereotypical and empowering representations of Black women: "As with the spiritual traditions of obeah, conjure, and hoodoo, visual media partake in both healing and harming practices. I assess cinematic renderings of the black priestess to discern which elements of film representation are cathartic and which continue to be problematic to the cultural health and wholeness of black women."[37] As important as it is to disarticulate the religious practices of Vodou from the negative images that have come to define it in the American popular imaginary, I think it is equally important to acknowledge the extent to which this is not possible, and the fact that Black American women are themselves not always unproblematic interlocutors with Caribbean religion and culture.

In addition to locating Haiti and the Caribbean as a key source of Black American women's vexed relationship to African diaspora religions and magic, I also center New Orleans for similar reasons. New Orleans is a nearer but no less exoticized site of spiritual exploration for Black American women, and because of its historic linkages to Haiti deserves an in-depth consideration of the ways in which its residents and visitors negotiate its oft-cited legacy of African connection. In the words of Welele Raymond-Noël, a Haitian drummer who visited New Orleans through an exchange sponsored by the New Orleans Jazz Fest in 2011, New Orleans and Haiti "are on the same mountaintop, so we look down at the plain in the same way."[38] Adding the lens of New Orleans to Vodou feminism leaves room for the quixotic, the zany, and the inauthentic, muddled as it is by white Vodou practitioners, by carnival traditions steeped more in Jim Crow segregation than Afro-Caribbean ritual, and by the city's long but lacunar relationship with Haiti. New Orleans' reality constantly frustrates its public image as a space of unadulterated Africanisms, and as America's first Haitian city (before patterns of migration shifted to Miami, New York, and Boston), it offers crucial insight into how Americans grapple with both desires and rejections of Haitian spiritual legacies.

This project begins in the interwar period in the wake of the U.S. occupation of Haiti (1915–34). This is by no means the birth of the American fascination with Haitian religious iconography and the figure of the voodoo queen—as early as 1854, Frances Hammond Pratt's story "La Belle Zoa; or the Insurrection of Hayti" features a Black woman prophetess and sorceress as an instrumental character in the revolution. And this is to say nothing of the many nineteenth-century texts inspired by the New Orleans priestess Marie Laveau, whose overlap and divergence with Haitian religious practice will be discussed in greater detail in chapter 5. However, the interwar period was the first time that Black American women were instrumental in shaping the reception and dissemination of Vodou imagery throughout American culture. Beginning with the protofeminisms of the Harlem Renaissance, this book moves through the birth of Black feminism as such and its renewed interest in African spiritual forms in the 1970s and 1980s. Underlying Black American women's spiritual explorations and claims of homecoming and ancestral knowledge lies a deep and sometimes unspoken pain: the idea that the Middle Passage is an irreparable severing, that death is final, that our ancestors suffered in vain, that we are forever robbed of each other. Vodou feminism provides no simple triumphalism, but neither does it plunge into despair. Diaspora is different from what anyone supposed, and luckier.

Chapter 1 traces the evolution of Katherine Dunham's relationship with Haiti through archival research and a consideration of her 1969 ethnographic memoir, *Island Possessed*. Beginning with the influence of the American occupation of Haiti on the Harlem Renaissance, it argues that primitivist discourses framing Vodou as an instinctive capacity latent in all people of African origins provided interwar Black artists like Dunham with a tantalizing possibility of Pan-African solidarity, through which they could mobilize their desire for connection with an obscured past and an imagined community in the present. When her 1930s fieldwork inevitably ran aground on the wall of cultural difference, however, Dunham's initial feelings of discomfort in Haiti transformed her writing into an interrogation of the supposedly innate and homogeneous nature of Blackness. The language and praxis of Vodou proved flexible enough to provide her with the vocabulary to articulate a more nuanced version of diasporic Blackness beyond her preconceived notions of an easy or automatic alliance between all Black people.

Chapter 2 also centers Haiti as a space that allows Black American women to interrogate their most commonly held values and mores, this time manifested in the friendship of playwright Lorraine Hansberry and singer Nina Simone, both queer women who were publicly heterosexual. I argue that both artists sublimated queer desires that they deemed socially inappropriate into their mutual interest in the history of revolutions across the diaspora, which contributed to the radical quality of their friendship — as Simone notes on her relationship with Hansberry, "We never talked about men or clothes or other such inconsequential things when we got together. It was always Marx, Lenin and revolution — real girls' talk." In Simone's 1974 album *It is Finished* and Hansberry's posthumously published play fragment, *Toussaint*, traces of the two women's revolutionary girls' talk manifests in their shared construction of the Caribbean as a space of non-normativity fluidity that did not yet exist in their America. In the album and the play, Simone and Hansberry theorize the possibility of future revolutions that break down the limitations of prescriptive gender roles and compulsory heterosexuality.

Chapter 3 considers the role of Black American women's engagements with Afro-diasporic religious systems more broadly to critique gender politics within Black communities, revealing internecine rifts in Black liberation ideologies. It puts poets Audre Lorde and Lucille Clifton in conversation with Black power ideologies of the 1970s and 1980s, discourses into which they are seldom scripted. For Lorde and Clifton, Afro-diasporic spirituality becomes both escape and antidote to a gender-restrictive Black nationalism which they could never want or hope to access. The virulent authenticity politics of the era and the dominion that these held over memories of Africa shunted both women onto spiritual paths deemed outside of the movement. In her poetry collection *The Black Unicorn* and in her essays collected in *Sister Outsider*, Lorde turned to African and diasporic pantheons of spirits for a version of revolution in which Black lesbians are the vanguard rather than the outliers. Meanwhile, in her unpublished spirit writings, Clifton turned to an ancestral practice of spirit communication that allowed her to position herself as an omniscient authority on the past, present, and future of Black people. Despite the nascent popularity of African-derived spiritualities among African Americans in the 1970s, they are rarely considered to be Black power ideologies. I argue that this is due to the masculinism at the heart of mid-twentieth-century iterations of Afrocentrism. The perceived divide between the spiritual and the political of the 1970s was really a divide between essentialized concepts of masculinity and femininity—a divide that Lorde and Clifton tried to suture.

Chapter 4 transitions from the Caribbean influence on Black feminist spirituality to the equally ambiguous and overdetermined influence of New Orleans. This chapter focuses on Luisah Teish's 1985 spiritual autobiography *Jambalaya: A Natural Woman's Handbook* and Toni Cade Bambara's 1980 novel *The Salt Eaters* to argue that New Orleans represented many of the pitfalls and possibilities of Third World feminist spiritual connections. Both texts work at the intersection between a burgeoning New Age spirituality and Third World women's movements that sought to consolidate different cultural traditions into a unified liberation front. In this chapter, I argue that Bambara, who posits that the Vodou spirit "Damballah is the first law of thermodynamics and is the Biblical wisdom and is the law of time," uses a Vodou epistemology as a universal philosophy of global balance, seeking to encompass people of color across racial, religious, and national lines. Far from being a cure-all, Bambara's Vodou epistemology reveals the simultaneous necessity and impossibility of a universal Third World spirituality.

Chapter 5 blends personal narrative and New Orleans cultural history to create a transhistorical theorization of Black feminists' search for mentors in the archive. The chapter compares Zora Neale Hurston's search for the nineteenth-century priestess Marie Laveau in New Orleans in *Mules and Men* (1928) with Walker's parallel search for Zora Neale Hurston's grave in Florida in 1973. While Hurston positions herself as an apprentice to Marie Laveau's fantastic and semifictive public legacy, Walker represents herself as a loving daughter speaking her mother's buried truth. In this chapter, I argue that both models of historical reclamation respond to unknowable histories of Black women's power and that their explorations shed light on the strategic use of much-denigrated terms like "silence" and "invisibility." Even in the face of lost or lacunar archives, the living can still access ancestral power through a respectful engagement with their opacity.

In the conclusion, I return to Dunham and Hurston as I argue that community can be achieved not through a return to a lost African ancestral wholeness but through a careful attention to the struggles of our more recent ancestors detailed throughout the book, whose ambivalence about community serves as a cartography of an affective landscape that has changed surprisingly little since Hurston and Dunham embarked on their Caribbean fieldwork.

It is my sincere hope that a fuller analysis of the lived experience and literary complexities of Black feminist icons will yield a greater range of possibilities for Black being in the present. Hurston herself, after dolefully confessing her shortcomings, also exalts her abundance: "But on the other hand . . . I have walked in storms with crowns of clouds above my head and zigzag lightning playing through my fingers. The gods of the upper air have uncovered their faces to my eyes. I have found out that my real home is in the water, and the earth is only my stepmother."[39] May we, her descendants, find ourselves at home in a Blackness that changes with each shore it meets.

CHAPTER ONE

An Ethics of Discomfort
Katherine Dunham's Vodou Belonging

In a backhanded review of Katherine Dunham's 1946 *Journey to Accompong*, which was based on Dunham's month of fieldwork among the Jamaican Maroons in 1935, Zora Neale Hurston congratulates Dunham on her achievement of "sustain[ing] the thin material to the end." "After all," Hurston goes on, "thirty days in a locality is not much in research and hardly affords enough time for the fieldworker to scratch the surface."[1] Yet Dunham herself never claimed that this book was comprehensive or definitive. Rather, the book is interspersed with the personal reflections of any tourist, amid various historical and ethnographic observations—feeling glad to escape her routines in America, feeling lonely, habituating herself to local standards of dress, and putting coconut oil on her sunburns. On the twelfth day she asks, humorously, "I wonder if this is what anthropologists call 'going native.'"[2] This statement's ironic positioning on day twelve of her journey—precipitated by such superficial details as changing her sleep schedule, drinking white rum instead of brown, and "disastrously" attempting to carry a tin of water on her head like a West Indian woman—all convey the ridiculousness of the idea of going native and redirect the reader's attention to her fragmentary perspective rather than her native omniscience. Hurston's aspersions on Dunham's lack of expertise miss the point of what Dunham's critique of expertise is as a concept.

Perhaps it is inevitable that the competing authenticities of these two women would clash. When they first crossed paths in the 1930s, Katherine Dunham was a glamorous midwesterner who would later be known for her popularizations of Afro-diasporic dance forms in American performance and cinema. Zora Neale Hurston was a charming southerner and student of anthropology who would come to be known as one of the greatest literary stylists of African American letters. They were what we would today call "frenemies." As African American women conducted pioneering ethnographic research in Jamaica and Haiti in the 1930s, their fieldwork overlapped both thematically and temporally, to such an extent that Hurston accused Dunham of stealing her research itinerary.[3] There was even some suspicion on Hurston's part that the Rosenwald Foundation, which reneged on a portion of its fellowship offer for her research and graduate education in 1935, simply used the intended funds for Dunham's research instead (Dunham did, indeed, travel to the Caribbean with a Rosenwald Fellowship that year). In 1936, when Hurston finally received funding from the Guggenheim Foundation to conduct her Caribbean research, she wrote to Henry Allen Moe, the secretary general of the foundation, that "Miss Catherine [sic] Dunham" was "a petty dancer of Chicago" and that "she stayed here [in Haiti] six months with infinitely less preparation than I have for the work."[4]

In a 2000 interview, an elderly Dunham is able to regard their rivalry with a sense of humor. While she acknowledges that in the 1930s she was jealous that Hurston "didn't care a thing about me" and that "she knew the other anthropologists better than I did," she also acknowledges the pettiness of their competition, in saying, "I don't know who told me that I was going to be the only little black girl in anthropology."[5] But Dunham's and Hurston's desires for exceptionalism were not intrinsic to their relationship; they were ingrained in American interwar conceptions of the fledgling identity category of "black woman anthropologist." In this economy of authenticity, the Caribbean became not just a space for spiritual and intellectual discovery for the two women but a place on which their ethnographic authority, and thus their careers and livelihoods, depended.

Their rivalry was exacerbated by the pressure to be the first participant ethnographic observer of hitherto undocumented Afro-diasporic rituals at a time when for white anthropologists, in the words of Halifu Osumare, "merely 'being there' with a pad and pencil was deemed enough participation."[6] Both women were considered the protégés of two of the leading white anthropologists of the day—Zora Neale Hurston as Franz Boas's student at Barnard, and Katherine Dunham as a mentee of Melville Herskovits. Boas, in his preface to Hurston's 1935 ethnography *Mules and Men*, assures the reader that Hurston "entered into the homely life of the southern Negro as one of them and was fully accepted as such by the companions of her childhood. Thus she has been able to penetrate through that affected demeanor by which the Negro excludes the White observer from effectively participating in his true inner life."[7] Historian Kate Ramsey notes that Herskovits had similar feelings about Dunham's ability to participate in Afro-diasporic ritual where a white anthropologist could only ever be an outside observer.[8] But the idea that a Black American anthropologist is welcomed unequivocally into the fold of a foreign community of Black people elides the struggle, work, and inevitable failures of diasporic community building. As Daphne Lamothe notes in her study of African American ethnographers of the Harlem Renaissance,

"A shared racial identity provided them with easier access to their subjects, and gave them an affinity with the experiences and feelings of those they observed, apparently allowing them to render folk culture more realistically and truthfully to their audience. At the same time, class, regional, and national differences could result in mutual incomprehension and distrust."[9] Despite the radical potentiality of the participant observers' gaze, early Black women anthropologists struggled to establish the necessary bonds of trust and understanding between themselves and their estranged diasporic kin at their fieldwork sites. Both Hurston and Dunham experienced a great deal of discomfort during their Haitian fieldwork, from gastric disturbances to scoldings from their informants. They were supposed to be greeted with open arms by their skin-folk abroad, but how could this be possible when they did not even consider themselves to be kinfolk at home?

Dunham's first research trip to Haiti, Jamaica, Trinidad, and Martinique in 1935–36 began from a feeling of diasporic similitude. In this sentiment, she was beholden both to her own desire for Pan-African community and to white demands for an embodied display of her inner Africanity. John Martin, a prominent dance critic and *New York Times* columnist in the 1920s and 1930s, wrote on "the essence of Negro dance" in a 1940 tribute to Katherine Dunham's work: "There is nothing pretentious about it; it is not designed to delve into philosophy or psychology, but to externalize the impulses of a high-spirited, rhythmic, and gracious race."[10] Martin's assessment of Dunham's dance reviews, which were the product of years of research in the West Indies, characterizes the stance of many white critical reviews of African American concert dance in the interwar period. These critics tried to relegate Black dance efforts to the ethnographic, that is to say, as an expression of ancestral racial characteristics rather than as a concerted intellectual effort to define and articulate identity out of the inconsistencies of diasporic cultures.[11]

Dunham herself, however, over the course of decades of immersion in Haitian Vodou, found the practice of ritual dance far from easy or natural. Rather than finding any insight into her ancestral impulses or any comforting realizations of her true African essence, Dunham's years of performing Afro-diasporic dance forms only increased her uncertainty of what constituted that African essence. In Haiti, she found not clarity but complication, not sameness but difference, not an African past but a Creolized present. The goal of her Haitian ethnographic *Island Possessed* is not to reveal but to disturb the notion of essentialized Blackness by positioning Dunham and the Vodou religion itself as Creolized products of uncomfortable truths and terrifying juxtapositions. Retrospection is Dunham's critical stance in *Island Possessed*, published nearly thirty years after her initial fieldwork: "the present diffused in the roundness of time is the way [she sees] time and events."[12] While many of Dunham's contemporaries enjoyed a momentary interest in Haiti during the interwar period, for her "the roundness of time" becomes a lifelong refractory lens that allows Dunham to both hold space for and move beyond the inevitable mistakes and misunderstandings of a Black American engaging with a country under constant attack from American imperialism.

In *Journey to Accompong*, published a decade after the Jamaican fieldwork on which it is based, Dunham is already beginning to use retrospection for pedagogical purposes. Using her youthful misconceptions as a cautionary tale, Dunham seeks to illustrate that, in the words of James Clifford, "identity, considered ethnographically, must always be mixed, relational, and inventive."[13] Among the Jamaican Maroons, Dunham describes her initial disappointment when her hosts want to listen to her American records rather than regaling her with traditional Jamaican music: "Here I am dying to hear wild exotic native music and watch weird ceremonies and I must sit up and listen to Duke Ellington, Cab Calloway, Benny Goodman, and Billie Holiday. . . . *Later* I learned to use these American idiom records to evoke native parallels."[14] This potent "later" holds within it a multitude of lessons learned: that Caribbean music is not static; that it exists in a dialogue with African American musical practice; that perhaps the demand that it be "wild" and "weird" and ethnically pure is racist and unreasonable. This politics of nonessentialism was a long and hard-won lesson precipitated, but by no means resolved, by Dunham's 1930s fieldwork. From the time of her 1930s fieldwork into the 1960s, Dunham and her dance company toured the world portraying the dance traditions of the African diaspora as complex and mutable. In the words of longtime dancer and her collaborator Vanoye Aikens, "No one had ever thought of Voodooism without thinking of something kinky before Katherine Dunham."[15] But Dunham herself seemed to view Caribbean ritual as "something kinky" in the early stages of her encounters with Haitian culture. And how could she not, given the preponderance of American materials written in her youth about the innate spookiness of Afrodiasporic spiritual practice? This spookiness in itself becomes an inheritance, the Magical Negro a common ancestor. The American Occupation of Haiti (1915–34) brought with it a flood of "voodoo" imagery that forever changed the landscape of Black American self-representation and formed the backdrop to Dunham's first trip to Haiti. Over the decades, this initial encounter was the fertile ground from which grew her crucial rejoinder to primitivism, tourism, Pan-Africanism, and any other "ism" that reveled in a flattening of transnational difference. Dunham learned in Haiti that difference bred, and necessitated, discomfort.[16]

The Tom-Tom Beats Back: Haiti Comes to Harlem

On July 28, 1915, a group of Haitians assassinated Vilbrun Guillaume Sam, then president of Haiti, in retaliation for his execution of nearly 200 political prisoners in the weeks previous. The embroidered tale of President Sam's death at the hands of angry Haitians—construed as an act of mob violence in which the crowd continued to brutalize Sam's corpse long after it was dead—provided crucial ideological fodder for the justification of the subsequent U.S. invasion.[17] The *New York Times* headline for July 29, 1915, reads, "Haitians Slay Their President; We Land Marines," with the tagline "Body Is Cut to Pieces," emphasizing the causal connection Americans sought to establish between Haitian savagery and the moral/pedagogical necessity of the occupation.[18] President Sam's murder came to stand in for an atavistic lust for violence, and for the fragility of Haitians' psychic and cultural self-control. This inaugural narrative of a Black Dionysiac went on to inform a genre of occupation-era literature by American soldiers and civilians in which Haitians were presented as slaves to debased ancestral and bodily impulses.

A whole genre of "voodoo" pulp fiction arose in the wake of the American occupation of Haiti, the most famous of which was William Seabrook's pseudoethnographic novel *The Magic Island*.[19] Despite Seabrook's insistence that "it happens that I like blacks. On the whole I like them better than whites," his texts exhibit the same revelry in racialized sex and violence as the most of virulent of anti-Black tracts.[20] In a description of a Vodou ceremony at which he claimed to be in attendance, for instance, he describes the worshippers as "writhing black bodies, blood-maddened, sex-maddened, god-maddened, drunken."[21] However, Seabrook's meditations after the ceremony are laced with a heady longing, in fact, for the spiritual fullness of the ritual he has just described: "What, after all were they doing . . . that was so different from things which occur in our own fashionable and expansive nightclubs, except that they were doing it more successfully? . . . There is nothing so stupid and pathetic as an orgy that doesn't quite come off. . . . Perhaps if we mixed a little true sacrificial blood in our synthetic cocktails and flavored them prayerfully with holy fire, our night clubs would become more orgiastically successful and become as sacred as temples were in the days of Priapus and Aphrodite."[22] What exactly does it mean to be "orgiastically successful"? It appears that the line between the Vodou ceremony and "an orgy that doesn't quite come off" is entirely cosmological. Seabrook's semiflippant allusion to sacrificial blood and ancient Greek temples would suggest that religious fervor is the line that separates African religious dance from American secular dance forms. For all its racism, Seabrook's text constructs a kind of Black Dionysiac aligned with a Western sacral inheritance from which the white denizens of Western nightclubs had been irreparably severed. In doing so, Seabrook constructs the Black Dionysiac as a potential balm to the spiritual wounds and amputations inflicted by interwar modernity.

The methodology of Vodou worship—specifically, of ecstatic possession heralded and induced by ritual dance—had a profound influence upon the entire American imaginary of the interwar period. The figure of the Black dancing body, possessed and ventriloquized by spirits, begins to appear in the dreams of Americans both Black and white during the interwar period, itself a kind of possession. But whether this spirit is construed a god or a demon, an ancestral impulse or a deliberate response to the conditions of modernity, is dependent entirely on the author's political and cosmological commitments. Magical and religious practice in Haiti served as framing metaphors for American meditations on whether Blackness was socially constructed or composed of inherited racialized tendencies. John H. Craige, a U.S. Marine who published a popular travel account of his time in Haiti in 1934, wrote of the various forms of psychic unease experienced by white Americans when confronted with Haitian religious practice as products of the Haitian landscape: "The old resisted. One sensed its spiritual resistance. We whites were vaguely uncomfortable. We experienced queer sensations, tense psychic currents. It was as though one could feel, dimly, a struggle of soul against soul. Ancients believed that each race and each place had its gods. At times one was tempted to believe that it was the old, mystic gods of the locality that brought these floods of indefinable, subconscious unrest. White men think queer thoughts and sometimes do queer deeds in the tropics."[23] Craige's unease was in large part due to the persistent sounds of drumming in the hills, which he describes as the backdrop of a "condition of nervous hysteria" which afflicted some of his fellow marines.[24] During the Haitian occupation, the anti-imperialist guerrillas known as Cacos used drums both as a means of communication and as a form of psychological warfare against the occupying forces, whose distress and unease upon hearing the constant drumbeats is itself a trope of occupation-era travelogues about Haiti.[25] Kate Ramsey points out the irony of the marines' simultaneous persecution of ritual drumming in Haiti and their practice of confiscating

An Ethics of Discomfort 19

drums and bringing them back to the United States as exotic trophies.[26] The travel of the drums raises the question, what happens when these terrifying local gods and the "queer sensations" they evoke are removed from the tropics and imported to America? Can the gods grow through concrete as easily as they sprout up in soil, and is the heart of the "modern" American (Black or white) a hospitable enough ground for the demands and machinations of these ancient gods?

Black performance in interwar Harlem explored these very questions. The interwar period saw a flowering of theatrical performances in which African American performers, writers, and choreographers danced the diaspora into being. All under the heading of "African" dance, these performances created their own genre of "African" dance in which African, West Indian, and African American traditions became interchangeable. While the source material of these performances came from a variety of national provenances, they invariably featured drumming and some element of the supernatural or religious themes as framing characteristics of diasporic musical expression. A whole genre of wildly successful "voodoo"-themed plays and operas sprung into being in the 1920s and 1930s, incorporating themes from Occupation-era rumors of zombies, human sacrifice, and possession in Haiti: Eugene O'Neil's *The Emperor Jones* (1920); Em Jo Basshe's *Earth* (1927), Harry Lawrence Freeman's *Voodoo* (1928), Shirley Graham Du Bois's *Tom-Tom* (1932); Clarence Cameron White's *Ouanga!* (1932), Asadata Dafora's *Kyunkor* (1934) and *Bassa Moona* (1936); Orson Welles's Works Progress Administration (WPA) production of a "voodoo" *Macbeth* with an all-Black cast (1936); and William Grant Still's *Troubled Island* (1949), whose libretto was partially written by Langston Hughes.[27] The genre was pioneered by Asadata Dafora, a choreographer of Sierra Leonian origin, who enjoyed a brief period of success as the poster child of this genre of "voodoo" plays. Dafora's popular 1934 opera *Kyunkor, Or The Witch Woman*, was a tom-tom-inflected dance performance depicting a fairy tale set in a rural African village in which lovers are separated and then reunited by the machinations of witches.[28] Dafora was also responsible for the choreography of Orson Welles's WPA stage production of "voodoo" *Macbeth*. Dafora's fingerprints on the two projects—one set in Africa, the other in Haiti—indicate that the common heritage of diasporic traditions is often bridged by a complex though geographically nonspecific symbology. My purpose in detailing these performances and traditions is to show the way in which African American, African, and West Indian dance traditions were deeply coentangled on the stage in interwar America. In other words, any representation of a specific Black culture onstage implicated all Black culture in a complex web of "shared" culture, creating a Pan-African community in the present while laying claim to an African inheritance from the past.

David F. Garcia argues that Dunham, like Dafora, used choreography "to broker cultural understanding—not, however, of Africa, nor for that matter of the origins of American Negro dances, but rather of these dances' universal qualities."[29] As the founder of one of the first African American dance companies, Ballet Nègre, in Chicago in 1930, Katherine Dunham had already been participating in and shaping the interwar fascination with diasporic dance traditions and their ritual importance when she received a Rosenwald Fellowship to conduct fieldwork on Caribbean dances in 1935 as part of her graduate study at University of Chicago. Though she was just twenty-six years old and had yet to achieve her later prominence as a choreographer, she knew well that ritual dance was often the crucible in which African ritual traditions could be both discovered and reinvented. Venturing into a complex field of representation created by the American occupation of Haiti and an interwar interest in the "primitive," Dunham very quickly found that the promise of diasporic solidarity that had led her to leave her Chicago home was not inherent in her relationship with Haitians. This is the beginning of Dunham's lifelong relationship with the island and the beginning of her discomfort with easy notions of kinship and belonging in the African diaspora.

What does it mean for dance to be the initial space of possibility for Dunham's diasporic belonging? The primal scene of diasporic movement is, of course, the forced migration of the Middle Passage and the practice of "dancing the slaves" on slave ships, wherein sick and exhausted men and women in chains brought up from the holds of the slave ship and forced to stretch their stiff limbs by dancing under the shadow of the whip. But, as dance scholar Katrina Hazzard-Gordon states in her eponymous chapter "Dancing under the Lash," dancing has significance in excess of the constraints and coercions responsible for its performance: "For most of the captive Africans, dancing was a cultural vehicle used to mediate between mankind and the deities. African captives on slave vessels attempted to evoke deities who could assist them in revolt and escape. Indeed, they might have attributed their failures to their inability to perform ceremonies properly, with appropriate religious objects and the aid of the entire community."[30] Hazzard-Gordon's conjecture gestures toward an anteriority to dance in bondage: dance in worship. Ritual dance, of course, cannot stand in as an Edenic practice developed in Mother Africa, or as a way of experiencing pleasure unsullied by bondage and community unmarred by ambivalence. However, the stakes of the attempt to reconstitute the elements of ritual dance in the context of New

World performance practices are these: if diasporic movement is an investigation into the way "to perform ceremonies properly," the result may be an ontology that peels back the layers of pain to reveal a more livable form of Blackness.

As Saidiya Hartman reminds us, the act of dancing in the context of slavery was so deeply tied to dehumanizing narratives of happy-go-lucky darkies content in their bondage that Black pleasure is forever haunted by the specter of complicity. However, Hartman does not rule out the possibility of pleasure in dance as a means of redress for "the body broken by the regime of work, the regularity of punishment, the persistence of torture, and the violence of rape and sexual exploitation."[31] The incompletion and impossibility of redress through dance does not invalidate the imperative to dance. Hartman's acknowledgment simply articulates a different but equally salient social utility of dance. Rather than the pleasures of performance constituting a means of redress in and of themselves, they become "an articulation of loss and longing for remedy and reparation."[32] This compelling note on the elegiac power of dance is an unanswered question dangling provocatively at the end of a chapter, forcing us to meditate upon the character of this mourning, of dance's dream deferred, and whether it shrivels or whether it explodes. The surge in interest in "African" dance practices in America in the 1920s and 1930s, however far removed they may be from the African context from which they are professed to originate, is an articulation of the loss of that African context. It is the diasporic person's grappling with the loss of history, the loss of kinship ties, the loss of the very rituals that would enable the diasporic person to conjure and mourn unburied and unmemorialized ancestors. The ethnographic, historical, and artistic explorations of dance as a conduit for Black identity were all part of a symphonic eulogy in a funeral that would never take place.

Katherine Dunham first arrived in Haiti in 1935, just one year after the end of the U.S. occupation. Unlike Hurston, who framed the occupation as the "the beginning of peace," Dunham is constantly and awkwardly reminded of the occupation's violence (and her unwitting complicity in it as an American person) by the Haitian women who form part of her "family" during her initiation into Haitian Vodou. One of these women, Madame Ezméry Dessalines, struggled to support five children, the first two having been "sired by some Marine long since forgotten."[33] Another, Cécile, had a disturbing party trick acquired during the occupation: "With a wide smile, gold teeth gleaming, Cécile would begin with 'Come here you f—g black bitch!' and gaily recite the list of endearing obscenities which constituted her English instructions from the Marines who had solicited her services a few years earlier."[34] Téoline, Dunham's spiritual mother during her initiation, highlights the unfairness that Dunham "should have something better than the others" by, under the guise of spirit possession, demanding that Dunham give her the corduroy skirt she was wearing. Dunham felt "humiliated and betrayed." Though she was assured that "Téoline had no control over her actions and wouldn't remember in a few hours what had happened," there was still "a cobweb of doubt that refused to be swept aside [when she] remembered Téoline fingering [her] skirt, asking about the material and if such a thing could be found in Haiti."[35] Like Dunham's ability to travel halfway around the world at will, the skirt was one of many things that could not be easily accessed by working-class Haitian women like Téoline. Even in a setting in which Vodou initiates are encouraged to think of one another as a family, the friction between Dunham and the Haitian women who constitute her spiritual family reveal that her family members are well aware that she, as an American, is a sibling favored by circumstance.

Far from a sense of comfortable belonging in a shared Afro-diasporic culture, as espoused by the American performance scene she had just left, Dunham's primary affective state at the beginning of her time in Haiti is one of discomfort. Whether she is drinking water from a scum- and tadpole-filled basin in the depths of a bokor's (conjure-man) temple or wearing a ceremonial headkerchief containing a mixture of "feathers, sacrificial food, liqueur, orgeat, [and] blood" for her Vodou initiation, she is constantly in a state of disgust, confusion, and embarrassment.[36] Ironically, even the Vodou *lwa* to whom Dunham is pledged is initially a source of revulsion; despite her marriage to Danbala,[37] a spirit who is represented as a snake, she admits: "I have never overcome a fastidiousness since childhood when near serpents."[38] Perhaps because of some of these emotions, one of her friends chastises her, after a particularly disastrous midnight excursion to the Haitian countryside, for being "thoughtless, obstinate, unkind, inconsiderate, and finally stupid in his estimation, to follow continually this obsession to get to the bottom of things."[39]

Though undoubtedly a part of every anthropologist's experience in the field, these admissions of personal failures are certainly out of place in an ethnography published in 1969, in a genre then dominated by scientific models of objectivity and observation mostly disseminated by white men. While often understated in her text, her moments of unease are always inflected by gender, as when, at her unwillingness to drink from a slime-covered basin in his temple, a sinister bokor in Léogane laughs "like any man might do upon discovering a weakness in a woman who thinks she has it well guarded."[40] In the context of her field research and her writing, Dunham's signs of disgust, confusion, or general lack of ethnographic mastery always bring to the surface cultural assumptions that equate femininity with weakness and irrationality. However, rather than disavowing this uncomfortable position in which she finds herself, Dunham crafts her entire narrative around it. In an effort to create a brand of ethnography that espouses "an essential kindness to humanity," Dunham makes discomfort an ethic.[41] The doubts and crises of authority that Dunham experiences as a woman of color following an unprecedented career path in a field that demands authority and mastery become the foundation of her practice. Dunham embraces discomfort because discomfort is not just something she *does* feel as a woman anthropologist, but something any outsider to a culture *should* feel. If the alternative to discomfort is a false sense of mastery or an easy elision of the power differentials between anthropologists and informants, Dunham both chooses and avows discomfort.

Dunham's discomfort revises and responds to interwar primitivist discourses of a comforting similitude in culture and psyche across the Black diaspora. For Dunham, discomfort becomes the sacrificial price of diasporic knowledge. Dunham comes to Haiti, after all, not just as an anthropologist investigating the ways of foreign peoples but as an African American following her own "awakened and undefined need" for a renewed connection to the lost and lacunar history of the Black Atlantic.[42] At every turn, Dunham refuses to embrace a sense of belonging she does not feel, to sink into the comfort of an oversimplified Afrocentric kinship that ignores language barriers, income disparities, and diverging systems of belief. Dunham comes to Haiti with a number of illusions about the possibilities of diasporic community, all of which she is disabused of by the long and arduous process of *lave tèt*, her initiation into Haitian Vodou. *Lave tèt* means literally "to wash one's head," but in Creole the word *tèt* also includes connotations of selfhood and mental capacities. I would like to propose the alternative translation of "washing one's mind" in preparation for spiritual encounter, in order to account for the process of discovery Dunham undergoes during this ceremony. Rather than cultivating a feeling of acceptance into a given community, as initiations are meant to do, Dunham's *lave tèt* purges her of any illusions about the simplicity and easiness of belonging to a community. Explaining the difficulties of the ceremony, Dunham provides an ironic rejoinder to those who would believe in the possibility of an easy entry into the community of Vodou: "It is conceivable that some Prête savant directly from 'Nan Guinée

[sic], still damp with sacrificial blood from his own temples and scarred with tribal markings and jangling gris-gris from neck to ankle, as is the custom in Africa, could so impart his 'belongingness' that taboos would fall, the way would be immediately opened, and centuries and oceans bridged in moments."[43] Of course, Dunham's tongue-in-cheek remark of "it is conceivable" highlights the ludicrousness of her imaginary "Prête savant." The very notion of an American, even a Black American, gaining easy access to one of the world's most complex belief systems becomes a kind of joke, in Dunham's formulation. And this joke stands in sharp contrast to the rigors of the *lave tèt* ceremony, which (mirroring the Middle Passage) requires her to lie on a dirt floor with her eight Haitian co-initiates for two days straight without moving, finding her eventually "at four in the morning, wearing a nightgown wet by someone else's urine, chilled, disconsolate, feeling none of the promised ecstasy, and no signs of it, alien to gods, people, and land."[44] This experience calls to mind the words of Katherine Dunham's erstwhile administrative assistant Maya Deren, who was inspired by Dunham to pursue her own ethnographic research in Haiti in the 1950s, as she describes in her observations of a ceremony for the ocean spirit Agwe: "What, in such a context, did it mean when, somewhere, someone would state that belief was comfort, that ritual 'released' the 'inhibitions'? Here the serviteur was a worker and his every movement, his every aspect, workmanlike."[45] Dunham's experience in her initiation ceremony illustrates Deren's point that being a part of Afro-diasporic religious traditions is far from effortless, even for those raised in the tradition. As Dunham would learn throughout the decades between her fieldwork and her reflections in *Island Possessed*, initiation was not just a ceremony, but a lifetime of service.

This is not to say that Dunham completely discards the primitivist coalition building that was in vogue during the time of her fieldwork. As I will discuss in the following sections, in *Island Possessed* Dunham seeks to suture together ideologies from the 1930s and later decades without completely discarding the Pan-African dreams of the primitivism of her youth. David Luis-Brown has argued that many Black writers and artists of the interwar period actively moved beyond the pejorative associations of primitivism through "alternative primitivism," which "aspires to utilize its transnational perspective in order to realize antiracist and anticolonialist aims."[46] For instance, one of the most potent and mutable symbols of a shared African heritage was the trope of the drum, known popularly as the tom-tom. In an American context, jazz music is often specifically linked to the ideological legacy of the tom-tom, despite the drum's relatively secondary role in jazz compositions.[47] In fact, there was some serious debate between white artists and intellectuals at the time regarding whether jazz was a fundamentally modern art form or whether it was an ethnographic curiosity not too far removed from the tribal music of Africa, hence the allusions to tom-toms.[48] Either way, this strict dichotomy elides the way in which African musical forms, "modern" as well as "primitive," are part of the same genealogy of critical resistance. As Langston Hughes phrases it, in his seminal 1926 essay "The Negro Artist and the Racial Mountain," African American music forms, specifically jazz, invoke "the eternal tom-tom beating in the Negro soul—the tom-tom of revolt against weariness in a white world, a world of subway trains, and work, work, work; the tom-tom of joy and laughter, and pain swallowed in a smile."[49] Hughes's playful invocation of both the tom-tom and jazz in the same breath invalidates the supposed divide between inheritance and artistry. Hughes constructs the tom-tom's history as an instrument of marronage and resistance and its linkage with jazz as a shared critique of the privations of racial capital. If the "primitives" did what the eternal beat of the tom-tom urged them to do—to dance and make merry and slake their lust indiscriminately with multiple partners—capitalism would surely crumble. Indeed, the beat of African drums—always labeled grandly as "tom-toms"—played a rebellious role in the interwar imaginary.

The tom-tom becomes a way of discussing the crisis of agency that the allure of African American performance comes to represent for white audiences. In Carl Van Vechten's famously sensationalist and exoticist work *Nigger Heaven*, the tom-tom serves as the call for the relinquishment of inhibitions and the reversion to primitive urges. In the climactic final scene of *Nigger Heaven*, in which the educated Black male protagonist is driven to murder in a nightclub, as "the music shivered and broke, crashed and smashed," the frenzied jazz band has an almost hallucinogenic effect, bending the reality of the scene into a confused mixture of Africa and Harlem, of past and present. "Jungle, jumble," writes Van Vechten, "waiters with shields, bearing poisoned wine: waiter-warriors."[50] The jazz band's function here is both historical and prophetic; it has the power not only to remind the cowed and captive "waiters" of a majestic past in which they were warriors but also to encourage them to reclaim the militarism of the past in order to break their present bonds. Van Vechten poses the question himself: "Might it not be possible that prejudice was gradually creating, automatically and unconsciously, a force that would eventually solidify, in outward opinion at least, a mass that might even assume an aggressive attitude?"[51] In the world of *Nigger Heaven*, Van Vechten explores music as the very force that, automatically and unconsciously, creates a cohesive Black proletariat that hurtles toward revolution, toward wholesale slaughter of the whites, toward the spirit of Dessalines which demands severed heads and burnt properties.[52] Even in Harlem, his conflation of tom-toms and jazz suggests, these things could happen.

What the Jungle Knows

Indeed, they did happen. The sudden transformation of a modern cabaret into a primordial jungle was something of a leitmotif in interwar literature, not only among white authors trafficking in primitivist tropes but among Black authors themselves. In her 1928 essay "How It Feels to Be Colored Me," Hurston describes her devolution into the very bacchanalian madness that Seabrook and Van Vechten fetishized, all while dancing in a decidedly modern Harlem nightclub: "I am in the jungle and living in the jungle way. My face is painted red and yellow and my body is painted blue. My pulse is throbbing like a war drum. I want to slaughter something—give pain, give death to what, I do not know."[53] Her unspecified and undirected rage rises to the surface as she reconnects with a desire at once ancestral and oneiric. The "jungle" becomes a psychic space of exploration of all the things that Hurston as a Black woman in 1920s America must repress to get through each day: the financial manipulations of her white patroness, Charlotte Osgood Mason; the weight of whiteness in her chosen career as an anthropologist; the fact that she is trying to have a spiritual experience in a nightclub accompanied by a bored white man rather than in an African religious ceremony. These material conditions, like her rage, are Hurston's generational inheritance, so it is only fitting that the cabaret moment gestures toward an ancestral mood rather than a specific feeling in the present tense.

This primitivist discourse of tom-toms, witch-doctors, and jungles was itself only a mask that pretended knowledge of the maelstrom of desires, practices, and people that went under the guise of Blackness in the interwar period. More than an identity, Blackness in the interwar period was a feeling of dissatisfaction with the status quo. It represents an alternative mode of being to the Western, capitalist, and colonialist ontologies whose credibility had been eroded by the Great War, the stock market crash, and the rise of fascism. In the words of Claude McKay, "If the Negro had to be defined, there was every reason to define him as a challenge rather than as a 'problem' to Western civilization."[54] A far cry from W. E. B. Du Bois's 1902 formulation "How does it feel to be a problem?," the interwar period produced the idea that perhaps a universal African ontology could be the antidote rather than the problem.[55] This is the promise of entering the jungle: that among the vines and creepers and poisonous flowers, Black persons can shed the psychic baggage of modernity to find their true selves before poverty, before indignation, before alienation, before "the problem." Clearly, the spirit was willing but the flesh was weak, as the metaphorical psychic jungle was a much less terrifying prospect than the actual phenomenon of spirit possession that these jungle musings mimic but do not replicate.

Dunham views the phenomenon of spirit possession as a constant source of anxiety and embarrassment throughout her first visit to Haiti. She admits that after her "'marriage' to Danbala," she "longed for some indication, some inkling of possession," a sentiment that, retrospectively, she "can now observe with some pity, even amusement."[56] Possession, in Dunham's youthful conception of the practice, is the ultimate marker of belonging. Her possession by Danbala would proclaim, both to observers and to herself, the authenticity of her belief in Vodou—the assumption being, of course, that possession is such a spectacular and nonconsensual display of belief that it could not possibly be feigned, and standing in direct contrast to Karen McCarthy Brown's conception of Vodou "possession-performance," which Brown uses "not to indicate that possession is playacting but to emphasize the theatrical quality of visits from the Vodou spirits."[57] Through possession, Dunham seeks clarity: "What part of me lived on the floor of the houngfor [temple], felt awareness seeping from the earth and people and things around me, and what part stood to one side taking notes?"[58] Possession would make her into the believer rather than the scientist in this formulation and would put to rest all those unsettling fears about whether or not she really "belonged." But she fears the relinquishment of self that possession would entail, wondering "what sort of spectacle I would make of myself if by chance possessed, what would be thought of me if I weren't."[59] Torn between the call of her estranged diasporic kin and her Western education, between a country that did not love her and a past she could not access, there was no clear path for Dunham.

The dilemma is also narrated in Nella Larsen's 1928 novel, *Quicksand*, demonstrating how the jungle trope was a psychic as well as a geographic dilemma. *Quicksand* is a protofeminist exploration of both the pitfalls and the promise of atavistic narratives of a universal Black psyche. In this novel, Larsen's restless mixed-race heroine Helga Crane hopscotches from an all-Black southern school to her native Chicago to Harlem to her mother's native Denmark and back to Harlem and then to an unnamed rural southern town, all in a futile search for belonging. Nella Larsen's critique is inextricable from the tenuousness of her Blackness and, indeed, the tenuousness of Blackness as a category in the 1920s and 1930s. As Larsen was the daughter of a working-class white Danish immigrant and a Black immigrant from the Danish West Indies (now the U.S. Virgin Islands), her life was marked by her inability to fully integrate into either Black or white society. In his critique of Larsen's earlier biographers, George Hutchinson debunks Larsen's posthumous reputation as a self-hating Black woman who "played up her Danish roots to gain status." Hutchinson argues that this figuration of Larsen is based on the essentialist presupposition that "psychic health . . . requires the child to develop a normative black racial identity, assimilating 'realistically' to the law of the color line."[60] She can be both Black and Danish, and also neither. Similarly, Hazel Carby argues compellingly for the complexity of Larsen's vision in *Quicksand*, in which the semiautobiographical heroine does not fit comfortably within rigid matrices of race, class, and gender, thus allowing her to critique, on the one hand, the hypocrisies of Black middle-class respectability politics, and on the other, a Black cultural politics that "glorified a limited vision, a vision which in its romantic evocation of the rural and the folk avoids some of the most crucial and urgent issues of cultural struggle."[61]

Like Dunham, Larsen was a figure of compromised authenticity, unable to enjoy the purported pleasures of a universalized Black psyche. In another notable jungle/cabaret scene, Helga Crane has a transcendent experience in a Harlem nightclub:

> For a while, Helga was oblivious of the reek of flesh, smoke, and alcohol, oblivious of the oblivion of other gyrating pairs, oblivious of the color, the noise, and the grand distorted childishness of it all. She was drugged, lifted, sustained, by the extraordinary music, blown out, ripped out, beaten out, by the joyous wild, murky orchestra. The essence of life seemed in bodily motion. And when suddenly the music died, she dragged herself back to the present with a conscious effort; and a shameful certainty that not only had she been in the jungle, but that she had enjoyed it, began to taunt her. She hardened her determination to get away. She wasn't, she told herself, a jungle creature.[62]

Helga's rejection of her "jungle" impulse should not be read as a rejection of Black community. Helga's self-fashioning throughout the novel is as much rooted in her occasional unconscious lapses into the beckoning arms of community as it is in a disavowal of kinship. Her constant emphasis on the fact that she has no family and no "people" stands in contradiction to the sentiment that she feels "as though she were shut up, boxed up, with hundreds of her race."⁶³ This middle passage metaphor of kinship—of strangers rather than family hemming the borders of one's subjectivity—is one in which a common Afro-diasporic destiny takes precedence over individual differences in language, class, and origin. Larsen constructs as tragic Helga's inability to see this kinship as anything other than a constraint, when occasionally (as in the jungle) the kinship erupts in unruly communion.

Notably, the jungle motif seems to appear most commonly in 1920s texts by Black women and queer Black men as a way to express socially unacceptable erotic desire. In addition to the jungle scenes by Hurston and Larsen, it also makes an appearance in the novels of Claude McKay and in Countee Cullen's magisterial 1925 poem, "Heritage." In "Heritage," Cullen links his closeted desires to an "African" jungle impulse whose "primal measures drip / Through my body, crying, "Strip!"⁶⁴ Reflecting the experience of Blackness in the Americas, these erotic characterizations of the jungle/dance floor express an African inheritance that manifests, not as a simple love of music and dance, but as a mess of heady and conflicting desires. A space where Blackness is not an essentialized common origin, but a meeting of identity's broken shards. For instance, on the heels of Helga's ecstatic experience on the dance floor in *Quicksand*, she feels shame in the possibility that she may be a jungle creature, as she observes the other denizens of the jungle, all united on the dance floor:

> For the hundredth time she marveled at the gradations within this oppressed race of hers. A dozen shades slid by. There was sooty black, shiny black, taupe, mahogany, bronze, copper, gold orange, yellow, peach, ivory, pinky white, pastry white. There was yellow hair, brown hair, black hair; straight hair, straightened hair, curly hair, crinkly hair, wooly hair. She saw black eyes in white faces, brown eyes in yellow faces, gray eyes in brown faces, blue eyes in tan faces. Africa, Europe, perhaps with a pinch of Asia, in a fantastic motley of ugliness and beauty, semi-barbaric, sophisticated, exotic, were here. But *she was blind to its charm* [emphasis added], purposely aloof and a little contemptuous and soon her interest in the moving mosaic waned.⁶⁵

Violent and complex histories of colonialism, rape, and migration are written on the varied Black bodies of this Harlem jungle. The sensual pleasure in this litany of their colors and textures is not unlike the pleasure Helga takes in her wardrobe. However, unlike the scenes in which Helga chooses to adorn herself in sumptuous fabrics, Helga is "blind" to the way in which she might put on the beauty of this assortment of moving colors; in other words, she refuses to identify with and thus become part of this particular community. It is the omniscient narrator who must interject her voice to alert the reader to a reality outside of Helga's realm of perception: that the elusive happiness for which she longs throughout the novel is right here on the dance floor. But because of the middle-class respectability injunctions that Helga critiques but cannot escape, Helga's pleasure in ambiguous and nonnormative presentations of Blackness is represented as a socially inappropriate desire that rises irrepressibly to the surface when her inhibitions are lowered. In other words, Helga is not dissimilar to Dunham in her inability to succumb to the vulnerability that embodied community requires.

In *Quicksand*'s infamous ending, Helga Crane (improbably, according to the novel's critics) abandons her cosmopolitan lifestyle to marry a repugnant southern pastor she meets at a nightmarish church revival. What Helga embraces at the revivalist meeting and in her subsequent marriage to the Reverend Mr. Pleasant Green is "the regaining of simple happiness, a happiness unburdened by the complexities of the lives she had known."[66] Her acceptance of this simple happiness serves as a foil to her disavowal of the pleasures of the jungle in the Harlem nightclub scene earlier in the novel. This acceptance comes in spite of her initial terror and repugnance at the scene of the revival, which she initially finds "foul, vile, and terrible, with its mixture of breaths, its contact of bodies, its concerted convulsions, all in a wild appeal for a single soul. Her soul."[67] The loss of self that Helga experiences at the revival prompts a tragic spiral into the reproductive nightmare at the end of the novel.

In the revival scene, Larsen links the respectability politics of marriage and reproduction with the quest for the "holiness of far-off simpler centuries" epitomized by reclamation efforts of an Edenic pre-diasporic Africa.[68] This scene stands in direct contrast to the "moving mosaic" of the dance floor, which is a celebration of opacity and difference, a proclamation that no century has ever been simpler. The moving mosaic catches uncertainty in its embrace by giving lie to the notions of an authentic, monolithic Blackness. The sinister quality of the revival scene and its grotesque representations of "the writhings and weepings" of the congregation comes from its greediness, its demand for conformity with one version of Blackness.[69] When Helga enters the room, her difference causes turmoil among the worshippers: "At the sight of the bare arms and neck growing out of the clinging red dress, a shudder shook the swaying man on her right. On the face of the dancing woman before her, a frown gathered. She shrieked: "A scarlet 'oman. Come to Jesus, you pore los' Jezebel!"[70] In this context, Helga's difference is something to be feared rather than incorporated. The true tragedy of Helga's capitulation to the will of the congregation rather than to the will of the "joyous, wild, murky orchestra" of the nightclub is the congregation's demand for her sameness rather than for her difference. The "moving mosaic" of the nightclub makes no such demands and allows her to experience her Blackness as multiple and complicated, outside the realm of biological prescriptions and reproductive injunctions. The colors of the jungle/dance floor—a space of love without respectability, sex without reproduction, and belonging without permanence—remains the only place in the novel where Helga's difference was appreciated.

If Larsen's novel is a cautionary tale of the dangers of believing in a monolithic Blackness, with glimmers of hope sparkling on the dance floor, Dunham's memoir is ultimately a roadmap through it. Like the experiences of Larsen, who writes of her fictional dance scene that "the essence of life seemed in bodily motion," Dunham's experiences with ritual dance become creolized spaces that allow multiple versions of Blackness to coexist and intermingle. Dunham uses dance to rework the uncompromising line she drew in her youth between sincere yet embarrassing possession and rational yet cold scientific observation. Ultimately she reconciles herself with her position "on a fringe border of belief and non-belief, because the two are so close."[71] Dancing becomes the way Dunham resolves this tension. In one of her greatest moments of ethnographic unease during her first trip to Haiti, she claims that her "dancing ha[s] saved [her] from disgrace."[72] Unable to feign possession by Danbala by eating the sacrificial offering of raw egg and flour, lying on the floor crying with bits of flour and egg plastered to her face, Dunham fears that the community will reject her difference. But she rises from the floor and begins to dance: "I danced out all my anger and unknown things and at myself for trying to know them, frustration at the rotten egg and weariness and strange mores."[73] At the end of the dance, she realizes everyone is looking at her with "affection and encouragement."[74] In this particular instance, the alternative to possession is not aloofness; the alternative to possession is itself a kind of spiritual transcendence. It is the kind of transcendence she longed for and did not achieve during her *lave tèt* ceremony: "The sheer joy of motion in concert, of harmony with self and others and the houngfor and Damballa and with all my friends and enemies past present and future."[75] Who can say that this "sheer joy of motion" that Dunham experiences in dance is different, not the same possession that she has observed in others? After all, ritual dance is an act that invites possession; the *yanvalou*, Dunham's favorite dance, is a dance meant to invoke and call Danbala into ceremony. Dancing complicates the notion that belief is a self-annihilating process inimical to the being of the rational anthropologist observer, as dancing cannot be characterized as either completely secular or completely religious in this context. Dunham's dance allows her to exist in the borderland between belief and disbelief, between belonging and unbelonging, between surrender and self-discovery; it allows her to revel in her liminal position.

This lesson is further solidified while Dunham is on tour in Rome in 1954, where she is "possessed of and carried out a thoroughly childish impulse" to light a candle in a cathedral for Legba instead of a Catholic saint. The word "possessed" is employed semi-ironically, indicating neither complete belief nor complete skepticism, as she sardonically catalogues the contrast of "hallowed soft-toned stained windows" and the "pious incantations" of the surrounding worshippers. Meanwhile, she speaks secretly to Legba in Haitian Creole, "to test the presence of certain beliefs in [her]self over and against superstition."[76] It is an act of fidelity to the *lwa* to pray to them in a place of worship of a religion that has at various points demonized and delegitimized them, to pray to the *lwa* in the presence of a god that demands worshippers abandon all other gods, and to pray to these dark gods and come away unscathed. In doing so, Dunham follows a long tradition of Vodou practitioners who are also Catholic and do not find the two forms of worship incompatible, but complementary parts of a creolized theological landscape that includes the spirits of colonizers as well as the spirits of the oppressed, a landscape where there is no possible return to a past in which African religious traditions are unentangled with European ones. It is no accident that Dunham prays in this moment to Legba, the spirit of the crossroads who has often been mischaracterized by Christians as a demonic figure; like him and the religious tradition to which he belongs, Dunham is pinioned between worlds but thence powerful.

In Dunham's thought, being at the crossroads of diaspora requires complex and embodied processes of cleansing and exorcism. Putting this into practice, when she buys the former plantation (and site of numerous revolutionary-era atrocities) of Habitation Leclerc as her Haitian place of residence in 1951, Dunham says, matter-of-factly, "I knew that there must be an exorcising."[77] Despite its supposed curse of eternal unease upon its owner—"The master of Leclerc will never be happy," she is told, multiple times—Dunham insists upon occupying this space of ghosts.[78] Although she admits that indeed "the mistress of Leclerc was not happy," Dunham remains obstinate in her desire to live there.[79] Dunham's continued residence at Habitation Leclerc and her general woes, attributed to the ghosts of tortured slaves, stem from a sense of responsibility to the ghosts themselves, one of whom appears to her as "a man, black, bare to the waist, hands tied behind his back, wearing only ragged trousers, kneel[ing] in the doorway and plead[ing] for help."[80] In order to exorcise Habitation Leclerc, Dunham calls on her friend Kam, an older and respected *mambo* who served as her mentor throughout Dunham's time in Haiti. Kam's exorcism of Dunham's home is completely devoid of magical pyrotechnics or visible manifestations of demonic struggle; rather, Kam spends much of her time sitting with closed eyes while "through her body were passing many evils, and she was sending them far out into the sea."[81] Kam's actions constitute a kind of methodology that Dunham seeks to emulate in the staging of her dancing, writing, and research. In her ethnographic research, Dunham uses her own body as a staging place for the evils of the slave trade to pass through in order to be spirited away. Hers are smaller, more interpersonal evils, but evils nonetheless: the drastic income and power disparities between peoples of color, patriarchal structures that both demand feminized labor and deny its importance, and all daily moments of cultural incomprehension and faux-pas that occur among any people trying to form a community in spite of language barriers and cultural differences.

After the Dance, the Drum Is Always Heavy: Dunham's "Record of Unevenness"

Throughout her decades of scholarship, dance, and travel, Dunham must carry the burden of her increased awareness of the fractures and prohibitions of diaspora. Her journey from blithe tourist to world-weary traveler is perfectly encapsulated in the Haitian proverb "After the dance, the drum is always heavy": after a good time, it is always tiresome to resume one's responsibilities.[82] In the surprising medium of a list of tips for cruise travelers, originally published in *Travel Magazine* in 1964, Dunham speaks of travel as "a time of unspoken obligation to know more, to return to suburbia better informed."[83] Charged with a sense of transnational duty, the retrospective Pan-Africanism that Dunham layers onto her experiences in *Island Possessed* becomes richer and more nuanced. Dunham admits upon one of her return trips to Haiti during the Duvalier regime, "They live there all year round. I for my part, felt sad and sick at the increased poverty, distressed at the lost melody of a wide eyed scholar."[84] Here, Dunham's longing for a diasporic community dissolves into despair at the material realities that keep diasporic communities mired in difference and contradiction. The Duvalier regime lends a dark filter to her retrospective lens. In *Island Possessed*, she contrasts the 1936 Mardi Gras celebrations in Pont Beudet, the town where her friend Stanley Reser ran a psychiatric clinic, with the 1962 Mardi Gras in Port-au-Prince, five years into François Duvalier's infamous regime.[85] The 1962 celebration is haunted by Duvalier's militiamen harassing civilians, and by the image of Duvalier himself—"Over it all the badly installed, unflattering portrait of 'Papa Doc' traced in electric bulbs winked and blinked," overshadowing the "meagerly draped floats."[86] Visually, this is a far cry from Dunham's 1936 film footage, which depicts elaborately designed papier-maché floats and dancers in immaculate white twisting their legs artfully to the beat of Reser's drum.[87] Dunham was deeply charmed by her participant role in the 1936 Mardi Gras: "I too was drawn into it. All of the things that you have ever been curious about + suppressed, dreamed of but not thought of—wished without being conscious of wishing. These you do know and find that your neighbor too has been wanting to do them." The queer valences of these closeted desires are even made explicit, though abstractly posed as a rhetorical question: "Can we say that the sex stimulation of two of the same sex is homosexuality, or is it merely a levelling [sic] down of all equations to a pure and simple sex, with neither man nor woman predominant?"[88]

Haiti of 1936 is, for Dunham, a space of endless ludic possibility, while Haiti of 1962 is a space of oppression and constraint. Dunham's sense of hurt is not just for the ways Duvalier's regime had changed Haitian life, but the way that she herself has changed. In the intervening decades, the possibility of knowing the great round world of diaspora is shattered into narrow localities. The idealistic dreams of the possibilities of diasporic connection become the more circumspect and drudging tasks of evaluating one's privilege, relinquishing fantasies of wholeness, and settling down to a life in which the only certainty is the understanding that no understanding will ever be enough. As Dunham posits, "The list of suggestions, cautions, advice, even rules governing getting the utmost from excursions into strange territories, grows as you increase in sensitivity and interest."[89] Unfortunately, the ignorance of rules that allowed the relatively anonymous young Dunham to engage in freewheeling public queerness had dissolved by the 1960s into a knowledge that prevented Dunham the international celebrity from doing the same under the watchful eyes of Papa Doc.

It is only after many years of discomfort and many lessons in diasporic complexity that Dunham finally feels a call to the African continent. As

Joanna Dee Das argues, "Dunham's perspective on Haiti as the keeper of the flame of blackness would profoundly influence her decision to visit sub-Saharan Africa until 1962."[90] It is no accident that Dunham was living in Senegal during the writing of *Island Possessed* in the 1960s. Far from being an idealized space of unity and primordial simplicity, Africa becomes a perspective that allows her to comprehend the nuances and differences of diaspora. The older Dunham, looking backward from Africa, is able to conceptualize the heterogeneity of belonging and dwell in its contradictions as an imperative to discover diasporic difference rather than despair in it. Haiti was only a small part of the mosaic of diasporic realities that youthful Dunham had sought to catch in her embrace after her 1930s fieldwork. An ever-present yet underresearched aspect of Dunham's spiritual landscape is her relationship with the orishas of Yoruba cosmology, funneled specifically through her interest in Cuba and Brazil. Her 1950 trip to Brazil famously involves the cancellation of her stay by the racist hotel managers at La Esplanada in São Paolo.[91] Outside of Rio de Janeiro, however, Dunham has another distasteful Brazilian experience: a candomblé ceremony at the temple of a priestess named Tia Lucia. Dunham seems put off by the "throat slitting, head severing, evisceration of animals" required by the ritual sacrifice of the ceremony, and she concludes, "Because I have never known in depth the Brazilian gods they remain *to me* alien, enigmatic, cruel and over exigent."[92] This crucial "to me" was inserted as an editing mark, indicating the Dunham was not unaware of her cursory knowledge of candomblé and her inability to make a value judgment based on one ritual.

Dunham's relationship with Afro-Cuban spirituality is slightly more extensive but equally vexed. According to the santera/scholar Marta Moreno Vega, Dunham visited Cuba in 1938, but this trip is not detailed in Dunham's archives or in any other scholarship about her.[93] Dunham's relationship to Cuba appeared to have been mediated mostly by three figures: the drummers Julio Mendoza and La Rosa Estrada and a New York–based santera called Rosita.[94] Dunham was so close to Rosita that she almost called *Island Possessed*, *Letter from Rosita*, after a scolding letter Rosita had sent her during its writing.[95] Rosita's letter, written in Spanish, is included in Dunham's archives along with the first draft of *Island Possessed*: "All of your affairs are backwards. You don't like to listen to advice. You use your head the way you want to use it. This isn't good for you. You have to listen. You go along like a train without stopping. This isn't good for you. You like to play with things that aren't good for you. . . . You boast about your head but your head is lost."[96] Rosita goes on to tell Dunham to give a kiss to Oggun, to break eggs in the street for Eleggua, and that she is a child of Ochun.[97] Rosita wants Dunham to placate the orishas because she is deeply worried that Dunham is mixing volatile spiritual traditions, that she is serving too many gods to serve any of them well. The inclusion of this rather damning letter suggests that the impetus for *Island Possessed* was more to showcase Dunham's confusion and culpability than it was about any kind of mastery or growth. While most of Dunham's relationship with Rosita and her sense of discomfort with the orishas were ultimately excised from the published version of *Island Possessed*, Rosita's concerns remain as the shadow text to *Island Possessed*. In the published version, Dunham writes that Rosita expresses concern that Dunham is "trafficking with African gods" while living in Senegal, to which Dunham's glib response is that it is "all the same thing." Surely, after nearly 300 pages of disaggregating diasporic connections and thirty years of serving the *lwa*, Dunham cannot possibly believe that all the spirits of the African diaspora are the same? But she tempers her response by citing her hope to study the Cuban spirits so that she can one day "bring some reconciliation into these wandering, jealous siblings of different nations but of the same ancestors."[98] After the many blows her research delivered to the notion of diasporic wholeness, Dunham in her sixties still held the lofty goal of laying to rest the "interpantheon jealousy" of the spirits of Africa and its diaspora.[99] Which, perhaps, is the same thing as laying to rest that same thing that caused the jealousy between herself and Hurston: the false equivalencies of diaspora, its tragic misunderstandings, the rotten tooth of antagonisms. Dunham's experiences in other countries, far from being irreconcilable with her love for Haiti and the *lwa*, are an integral part of her diasporic vision. The fact that these forays into other cultural contexts never took on the depth and seriousness of her commitment to Haiti does not mean that her vision was wrong; it just means that her vision was honest.

Take as another example the uncomfortable fact that following the 1951 exorcism of Leclerc, Dunham turned the spiritually cleansed site into a luxury resort ten years later. As Dee Das notes, Dunham's ownership of Habitation Leclerc began with an act of imperialism, enabled by a law imposed by the U.S. occupation allowing foreign land ownership in Haiti.[100] Until the 1980s, Dunham presided over swimming pools and cocktails and putatively authentic Vodou ceremonies on Leclerc and adjacent properties. One 1970s advertisement for Habitation Leclerc read, "In the colonial tropics, Habitation Leclerc, once Residence of Pauline Bonaparte reconstructed by John Pratt and Katherine Dunham, offers apartments decorated in the style of the Empire with the added attraction of modern conveniences."[101] Gone is the history of colonial brutality and the Black women's labor of laying unquiet spirits to rest. The exorcised history becomes a quaint architectural legacy, and the exorcism itself becomes a tool make the land fit for capitalist incorporation. And although Dunham cannot take complete responsibility for Habitation Leclerc's marketing, since she leased the property to a French real estate developer in 1972, Dee Das argues that it permanently influenced her reputation in Haiti: "For many Haitians today, this is the Dunham they remember: mysterious, closed off, and catering exclusively to Europeans and Americans."[102] However, in 1992, at eighty-two years of age, Dunham went on a forty-seven-day hunger-strike in protest of the George H. W. Bush government's policy of refusing Haitian refugees fleeing political instability in Haiti. Though it did not change the official government stance toward Haitian refugees, hers was a highly visible effort that succeeded in raising awareness about the unfair treatment and stigmatization of Haitian immigrants that had been a problem since the onset of the AIDS crisis. Dunham's hunger strike, in addition to seriously putting her health in jeopardy, also came at a time of financial instability that left her struggling to pay her medical bills incurred because of the hunger strike.[103] Taken together — the exploitative colonial nostalgia of Habitation Leclerc's 1970s marketing and her 1992 hunger strike — Dunham's Haitian activities illustrate what Dee Das terms as her "record of unevenness."[104] Dunham's life continues to stand as testament to the notion that diaspora itself is uneven in its privileges and experiences. Today, all that remains of the formerly grand Habitation Leclerc, which was mostly destroyed in the 2010 earthquake, is the center pole of Dunham's temple, a thick wooden pillar with the ghost of a green snake etched up its length. A center pole, called the *poto mitan*, occupies a central spatial and spiritual position in every Vodou temple: it is the physical object through which the spirits enter the space.[105] Perhaps Dunham's project was necessarily incomplete, but the spirits have seen fit to leave the *poto mitan* standing as a monument not to Dunham's success but to the grandeur of her goals, and as a gateway for them to return should she ever try again.

Dunham tried to have it all — discomfort *and* belonging, universalism *and* nuance. This is why she argues that "one can, with good fortune and great care serve a number of loves and more than one master[,] I know, and the tranquility with which they live under the same roof depends in no small degree on the love and attention we ourselves feel for these separate drives."[106] This overextension to a variety of spiritual traditions, though it is precisely what Rosita counseled her against, is what fueled many of Dunham's moments of diasporic connection as well as some of her most glaring inconsistencies. Ultimately, *Island Possessed* is a reformulation of the problem of diasporic community building, not its cure. Dunham's informants assure her, "Anyone issuing from anyone remotely joined in kinship with 'Nan Guinée, from Africa, is potentially 'vaudun.' If they do not practice it, it is because of ignorance, and those of us black people carried from Africa to other parts of the world, especially to the United States, are known to be in total ignorance of many truths."[107] Throughout her time in Haiti, Dunham's informants express admiration for her commitments to their religion, telling her, "It was important that I carry the meaning of the true vaudun to my people in that other country [the United States]."[108] Dunham's text does so, though not in the form of "songs and litanies and instructions" her "well-meaning informants" intended.[109] In *Island Possessed*, Dunham does not bring back the key to a diasporic belonging that would suture the wounds of the Middle Passage. Rather, she brings back a deeper knowledge about "blackness in the sense of spirit, a charismatic intangible."[110]

This knowledge is not an empty comfort, but "of utmost importance to the cult [of Vodou] itself."[111] Vodou itself constantly troubles and frustrates any attempt to draw a distinction between ancestral impulses and contemporary Black desires. Thinking through the lens of Vodou is a particular way of relating to the opacity of history and the crisis of filiation in Black culture; namely, Vodou conjures an Africa whose tenuous factuality makes it no less culturally and spiritually salient. Practitioners of Vodou would not ordinarily refer to themselves as practicing Vodou; they would rather term themselves as servitors of the spirits or devotees of the mysteries of Ginen, the Haitian Creole name for Africa. In Haitian Vodou, *Ginen* also comes to stand in as the geographical location of the afterlife.[112] It is more accurate, therefore, to characterize Vodou as a system of knowledge committed to negotiating ancestral desires without resorting to simplistic narratives of authenticity. It is a New World relationship with a longed-for and lacunar memory of Africa and of less distant relatives crushed in the machinery of racial capital in the Americas. Vodou derives its power not from an ability to offer a simple return to a quasi-fictive origin Edenic Africa, but in its ability to sing a diasporic song in the present. The songs, rituals, and incantations Dunham was supposed to import to the United States, then, are not spells to resurrect a past sense of belonging, but fragile threads of a creolized web being spun in the present, carefully, uncertainly, between Africa and the Americas.

CHAPTER TWO

Girls' Talk

Revolutionary Destinies in Hansberry and Simone

Nina Simone had flowers on her wrists and Lorraine Hansberry on her mind. It was the last song of the night in Simone's performance at Morehouse College in June of 1969, a song "which was given to us to be given to you by Lorraine Hansberry, who has long since left us, and she was my dear friend." Instead of "To Be Young, Gifted, Black," the song she named in honor of Hansberry, she begins to play "Take Me to the Water." It is an old song, a spiritual, a baptismal hymn, but it is new in her hands. Departing from the traditional version, she begins to mold the song in her own image, in that inexorable way that has made her covers famous. Scatting gently between each line, she departs from the traditional lines ("Take me to the water / To be baptized" and "None but the righteous / Shall see God") with which she starts. Playfully, irreverently, she begins to improvise: "And I don't mind if it's turbulent / I don't mind of it's green / I don't mind if it's cum / I don't mind if it's blue / But as long as it's water / Then I feel at home / It soothes me and moves me / It soothes me and moves me / Got to have it / It cools me right down." By the end of her improvisation she is laughing. She abandons her piano and lets the drummers do the work, dancing instead—her arms sinuous, her shoulders bucking, like a dance for a ritual that has yet to be named.[1] Lorraine Hansberry had been dead for four years when Simone invoked her in the Morehouse performance. The two women had shared a brief but potent friendship in the first half of the 1960s, cut short by Hansberry's death in 1965. The Morehouse performance brings up more questions than answers, including, Why is this a fitting tribute for her friend Lorraine Hansberry? Why would Hansberry, a decidedly secular thinker, "give" her friend Simone this spiritual-turned-erotic celebration of water? And why did it necessitate a dance?

The question of spirituality was a primary divergence in the two woman's visions. Simone's posthumous casting of Hansberry as a kind of patron saint, as well as Simone's deep rootedness in Black spiritual traditions, mobilized notions of an afterlife that Hansberry undoubtedly did not believe in. However, their worldviews were not so divergent that they did not share a belief that motivated human beings can, will, and must change the world. One of

Hansberry's characters describes himself as "a fool who believes that death is waste and love is sweet and that the earth turns and men change every day and that rivers run and that people want to be better than they are and that flowers smell good and that I hurt terribly today, and that hurt is desperation and desperation is—energy and energy can move things."[2] Though Hansberry evinces a kind of secular humanism, it is undeniable from her often exalted language about human potentiality that belief is important to her as an act if not as a religious creed. In *Blackpentacostal Breath*, Ashon Crawley makes the argument that despite the homophobia, transphobia, classism, and sexism that exist in Black church spaces as much as in the world around them, there is still futurity in the act of belief. "Belief," Crawley says, "when borne out through certain aesthetic behaviors, is considered to be blackness itself. Whiteness is considered the absence of such purportedly primitivist behaviors, and thus, a lack of belief that moves the flesh."[3] Nina Simone's scripting of herself and her dead friend Lorraine into a religious tradition inhospitable to both of them lays a profane claim to the power of belief beyond human gatekeeping, even for people whose politics, sexualities, and experiences would place them on the fringe of faith communities.

Furthermore, Hansberry's archive reveals a hitherto unexplored interest in Haitian spirituality. As Soyica Diggs Colbert has noted in her intellectual biography of Hansberry, "her unpublished work dwarfs the volume of the work in print. Additionally, much of the unpublished work remains unfinished. To wade in the waters of the Hansberry archive and return with a cohesive narrative requires stitching together details, ideas, lines of thought, and historical contexts that were, for the most part, left undone."[4] To reconstruct Hansberry's ideas about Haiti, as I attempt to do in this chapter, it is necessary to scour her unfinished and unproduced work. In Hansberry's little-known adapted screenplay of the Haitian novel *Masters of the Dew*, which was contracted and then dropped by the production company MO-PIX in 1961, there are tantalizing glimpses into Hansberry's interest in Haiti and her own spiritual temperament. The screenplay includes a Vodou ceremony for the spirit Legba, which Hansberry renders as a processional with women dancers in white and "the pulsing stirring rhythms of the congo ceremonial drums, which are, in turn, punctuated by the clash of cymbals." Hansberry adds a footnote to the script: "The writer has seen this particular dance performed a number of times and it is a thing of beauty in its authentic form. In production it would be a disservice to have it merely approximated but should be, like any other culturally specific allusions in the script, presented only on the basis of authoritative Haitian cultural consultation."[5] Hansberry then suggests the cultural consultation services of Jean-Léon Destiné, a pioneering Haitian dancer who played an integral role in popularizing Haitian folkloric dance in the United States. It is possible that Hansberry's knowledge of the dance came directly from watching Destiné's performances, in which the line between religion and folklore was intentionally blurred for an American audience.[6]

It makes sense that Hansberry would be drawn to Langston Hughes and Mercer Cook's 1947 translation of Jacques Roumain's novel, which includes many of the hallmarks of Hansberry's dramatic interests: Marxism, charismatic Black male leadership, and a historical and cultural setting far removed from her own. Like Hansberry, Jacques Roumain's Marxism makes him a materialist, and his original novel portrays Vodou with some ambivalence.[7] The protagonist, Manuel, is a Haitian worker radicalized by his time in Cuba, and when he returns to Haiti, he is saddened by his community's feeling of impotence before the whims of the *lwa*. In Roumain's original description of the Vodou ceremony, he espouses a familiar "opiate of the masses" stance regarding Haitian religion: "The peasants forgot their troubles. Dancing and drinking anesthetized them—swept away their shipwrecked souls to drown in those regions of unreality and danger where the fierce forces of the African gods lay in wait."[8] In Hansberry's screenplay, her own, similar ambivalence about spirituality is a palimpsest to her descriptions of Manuel's dilemma: "His thoughts are cut by his active contempt for the thought that the "supernatural" affect the destiny of material world. He had been out in that world for years and has come to believe that virtually everything which transforms the world of man is done by the hand and not the prayer of man. At the same time, he is of the flesh and spirit of these people, and knows a great love for them. His mothers [sic] face dances close to him." Eventually, in Hansberry's version, Manuel begins to dance, "slowly, almost thoughtfully at first; having very much the same experience he had with the first taste of a native mango. He begins to dance more and more energetically, throwing himself into it finally."[9] Hansberry's vivid description of Manuel's thought process—giving into the power of the dance out of love for his mother and his people—is much more detailed than in the original novel. Despite the fact that both Roumain's and Hansberry's Manuel ultimately disavows the influence of the spirits as "monkeyshine," for Hansberry, the allure of the people's embodied spirituality remains sweet and tempting as a bruised Haitian mango she cannot bring herself to discard.[10]

A careful attention to Hansberry's Haitian writings reveals the symbiotic lines of influence between Hansberry and Simone. Their friendship, according to Simone's narration, was instrumental to Simone's coming to consciousness as a revolutionary. The two women "never talked about men or clothes or other such inconsequential things when [they] got together. It was always Marx, Lenin and revolution—real girls' talk."[11] Though there is no such effusive record of Hansberry's thoughts on their friendship, Hansberry's turn to music and spirituality in some of her unpublished and unfinished work shows that as Hansberry was radicalizing Simone, Simone was also pressing Hansberry to consider the revolutionary power of music and dance. Hansberry, after all, initially conceived of her unpublished Haitian revolutionary drama, *Toussaint*, as a "Musical Drama in 7 scenes" with multiple songs and dance sequences.[12] Impulsive where Hansberry is methodical, spiritual where Hansberry is secular, emotional where Hansberry is restrained, Simone at first glance seems like an unlikely protégée of Hansberry. But both women, in their way, believed that it was possible to change the world now— and not just in the feel-good, amorphous sense that the word "revolution" has come to take on, but in the sense of a tangible change in regime and ideology. Revolution was necessitated not just by their Blackness riding the tide of 1950s and 1960s Black liberation, but by their covert queerness. As queer Black women, they shared a revolutionary sensibility that demanded change beyond integration and assimilation.

Hansberry has left behind clear written traces of her queerness, well excavated and documented by the scholarly work of Kevin Mumford, Imani Perry, and Soyica Diggs Colbert.[13] Simone's archive is more tenuous—she is frequently cited as a "bisexual" historical figure, but she never publicly used this term to describe herself and she never released any songs or autobiographical materials about the subject. In the 2015 documentary *The Amazing Nina Simone*, her brother Sam Waymon corroborates that Simone had relationships with women as early as the 1950s. This documentary also reveals that in the 1970s she was briefly in a relationship with Marie-Christine Dunham Pratt, Katherine Dunham's only child.[14] Although I do not argue that the relationship between Simone and Hansberry was anything other than a friendship, I do argue that their queerness was something they shared, and that their sense of their own non-normativity drew their revolutionary visions away from American gradualism and toward anticolonial revolution in Africa and the Caribbean.

In an interview the day after the Morehouse performance, the interviewer asked Simone why she had danced. She replied, "When I get moved onstage, moved to a point where I have to get away from the piano and move to the rhythm, what comes out is what you see. Its relationship to Africa is the same as my relationship to Africa: I can't define it. . . . I got very carried away last night. I don't think I've ever done a dance like that before. Except I've seen it done before, where it was almost a thing where you couldn't balance yourself."[15] She compares her dancing to women shouting in the Holy Roller churches where she used to play piano as a child in North Carolina. There are also resonances with African diaspora religions in which the sense of being "tipsy" or off-balance is a sign of coming spirit possession. The spirit of Hansberry puts Simone in a retrospective mood, pulling her back to their time together, back to her own childhood, and even further back to ancestral memories of Haiti and Africa. And this is no coincidence—it was from Hansberry's historically grounded politics that Simone learned that, in the words of Saidiya Hartman, "history is how the secular world attends to the dead."[16] Answering Hansberry's call, Simone's response attends to the dead in her own, spiritual, way. Across time, both women share an interest in the deep past of the Black experience, and mine this past for its spiritual and sexual potential in the present.

A Woman Called Destiny: Lesbianism in Lorraine Hansberry's Works

In her later plays, Hansberry is known for an idealism that sometimes borders on the didactic. Julius Lester, in his introduction to the edited collection of Hansberry's last plays, says that her short play *What Use Are Flowers?*—about a crusty former university professor who teaches a group of feral children to appreciate art after the apocalypse—"is not a good play." The play's staging of the feral children learning language and gender roles and eventually singing a choral arrangement of "Ode to Joy" can seem like a contrived and moralizing vision of the human desire for art and beauty. As Lester also notes, however, Hansberry's zealous defense of revolutionary art, quaint though it may seem in retrospect, is an attitude of engagement that formed a stark contrast to the political disengagement of some of her peers, former Communists who had been burned by McCarthyism and the various repressions of the 1950s. Lester holds that "while *What Use Are Flowers?* is a momentary failure of craft, it is not a failure of vision."[17]

Despite the persecution of the 1950s that marked her too-short adult life, Hansberry remained clear-eyed and committed to art in the service of revolution—by no means a universal standpoint among her contemporaries. In her play *The Sign in Sidney Brustein's Window*, Hansberry tries to exhort the white intellectuals of the play—who stand in for her friends, lovers, neighbors, and interlocutors in Greenwich Village, where she lived at the time—to shed their political cowardice disguised as apathy. *The Sign in Sidney Brustein's Window* portrays the stagnation of the Western intellectual through the plight of a gay man, an existentialist playwright named David. Although David, like most of the play's characters, is white, his paradox rings true. Sidney, the titular character and himself a Greenwich village intellectual, exhorts David: "David, you have now written fourteen plays about not caring, about the isolation of the soul of man, the alienation of the human spirit, the desolation of all love, all possible communication. When what you really want to say is that you are ravaged by a society that will not sanctify your particular sexuality!" When David protests that he, as a gay man, is not the one Sidney should be critiquing, Sidney does not relent: "If somebody insults you—sock 'im in the jaw! If you don't like the sex laws, attack 'em, I think they stink! You wanna get up a petition? I'll sign it. Love little fishes if you want! But, David, please get over the notion that your particular 'thing' is something that only the deepest, saddest, most nobly tortured can know about. It ain't—it's just one kind of sex—that's all. And, in my opinion the universe turns regardless."[18] Sidney's words echo the arc of Hansberry's oeuvre, bending toward the idea that mere existence is not resistance in itself, that revolutionary art is necessary. But all this is easy for Sidney to say—he is a white man, and his statement is undergirded by his own failure to take a significant political stand (all he does is place a sign in his window in support of a "progressive" mayoral candidate who he later finds out is corrupt). Hansberry herself is also implicated in this nexus of action and hesitation—while outspoken on civil rights and anti-imperialism, her statements on gay rights were comparatively oblique, with none of the ease and bravado of Sidney Brustein's uninvested freedom. What does it mean to make revolutionary art with skin in the game?

In an essay publicizing *The Sign in Sidney Brustein's Window*, Hansberry characterizes her political moment as a time of bad faith aestheticism and moral bankruptcy among the American intelligentsia: "By the 1960's few enough American intellectuals had it within them to be ashamed that their discovery of the 'betrayal' of the Cuban Revolution by Castro just happened to coincide with the change of heart of official American government policy."[19] Her callout of the moral bankruptcy of white liberalism would be noteworthy even today. For her part, Hansberry, like her mentors W. E. B. Du Bois and Paul Robeson, had her passport revoked for her Communist sympathies. The FBI began surveilling her as early as 1952, when she attended a conference in Uruguay deemed subversive by the U.S. State Department.[20]

No one knew better than Hansberry the daily violence of McCarthy-era politics for one deemed politically or personally deviant. As early as 1950, Republican senator Kenneth Wherry told the American public that it was impossible to "separate homosexuals from subversives" and that it was necessary to protect "seaports and cities" against the "conspiracy of subversives and moral perverts."[21] In her study of lesbian life in twentieth-century America, Lillian Faderman argues, "If political conformity was essential to national security, sexual conformity came to be considered, by some mystifying twist of logic by those in authority, as no less essential."[22] Scholars have noted the way that "Communist" and "queer" became interchangeable terms of deviance in the Cold War fearmongering of the 1950s, and Hansberry was both.

Hansberry was publicly circumspect about her own sexuality. Although the witch-hunts of the 1950s resulted in higher numbers of arrests and firings of gay men, it also had real social and economic consequences for accused lesbians and created a climate of fear, distrust, and secrecy across all sectors of the queer community. Hansberry, after all, died in 1965, before the outspoken Black lesbianism of her agemate Audre Lorde, or of the generation that came after, which included Barbara Smith and Cheryl Clarke. Though I think the term "closeted" is a false binary that elides the complexity of Hansberry's range of choices regarding her sexuality, she certainly made choices to minimize the risk attending her sexuality, like writing her lesbian short fiction under a pseudonym. Choices like this were in response to the very real risks plaguing homophile publications and the organizations that released them. Just four years before Hansberry published her first story in ONE magazine, its copies were confiscated by the Postmaster General of Los Angeles because a lesbian story was deemed pornographic; and Daughters of Bilitis, in whose publication The Ladder Hansberry published her first admissions of queerness, was being closely monitored by the FBI.[23] When compared with her outspoken support of Black revolutionary causes, her queer politics may seem quite restrained. Even as she was dying of pancreatic cancer, she said to Nina Simone, "I must go down to the south. I've been a revolutionary all my life but I've got to go down there to find out just what kind of revolutionary I am."[24] What kind of Black revolutionary she was is evident from her published plays and her galvanizing presence in Leftist publishing and organizing of the 1950s and 1960s. What kind of queer revolutionary she was less transparent.

Trapped between racist gay liberation and homophobic Black nationalism, Hansberry's Black queerness found an outlet in her interpersonal relationships. She is not remembered for her relationships with other Black women—more famous was her friendship with James Baldwin and for her loving but complicated relationship with Robert Nemiroff, her tireless literary executor and ex-husband, with whom she remained close even after their divorce and her engagement in queer relationships during their marriage. Her plays themselves often center on men and white women; *A Raisin in the Sun* is her only produced play to include Black women characters in significant speaking roles.[25] In *Looking for Lorraine*, Perry speculates, "Maybe it was because Lorraine wanted to do things that were usually reserved for men—write about politics, write grand plays, lecture on street corners, and the like—that she more often cast the heroic in male archetypes."[26] I agree with Perry that Hansberry was hyperconscious of the masculinist contours of her world, and that she often chose mimicry to access it. In the case of *The Sign in Sidney Brustein's Window*, Hansberry anticipates reactions to the play's lack of attention to "the Negro question," and explains, "I write plays about various matters which have both Negro and white characters in them, and there is really nothing else that I can think of to say about the matter."[27] This direct evasion of the implications of writing a work featuring predominantly white characters is a complement to Baldwin's famous assertion of his dilemma in writing queerness in *Giovanni's Room*, and why he did not address "the Negro problem": "There was no room for it."[28] In many of Hansberry's plays, Black womanhood is the thing there is no room for.

Cheryl Higashida has called attention to Hansberry's positioning of "lesbian desire as a site for undoing the intertwining of militarization, U.S. Cold War nationalism, and heteropatriarchy" and her grappling with feminist themes in two early, unproduced plays—"Flowers for the General" and "Apples of Autumn," both of which feature troubled white lesbians as characters.[29] Though many of her plays include queer characters and implications, most of Hansberry's explicitly queer content was written under a pseudonym, and rarely featured Black characters consensually engaging in queer intimacy.[30] Despite Hansberry's commitment to humanizing white characters across her oeuvre, there is one dark spot: her representation of interracial queer relationships as complex, sordid, and inextricable from histories of slavery and colonialism. In *Les Blancs*, for example, it is strongly implied that the mixed-race teenager Eric is abused by Willy Dekoven, a white doctor who keeps him well-supplied in alcohol and "women's make-up." In her unpublished play *The Marrow of Tradition*, based on the 1901 novel by Charles Chesnutt, a white male aristocrat disguises himself as an indigent Black woman to flirt with a Black male servant.[31] And in the unpublished play fragment *Toussaint*, Hansberry tells the tale of a slave mistress sexually assaulting an enslaved woman. Perhaps all of these eager white queers and victimized Black bodies are a beard for Hansberry's own complicated desire. Not only was her heterosexual marriage with a white man, but her known lesbian relationships also appeared to be with white women.[32]

The complications of Hansberry's personal life are refracted in her plays and fiction. Perry speculates that "Apart from her pseudonymous fiction, Lorraine didn't spend much time writing about women's beauty. Maybe she worried that it would sound frivolous (or even too feminine) in comparison to the way many of her literary heroes wrote character descriptions. Perhaps she worried that her attentiveness to female beauty might be too revelatory."[33] Another strange element of Hansberry's lesbian fiction, according to Perry, was that, like the social lesbian scene Hansberry participated in, the world of the stories was "overwhelmingly white." Again, Perry adopts a conjectural tone to speculate that "it might have been the case that" Hansberry was "depicting a world that seemed to have not yet made space for a woman like her, not really." Hansberry was, above all, a utopian and revolutionary thinker. The odd closeting of feminine and sapphic imagery from her public works is not an act of shame but an act of self-protection as she, quietly and secretly, built the foundation for a world that could house her pleasure.

Famously, Hansberry became a member of the Daughters of Bilitis, the first homophile organization (as such groups were called at the time) to focus specifically on advocacy for lesbian women. From its founding in 1956, it sought to be an integrated organization, and it counted Latina and Black lesbians among its leadership and as contributors to *The Ladder*, its official publication. However, individual Black women also reported a hostile environment at Daughters of Bilitis meetings, including one on Manhattan's Lower East Side, where Hansberry lived.[34] In 1957, when Hansberry wrote a letter of support to the Daughters of Bilitis, which was published in the eighth issue of *The Ladder*, she said, "I'm glad as heck you exist." However, in 1958, when the founders of Daughters of Bilitis traveled to New York to promote their organization, Hansberry met with them but declined to get more involved.[35] Hansberry's letter to *The Ladder* betrays her deep ambivalence about issues of gradualism and respectability within the gay rights movement. In diplomatic, careful language, she praises the organization as a "fine, elementary step in a rewarding direction."[36] The politeness of her tone masks the fact that saying something is "fine" and "elementary" is hardly high praise. She continues in this vein of veiled critique: "I could not help but be encouraged and relieved by one of the almost subsidiary points under Point I of your declaration of purpose, "(to advocate) a mode of behavior and dress acceptable to society. As one raised in a cultural experience (I am a Negro) where those within were and are forever lecturing to their fellows about how to appear acceptable to the dominant social group, I know something about the shallowness of such a view as an end in itself."[37]

On the one hand, she is "encouraged and relieved" by the Daughters of Bilitis' self-professed commitment to ensuring that its lesbian members uphold a normative standard in order to be palatable to straight society. Yet she labels the viewpoint as "shallow" when assimilation becomes a goal in itself rather than a pragmatic pathway to the day when "the 'discreet' Lesbian will not turn her head on the streets at the sight of the 'butch' strolling hand in hand with her friend in their trousers and definitive haircuts." The goal is not a world of "discreet Lesbians," but rather a world in which butches can exist without stigma. A different world, in other words.

Hansberry's poignant parenthetical—"I am a Negro"—sets her apart from the majority of the magazine's readership as someone with intimate knowledge of the pitfalls of respectability as a basis for equal rights. Even Nobel Peace Prize winner and UN diplomat Ralph Bunche, she points out, "with all his clean fingernails, degrees, and, of course, undeniable service to the human race, could still be insulted, denied a hotel room or meals in many parts of our country. (Not to mention the possibility of being lynched on a lonely Georgia road for perhaps having demanded a class of water in the wrong place.)"[38] In her subtle way, Hansberry is attempting to push the nascent gay rights movement leftward by narrating a natural trajectory from respectability politics to a politics of non-normativity which exists more in aspiration than in fact among Black people. Speaking from a personal rather than a racial moral high ground, Hansberry informs *The Ladder*'s readership that she has "long since passed the period when [she] felt personal discomfort at the sight of an ill-dressed or illiterate Negro. Social awareness has taught [her] where to lay the blame." This transition from discomfort to social awareness is one that cannot be attributed to Hansberry's status as "a Negro"; rather, it is her unique positionality as a Black queer woman that allows her to see that, as Soyica Diggs Colbert argues, "assimilation reinscribed norms that were historically grounded in a limited understanding of what it means to be human, and even those who assimilated most successfully would never be physically safe."[39]

Hansberry's queer short fiction, despite centering white lesbian characters, is a meaningful exploration of the potential alliances—and the heartbreaking betrayals—between marginalized identity categories. "The Anticipation of

Eve," published in *ONE* magazine in 1957, is a delightfully dark first-person narrative of an almost coming out. Rita, the white lesbian protagonist, goes to dinner hoping to tell her well-meaning but hopelessly heteronormative cousins that her "roommate" Eve is, in fact, her girlfriend. Because her cousin Sel and her husband David are fairly progressive by 1950s standards—in the past, they had come to the defense of a teacher obliged to shave his beard because the administration "thought it was bohemian and unbecoming to the teacher profession," and they had spoken out in defense of an interracial couple facing housing discriminations—Rita thinks it might be all right to tell them.[40] But when David speaks about a gay male colleague with disgust, Rita not only changes her mind about coming out but feigns disgust as well. " How horrible!" she exclaims, hating herself.[41] She sees David transformed, monstrously, by his homophobia: "Suddenly it all seemed so remote and alien; something that might, after all, in spite of beards and Negro equality, turn the simple good face into something hostile and painful and yes, frightened."[42] Most heartbreaking of all is not David's ultimately unsurprising homophobia, but Rita's own betrayal of a queer stranger, which she likens to those "moments on the battlefield, instants, when a man can feel only relief when he sees his buddy fall instead of himself."[43] Though, as Imani Perry has noted, the story has some autobiographical elements, "The Anticipation of Eve" makes a deliberate choice in projecting Hansberry's own anxieties about coming out into a white woman's body.[44] By translating the experience of coming out to a white woman's body rather than her own, Hansberry demonstrates that the retreat into privilege is a learned racial habit. She that shows the way that white people can retreat into whiteness at the least sign of danger is similar to, and entangled with, the way some queer people can pass for straight.

"Chanson du Konallis," published in *The Ladder* in 1958, is an even more stark example of this. The story is a strange and oneiric snapshot of an upper-class white woman with the intentionally overblown name Konalia (Konnie) Martin Whitside-Heplin, III (described as having ancestors who "almost made it over on the Mayflower"), sitting next to her husband in a jazz club and salivating over Mirine, an African American jazz singer fresh from a stint in the prewar Paris jazz clubs.[45] For Konnie, the pull of queer desire "had happened before in life. On the street; parties; in classes in school years back; the thing of being surrounded by many people and suddenly finding another girl's or woman's eyes, commanding one, holding one's own."[46] Looking at Mirine, she calibrates her racial rubric of attraction, building an elaborate daydream featuring Mirine as Cleopatra, then, "not Cleopatra, she was Greek or something. This particular queen would be darker—like the Nile without moonlight; with high cheek bones and—full, impossibly sensuous lips—like—like—like her!"[47] This transition from Cleopatra to Nefertiti, however, is precarious ground. Voyeurism being the refuge of whiteness and heteronormativity, she is accustomed to holding multiple cognitive possibilities in dissonance; neither her whiteness nor her sexuality is challenged by her fantasy. When her husband asks if she wants to meet Mirine, she refuses, retreating into a snobbishness that is not entirely feigned yet not honest either, hearing that "her own voice . . . was marvelously normal, cool, proper, the essence of disdain."[48] Yet her internal monologue rages against her outward indifference, oscillating between rebellion and complacency: "*Pleasure*. Why had pleasure so frightened her in the past? Why must one constantly run from it? Control it? Who were all those dead people who were deciding things from their graves? All those generations of high respected poor old souls who had done this or that in their lives; founded this or that. What had they to do with her! Why was she so bound to them? Who made them right about everything?"[49]

Konnie's diatribe is immature and, ultimately, thrust aside by her perceived social obligations. These ancestors who "founded this or that" have everything to do with her: the things they have founded are the basis of her social position and all her worldly comforts. Later, she chides herself, "upbringing had come to a pretty pass indeed when she could actually sit around like—like—well, one of those women, ogling colored girl singers!"[50] Pleasure is the necessary sacrifice she must make for continuing to be a part of whiteness and straightness. She ultimately decides that she is not one of "those women" and sides definitively with her forebears.

Hansberry's published lesbian stories are, in different ways, about the petty betrayals and the emotional dishonesty that it takes to get through the day as a queer person in 1950s America. Hansberry's queer stories represent a veneer of normativity beneath which roils the hot bile of shame and frustrated desire. She does not exactly traffic in a genre of queer tragedy—in the case of Rita and Eve in "The Anticipation of Eve," union is possible even if a public reckoning is not. The same cannot be said for Konnie and Mirine's interracial flirtation, however. Not even star-crossed lovers, the repressed white woman and the mysterious Black jazz singer are, unlike Rita and Eve, a pairing that could never be consummated because of the sedimented layers of race, class, and history that overlay their meeting. Hansberry's representation of interracial queer relationships sheds light on how much the world would have to change to allow even the possibility of a lesbian relationship that escapes the same violence and power imbalances of straight relationships.

Toussaint is Hansberry's only play to feature women's same-sex desire, although the setting in which it is explored is somewhat surprising. Like *Les Blancs*, it concerns a revolution in another country, but unlike *Les Blancs*, which takes place in the fictional country of Zatembe, *Toussaint* has aspirations of historical accuracy in its retelling of the life of Haitian revolutionary hero Toussaint Louverture. Hansberry appears to have conducted extensive research on the Haitian Revolution and colonial life in Saint-Domingue in what promised to be a play of epic scope. However, Hansberry died before she could complete the play, and one of the existing fragments, ostensibly the first scene of the play, describes not the heroics of Toussaint but the depravity of a white slave mistress sexually assaulting an enslaved woman. Why, of all Hansberry's plays, is this the only one to center lesbianism? And why is lesbianism centered in this particular way?

The fragment is largely framed as a conversation between Toussaint's fictional enslaver, Bayon de Bergier, and his wife Lucie. It appears to be an old and well-trod argument: Lucie attacks Bayon for his enduring love of an enslaved woman, on whose grave he has just laid flowers. Lucie's tone is venomously clearsighted; Bayon's is one of exhausted resignation to what he clearly views as his wife's hysteria. In the background, one of his enslaved children plays a minuet on the piano offstage, punctuated occasionally by the sounds of a cracking whip and screams of pain as Toussaint beats someone in his capacity as overseer. As Lucie and Bayon circle one another like lions, Lucie quotes the insults Bayon has leveled at her family in order to knock him off his moral pedestal: "Do you really think that one may ever forget hearing one's ancestors described as 'the baggage of the Paris gutters?' 'The prostitutes and refuse of the prisons of France dumped in that Bay out there . . . to begin a new and festering civilization!'"[51] In this, Hansberry's research has clearly included the writings of Médéric Louis Elie Moreau de Saint-Méry, whose influential eighteenth-century writings asserted through a protoeugenicist logic that white Creoles suffered from poor breeding and an unhealthy climate, and thus that Creole women had "a penchant for brutal domination, of which they acquire the habit at a tender age" ("ce penchant pour une domination sévère, dont elles contractent l'habitude dès l'âge le plus tendre"). Saint-Méry also narrates that "there is nothing like the rage of a Creole woman who punishes a slave whom her husband has perhaps forced to dig up the marriage bed. In her jealous fury she only invents things to satisfy her vengeance" ("Rien n'égale la colère d'une femme Créole qui punit l'esclave que son époux a peut-être forcée de fouiller le lit nuptial. Dans sa fureur jalouse elle ne fait qu'inventer pour assouvir sa vengeance").[52] Saint-Méry's oft-cited text provides a geographically determinist narrative of white Creole degeneracy, a narrative that Lucie corroborates but also subverts by representing her stifled longings in the face of her husband's coldness and hypocrisy. She is simultaneously a victim of a eugenicist patriarchy and an active aggressor in a slaveholding society.

In perhaps the most embodied queer content in any of Hansberry's works, halfway through the scene an enslaved woman named Destine enters the room at Lucie's behest. Lucie commands Destine to give her a massage while she sits "half-naked." Her mood fluctuates from pleasure at the massage to capricious rage at Destine, whom she pinches, strikes, and shouts at. Inexplicably, however, her mood shifts, and Hansberry's stage directions capture the erotic physicality beneath the spoken words: "How beautiful your hands are . . . (*She catches one of the hands on her shoulder and holds it and looks at it.*) How lovely you are . . . (*Turning to face the slave.*) Your body was molded by the Gods—(*She puts her hands caressingly down the sides of the other woman's body. Her husband re-enters, gets an article he had forgotten, and looks at her with disgust.*)"[53] It is impossible not to juxtapose Lucie's actions with those of her husband, whom she has just taunted for his love of an enslaved woman whose grave he visits religiously, tracking the mud from the grave into their shared bedroom. Neither is exempt from the coercive matrix of plantation intimacy, and Lucie's white womanhood does not make her actions any less exploitative than her husband's; in fact, the blatant utilitarianism of her abuse suggests a level of cruelty seldom documented among white women slaveholders. In accounting for the lack of archives around white women's abuse of enslaved women, historian Lamonte Aidoo argues, "The narrative of white women's virtue was both a prison and a veil, but also a source of power as it relates to black women, enabling extreme and unchecked forms of cruelty that were not much different from those committed by their husbands, sons, and brothers. If white mistresses did abuse slave women, their mythical virtue would protect them, just as being white and male protected slave-master rapists."[54] Hansberry was well ahead of her time in her conceptualization of white women's cruelty as a natural function of their limited but still potent power within slave societies, not as an anomalous case of sociopathy among the gentler sex.

The figure of the sadistic plantation mistress is a trope in itself in the literature and legends of enslavement. Central figures in contemporary novels like Marlon James's *The Book of Night Women* (2009) and Valerie Martin's

Property (2003) have countered the fainting benevolence of Scarlett O'Hara by featuring white women slaveholders whose appetites for violence rival or surpass men's. These were based on the stories of real plantation mistresses and the transnational appetite for lurid stories of women slaveholders' cruelty, as evidenced by the circulation of the legend of the eighteenth-century Jamaican plantation owner Annie Palmer—rumored to be a "white witch" who kept enslaved people in check with her knowledge of obeah—and the equally enduring story of Delphine LaLaurie, a nineteenth-century New Orleans "socialite and serial killer" whose torture of enslaved people in her household is still the fodder for many a moonlit ghost tour.[55] In those cases, white women slaveholders' cruelty is represented as somehow sensational or anomalous, when in fact it was utterly quotidian. For instance, Stephanie E. Jones-Rogers has used her historical research to counter the assumptions of largely male historians that enslaved women working in brothels owned by white women might have chosen to do so, while "when historians discuss white *men's* involvement in the fancy trade, they do not frame the sale of enslaved women for the purpose of sexual labor, or the men's perpetration of sexual coercion and violence against these women, in the same way."[56] Hazel Carby's argument that the cult of true womanhood in antebellum America had real consequences for the treatment of Black women may have become an accepted part of Black feminist scholarship, but the gap in historical theorizations of white women's cruelty reveals that the cult of true womanhood is alive and well in scholarship.

Little historical scholarship has considered the possibility of lesbian sexual assault committed by white women on enslaved Black women, presumably because of a continued presumption of white women's inherent innocence. There are a few notable exceptions of pathbreaking research on this issue. One is Nell Irvin Painter's assertion that for Sojourner Truth, "sexual abuse came from her mistress Sally Dumont, and Truth could tell about it only obliquely."[57] Another is the work of Lamonte Aidoo, whose study of sexual violence in Brazil delves into Brazilian inquisition records to reveal five incidents of interracial "female sodomy" between white women and Black women and girls in the sixteenth century, as well as adjacent practices well into the nineteenth century. Despite the distinctive nature of this cultural context, I argue that Aidoo's exploration of how lesbian sex with enslaved women provided "the opportunity for white women to explore dominance" rings true for Hansberry's fictional context.[58] Lucie's massage, for instance, evokes the Brazilian practice of *cafuné*, a grooming ritual in which an enslaved woman would rub the scalp of her mistress in a fashion so homoerotic that multiple nineteenth-century writers were disturbed and disgusted by its blatant sexual overtones.[59] Part of the problem of this practice involved the mistress's obvious enjoyment, which male observers found to be too unreliant on heterosexual reproduction to be tolerated. However, Aidoo cautions against the urge to romanticize this act as a form of lesbian resistance: "The mistress's pleasure—the notion of sex as an act of intimacy—conceals the power dynamic at work. White pleasure obscures Black captivity and injury and becomes a false equalizer."[60]

When Bayon reenters the room and regards Lucie's massage with disgust, Lucie shouts at him, "My pleasures are my own—monster! monster!"[61] But that is just the thing: her pleasures are not her own. Hansberry herself was purportedly ascetic in her own tastes, denying herself the pleasures of beautiful dresses and material goods.[62] An important part of her politics was the idea that pleasure is political, and that it often comes at the expense of someone else. Lucie also uses the language of "pleasure" when she asks her husband if he thinks Toussaint "gets pleasure" from driving the other enslaved people. They disagree, and Lucie observes that she has seen no pleasure in Toussaint's administration of corporal punishment; Bayon says, "Of course he does."[63] Lucie's pleasures are beholden to the concentric rings of domination in her Creole world, with her husband at the center, then her, then Toussaint whipping his fellow bondsmen in the field, then these enslaved women who are dead, gone, or trapped in the wake. The mistress and the slave, the piano and the screams, desire and disgust, are all braided together in one ugly rope. What is pleasure in such a world of domination, where one person's pleasure always seems to be at the expense of someone else's? What kind of world would have to exist to allow for Destine's pleasure?

Discussing this play in 1961, it is clear that Hansberry was striving toward a transhistorical message that resonates in the twentieth century despite its eighteenth-century setting: "What I think a dramatist has to do is to thoroughly inundate himself or herself in an awareness of the realities of the historical time period and then dismiss it, and then become absolutely dedicated to the idea that what you are going to do is create human beings whom you know in your own time."[64] If Lucie and Destine are ultimately people that Hansberry "knows" in an emotional sense, Hansberry's concern is drawing a historical trajectory of extant power dynamics in lesbian interracial relationships, an urgent questioning of what intimacy can be in bondage and in freedom. Her questions foreshadow the 1982 anthology *Against Sadomasochism: A Radical Feminist Analysis*, in which both Audre Lorde and Alice Walker critique sadomasochism from a Black lesbian feminist perspective. Although this critique has been underanalyzed or excised from the history of Black feminism, Sharon Holland argues that "absenting these somewhat conservative Black feminist opinions from the women of color intellectual production performs damaging work" within queer studies because it represents a concerted effort by Black feminists to bring historical specificity to bear on the self-involvement of a theory without praxis.[65] In Walker's essay in particular, the historical embeddedness of the master/mistress-slave dynamic between Black and white partners makes consensual sadomasochism repugnant, even between women. Audre Lorde similarly rejects sadomasochism between lesbians, arguing, "I'm not questioning anyone's right to live. I'm saying we must observe the implications of our lives. If what we are talking about is feminism, then the personal is political and we can subject everything in our lives to scrutiny. . . . You cannot corral any aspect within your life, divorce its implications, whether it's what you eat for breakfast or how you say good-bye. This is what integrity is."[66] As with her agemate Audre Lorde, Hansberry's personal intimacies with white women do not undermine the level of scrutiny she places on interracial relationships in her lesbian writing, depicting a violent world in which consent is never a factor. No interracial relationship is ever represented consensually because in Hansberry's world, as in the following decades that she never got to see, the conditions of possibility did not yet exist for sex devoid of history.

In *Toussaint*, Hansberry makes a case for destroying this world utterly. The epigraph of *Toussaint* is attributed to Toussaint Louverture: "I must warn you that to remain with me means to remain with your race and its cause, to remain in the Land of the Mountains, and to regard the Land of the Mountains as the Mother of the Earth. We must remold human relations here—we must alter human society here—and from here, liberty will go out to the whole world."[67] Though on a surface level the content of the epigraph and the play itself provide just another fetishization of masculine leadership, freedom radiates outward from this feminized Haiti. The epigraph targets "society" and "human relations" rather than the narrower goals of colonization and enslavement. This framing implicitly centers the interpersonal and the feminine in a revolution that has been remembered for the military achievements of predominantly male revolutionary figures. Lucie implies that the previous occupant of Destine's role, a woman named Delira, ran away. She asks Destine, rhetorically, "But then . . . you will all do it some day, won't you? . . . Run off to the hills . . . to return with fire and machete?"[68] Unusually for Hansberry, who often depicts male revolutionaries at the center of the action in her other plays, she depicts the female victims of lesbian sexual abuse as the revolutionary vanguard, coming down from the hills to change the society that has robbed them of the possibility for desire or pleasure.

This is illustrated by a fragment found among Hansberry's drafts of *Toussaint*, labeled as an "optional" insert to the play. It is simply Lucie, addressing Destine: "How tired I am of all of it, Destine. Why can't there be peace . . . Such a lovely il [sic] island . . . How tired I am of hearing it reviled . . . it should be someplace where dreams are dreamed and lovers rule . . . Sing me something beautiful, Destine . . . something beautiful about Saint Domingue. [Destine obeys and sings african [sic] song. Lucie listens and then joins it in a duet]."[69] It is telling that the duet was never recorded. The duet and the peace and beauty Lucie imagines are impossible in a world where Destine's voice cannot be heard. No matter the sentiment behind it, Lucie's desire to sing with Destine can only ever be a command, an act of coercion rather than an act of love. Dreams will never be dreamed in the colony of Saint-Domingue; only in a free Haiti, a country without Lucie, can the dreaming begin. Another archival fragment, a handwritten poem (or perhaps a song?) titled "Toussaint" begins, "When all these joys are true / There will be things to do."[70] The messianic scene of the Haitian Revolution is meant to make these joys true by clearing the path for all kinds of freedom, and not just from slavery. It will also end Lucie's imposition of her desire on Destine, and possibly clear the path for Destine's own desire. Until the revolution comes, there will be no possibility of consent between interracial sexual partners. Significantly, Destine is the feminine form of the French word for "destiny." Hansberry's play fragment ends with the image of Destine, both foreboding and promising: "(*She goes on stolidly massaging the flesh with her face fixed like a mask, as the light converges on mistress and slave, and the minuet and the cries of human pain continue . . .*)."[71] Destine herself stands in for the kind of human relations that are destined to end.

In some ways, the character of Konnie from Hansberry's earlier story, "Chanson du Konallis," is a descendant of Lucie de Bergier. An unhappy white woman who uses her own social power to snatch coercive pleasure from the bodies of Black women at work. Konnie's slaveholding ancestors are alluded to but not overtly outed: "Her family had grown reserve in Virginia for generations and she was a true harvest."[72] By framing Konnie's "reserve" and her very self as a "crop" of a Virginian plantocracy, Hansberry alludes to white femininity as a result of the exploitation of Black bodies. Konnie gets to have her "reserve" because of the work of invisibilized Black women whose excesses were defined in opposition to it. And Mirine is a descendant of

Destine: opaque, closed, withholding even as her work gives the illusion of availability for consumption. But unlike Destine, Mirine is allowed to refuse the white woman's voyeuristic, imbalanced sense of pleasure. When Konnie's husband compliments her French and asks if she studied French as a child, Mirine replies with "cool, dry, indifference, 'On a sharecropper's farm in Georgia?'"[73] Though the structural power dynamics do not seem to have changed much, Mirine's insolence is a tool in her arsenal that was not afforded to her ancestors (at least, not without the threat of severe bodily harm).[74] Mirine's powerful assertion of indifference strikes Konnie as an affront on her whiteness: "Konnie would have let herself laugh ordinarily, but something in her consciously rebelled at the insolence that she felt exuded from the woman. She hardly represented the Old South or any of that, but really! There were just some things one maintained. Tradition, it was true, was almost mystical in the way it bound one. But, nonetheless, it *did* bind one, thank God!"[75] Juxtaposing the descendant of Virginia planters with the child of Georgia sharecroppers allows Hansberry to highlight how little has changed since the eighteenth-century abuses of Lucie de Bergier. Konnie still demands the submission and availability of Black women as her birthright, as a thing "one maintained." All that has changed in the intervening centuries is the Black woman's increased capacity for haughtiness, a powerful emotional tool that, in the absence of structural power, has the power to show that the "tradition" to which Konnie finds herself bound is a cage with an open door.

By visiting the table, Mirine gives Konnie the chance to form a new kind of intimacy, one that is not rooted in histories of coercion. Konnie, of course, declines. She allows her husband to do most of the talking while she merely admires Mirine through her mask of feigned indifference. Mirine makes conversation for a time, then admits to Konnie, in a statement loaded with indictment, that she came over "because out there the lights play tricks on the faces of those who watch—you seemed like someone I knew once. In Paris. It was a mistake of course." In this case, it is a Black woman who confronts a white woman about her failure to acknowledge the potentiality of her pleasure—to be a lesbian she could know, to be a partner in building a world for their own pleasure. At the end of the evening, Konnie reflects on how Mirine had called their interaction "pleasant": "Pleasant, she had said, *pleasant*. It had not been pleasant at all; if anything, in those terms, it had been downright unpleasant. But the other—it had been so full of the other—*plaisir*."[76] Although the French word *plaisir* does not exactly hold the transcendent meaning with which Hansberry imbues it, she reserves the possibility of an unnamed feeling beyond mere pleasure.[77] Perhaps she means the erotic in the Lordean sense, or perhaps she means, very simply, two women mutually invested in the other's pleasure. And perhaps this ineffable feeling was more likely to be found between two Black women.

After all, the compulsory heterosexuality that Hansberry diagnoses throughout her work was, for Black women, a product of a slave society that reproduced value through enslaved women's childbearing capacities. In *Thiefing Sugar*, Omise'eke Natasha Tinsley points out the radical potential of eroticism between enslaved women who must literally steal their own commodified bodies for their personal use, in the same way they might steal a bit of the sugar cane they had harvested but did not own.[78] In considering the dialogic relationship between Hansberry and Simone, I find evidence of this *plaisir* between two Black women stealing themselves back from a world that wished to define them based on their deviance.

"The Historical Destiny of My People": Simone's Diasporic Spiritual Geographies

In the background there is Nina Simone, beckoning, weaving a new possibility. Amid Hansberry's struggles with masculinity and with white femininity, Nina Simone was a crooked Black note. Imani Perry has recently drawn attention to Hansberry's relationship with Nina Simone in the final three years of Hansberry's life. Though they did not have long together, Hansberry is palpable throughout the remainder of Simone's career. Many of Simone's performances throughout the 1960s and 1970s began with an invocation of Lorraine, "who is gone now but was my dear, dear friend."[79] Hansberry's entrance into Simone's life—with her real girl's talk of revolution and change—precipitated alternative timelines to Simone's rigidly constructed career and relationships.

Simone had her own demons of masculinity, combating her self-professed love of patriarchal authority in her personal life even as the content of her music explored "how it feels to be free." In her autobiography, for instance, Simone narrates how her second husband Andrew Stroud, who would also become her manager, was hesitant to tell her that he was a police officer when they first met, but when he did she "just squealed and liked him more."[80] In their relationship, Simone endured many forms of abuse from Stroud, from a brutal beating on the night of their engagement, to financial manipulation such that at the height of her career she did not know how much money she made, and the way he "worked [her] like a carthorse, one-night show after one-night show."[81] After their divorce, Simone still expressed some ambivalence about Stroud, and formed relationships with similarly patriarchal men in her transnational travels after her divorce. Describing her affair with Errol Barrow, the prime minister of Barbados when she lived there in the 1970s, "I was his courtesan and he my pasha."[82] Later, courting a rich Liberian septuagenarian who tried to convince her to marry him, she claims she cannot resist him because "he is like a Liberian Rhett Butler."[83] But Lorraine—Lorraine was different. Simone feels that need to clarify that "Lorraine was a girlfriend, a friend of my own, rather than one [she] shared with Andy." Lorraine was a person and space apart from the carousel of straight men and the security they represented for Simone. Simone had chosen to marry Stroud because, in her words, she "wanted to be a wife and mother instead of a performing machine." This dogged pursuit of heteronormativity—in my mind, the relationship analogue to her ambitions to be a concert pianist—rigged against her from the start. When she was married to Stroud, he kept a blackboard in their kitchen on which he wrote, "Nina will be a rich black bitch by . . ." However, "the last part was always changing; he'd write 'Xmas '63' on it until November 1963 when he'd replace it with 'Easter '65' or some other mythical deadline."[84] The date never arrived; in fact, after their divorce Simone sometimes had to rely on friends, lovers, and a new roster of performance gigs just to get by. In contrast to the mirage of heterosexual bliss, revolution was a different kind of timeline.

Simone had spent her life before her friendship with Hansberry and her entrance into the civil rights movement living on someone else's timeline. After years of grueling training in classical piano, when she was denied admission to Philadelphia's Curtis Institute of Music in 1950 (allegedly because of her race), she was thrown off the course of respectability, gradualism, and the politics she would label as "too slow" in her 1963 song "Mississippi Goddam." Even after her first hit record in 1958, Simone still aspired to make the money necessary to resume her classical music education. From her first performances at the Midtown Bar in Atlantic City, her "attitude to performing was that of a classically trained musician: when you play you give all your concentration because it deserves total respect, and an audience should sit still and be quiet. . . . My attitude to live audiences was formed there at the Midtown and it's never changed, no matter who the audience or how big the concert hall."[85] But this is not quite true; with her political coming to consciousness, her relationship to her audience changed as well. Although she still demanded a mutual respect from her audiences, she no longer deplored the lack of musical education that led to a veneration of popular songs.

Rather, in the 1960s, "My music was dedicated to a purpose more important than classical music's pursuit of excellence; it was dedicated to the fight for freedom and the historical destiny of my people. I felt a fierce pride when I thought about what we were all doing together."[86] Perhaps it was not she who had changed, but the audience. The rallies and marches at which she played in the mid-1960s were often young southern Black people "who risked their lives every day, [and] I had no choice but to line up alongside them. You can call it what you like, but to me it was destiny." These "kids out in the backwoods" were the ones who taught her a different story than the twice-as-good-for-half-as-much she had been living in her life as a classical pianist.[87]

In the 1963 Carnegie Hall performance that is said to have kicked off Nina Simone's transition from classical musician and singer of jazz standard to fiery civil rights activist, she performed "Pirate Jenny," a song from Bertolt Brecht's *The Three-Penny Opera*. In it, Imani Perry argues that "she is pirating the Middle Massage and claiming her freedom," while Ruth Feldstein says it is a "a song about race, class, and gender relations in the American South."[88] Either way, the image of a Black woman scrubbing the floors in a "crummy Southern town" and sailing away on a "black freighter" that kills everyone who has wronged her is a Black revolutionary revenge drama for the ages. Galled witnesses of Simone's performance of "Pirate Jenny" also remember her choosing a random white man in the audience and pointing to him as she sings the pivotal line of the song—"Kill them now or later?"—in a harsh, menacing whisper. Then shouting, "Right now!" A sublime cover artist, Simone transformed this song, as she did with many covers, into a unique statement of her own positionality by changing relatively few words from the original: the reference to the southern town, a touch of African American vernacular at the end when she declaims, "Then they'll pile up the bodies / And I'll say, / That'll learn ya!" The song shifts subtly back and forth between present and future tense, signifying both the unrealized dream of revolution and the groundwork that is already laid for it in the present.[89]

In conversation with Toussaint, Simone's "Pirate Jenny" reads as an apocalyptic sequel to act 1, scene 1 of *Toussaint*, a rejoinder written in Destine's voice. Though Simone's vision of revolution was different in tone than Hansberry's, they share a conviction that revolution is urgent, and that Black women are at the heart of it. An understudied song that raises similar themes is the song "Dambala," which invokes the Haitian snake spirit Danbala to enact a cosmic revenge upon the architects of racial capitalism: "You slavers will know what it's like to be a slave / Slave to your mind / Slave to your race / You won't go to heaven / You won't go to hell / You remain in your graves /

Girls' Talk

With the stench and the smell / Oh Dambala come Dambala."[90] The song makes liberal, haunting use of the sitar, played by her longtime guitarist Al Schackman, implying the influence of Eastern religions as well as Haitian revolutionary spirituality on Simone's spiritual landscape. Unlike Hansberry, Simone was informed by a variety of religious traditions interested in the karmic implications of revolution, giving her revolutionary meditations a distinctly cosmic feeling.

Simone's coming out as a radical in 1963, especially her first performance of "Mississippi Goddam" at Carnegie Hall, is well known and well documented. In this year, after the murder of Medgar Evers and the 16th Street Baptist Church bombing, Simone awakened to the realities of being Black in America, but she feels it is necessary to note that "it wasn't an intellectual connection of the type Lorraine had been repeating to me over and over." Rather, "In church language, the Truth entered into me and I 'came through.'"[91] Simone's transition from showtunes to freedom songs in 1963 has become a part of her mythology, but the religious language she uses to describe her "conversion" has not. Like her friend James Baldwin, and other Black intellectuals like Zora Neale Hurston, Simone was the daughter of a preacher. However, it was Nina Simone's mother, not her father, who was a respected Methodist minister much in demand on the revival circuit.[92] The influence of Simone's early days (starting at three and a half years old) playing piano for her mother's church services is evident in songs like "Sinnerman" and "Take Me to the Water" but also in a feminist spiritual sensibility throughout Simone's work. Despite a complicated relationship with both Christianity and her mother herself, Simone felt that her civil rights music "could finally answer Momma's great unasked question, 'Why do you sing out in the world when you could be praising God?'"[93] Too little theorizing has been done about the way Simone describes her post-1963 performances in mythical terms, describing her relationship with an audience of her people as "mass hypnosis." "Whatever it was that happened out there under the lights," she said, "it mostly came from God, and I was just a place along the line He was moving on."[94] Though her spirituality is not scrutable as stemming from any single tradition, Simone's artistic practice is undoubtedly a spiritual one. Despite the fact that her various unorthodoxies precluded her from participating in her mother's version of Christianity, Simone made her own medicinal cocktail from a blend of Christian, African, and New Age religious practice. As Kinitra Brooks has argued, Simone's performances "expand folkloric horror within a musical context to conjure the supernatural out of the deceptively ordinary."[95]

Simone's music is often thought of as delivering a corrective or an alternative to the Christian songs of 1960s nonviolent activism.[96] Ruth Feldstein argues that her 1964 *In Concert* album "questioned patient nonviolence, Christianity, the interracial folk revival and the related celebration of freedom songs, and white-defined images of blacks."[97] Feldstein identifies three songs in particular from this album as expressions of a nascent Black women's revolutionary consciousness: "Pirate Jenny," "Go Limp," and "Mississippi Goddam." In *The Witch's Flight*, Kara Keeling argues that the cinematic appearance of the Black Panthers at the California State capitol in 1967 challenged dominant American notions of what Black people could be like. "How could slavery, share-cropping, silent suffering, gospel singing, Aunt Jemima, Uncle Tom, Topsy, 'We Shall Overcome,' cotton picking, illiteracy, 'massa lovin,' cannibalism, watermelon-seed spittin', white-woman chasing, nonviolent resisting, Mammy, and Jezebel give way to blacks with guns?"[98] Keeling's litany of Black impossibility—the weight of white supremacy still heavy despite its contradictory and ludicrous amalgam of what Black is—had already been ruptured by the cinematic appearance of Simone herself. If Keeling's litany highlights the uncomfortable social juxtaposition of "nonviolent resisting" with "Uncle Tom," Simone's freedom songs shed light on counterperspectives to the institutional memory of 1960s civil rights struggles, which contained a glorious multitude of perspectives and attitudes toward violence, revolution, sex, and respectability. All that complexity that "silent suffering, gospel singing" does not cover.

In contrast to the church-sprung freedom songs that have come to define public memory of the civil rights movement and its soundtrack, Simone's songs were anthems against the very kind of gradualism by which the movement of the early 1960s has (unfairly) been remembered. As Feldstein argues, Simone's civil rights songs departed from "the process of canon formation that took place in the mid-1960s [which] reinforced a myth that 'authentic' civil rights music in the period before 1965 meant rural, grassroots, church-inspired freedom songs."[99] Similarly, in Simone's youth her mother had established a dichotomy between sacred and profane music: "Momma had a name for any sort of music that wasn't religious, that was 'of the world.' She called it 'real music.' If I played a tune I'd heard somewhere she'd say: 'Don't play any of those real songs.' For a long time I thought that 'real' was the name of a style of music, like 'blues' or 'gospel.'"[100] Ironically, Simone does make the real into its own style of music as she comes into her role as a civil rights singer whose lyrics grapple with the "real" problems of racial violence and political disenfranchisement. Simone's freedom songs may not have the long religious histories of freedom hymns like "We Shall Not Be Moved," but they have their own spiritual histories. They are real music, hymns of the real nuances and messy desires of a people who want pleasure rather than martyrdom.

Despite her mother's disproval and her own unorthodoxy, Simone insists upon making her own divine connections and highlighting her southern spiritual heritage throughout her career. In her autobiography, she attributes many of her most beloved concert techniques—notably her improvisations and her call-and-response relationship to the audience—as coming from her mother's Methodist services and the charismatic Holy Roller churches she also attended as a child. These musical forms help lend context to the spiritual atmosphere Simone tries to create in her concerts: "Gospel taught me about improvisation, how to shape music in response to an audience and how to shape the mood of the audience in response to my music. When I played I could take a congregation where I wanted—calm them down or lift them up until they became completely lost in the music and atmosphere."[101] The live album *It Is Finished* (1974) is a potent example of the continued influence of the Black church on Simone's concert techniques even during a time when she had seemingly turned to diasporic culture. Disappointed by the transition of the civil rights movement from "What do we want?" to "What can we get?"[102] Simone turned, in the 1970s and 1980s, from the national liberation to global and cosmic liberation. The album was recorded in New York during a time when she was living primarily in Barbados and experimenting with Caribbean musical forms generally, recording two covers of songs by the Bahamian musician Exuma: "Dambala" and "Obeah Woman." Both songs are utterly transformed, as always, for Simone's purposes. "Obeah Woman" in particular, which in its original version is a mythical history of Exuma's birth and life and is called "Exuma, The Obeah Man," is more of a nod to Exuma than a direct cover of the original. The songs are similar in content if not in lyrics and melody, full of mythical braggadocio and pride in origins. Neither version of the song rejects the singer's rural origins as provincial or unimportant, be it Exuma's birth on a small island in the Bahamas or Simone's birth in rural western North Carolina. Though Exuma positions himself as a mythical figure who "came down on a lightning bolt" and "had fire and brimstone coming out of [his] mouth" when he was born, he also takes pains to say in one of the verses that "Tony McKay was my given name / Given on Cat Island where my mama felt the pain."[103] Likewise, Simone hearkens back to her North Carolina upbringing when she, as the little girl named Eunice Waymon, used to play the piano in church. She does not exactly reclaim the name she abandoned in favor of her stage name (which she had initially adopted so that her mother wouldn't know that she was singing secular music), but she does lay claim to her mother's music.

The song begins, "Gonna take my time / Getting this one together / Gotta go home now / Gotta go home yea / You know about the holy roller church? / Ain't that where it started? / Ha ha I know / We've outgrown it now / I like money / I like fine clothes / I like all of it / But I know where my roots are / You hear me?" The song, which toes a line between speaking and singing over a martial backdrop of percussion, uses the Black Pentecostal aesthetic practice of testifying. In *Blackpentecostal Breath*, Ashon Crawley describes testimony: "The testimonies are song's punctuatory irruption. The testimonies do not necessarily interrupt but introduce a new path by which the Saints could flow; they are integral to the improvisational structure. . . . The point is not to begin and end songs or to begin and end testimonies. One is not in one song then another, in one testimony and then another. Rather the entire performance is to create a mood, to create an atmosphere, to create an environment where interruption is desired, where sporadic, spirited encounter happens."[104] This description of testimony is strikingly similar to Simone's description of how she shapes the mood of her audience through improvisation. The mood of "Obeah Woman" is one of diasporic fluidity, in which Simone can be both a child of the Holy Roller churches and a powerful non-Christian spiritual figure dubbed obeah woman by "you people from the islands." Obeah is a set of magical practices in the Anglophone West Indies that holds that its practitioners can manipulate the physical world through herbs, charms, and spellwork. Though testifying often centers on a redemption narrative in which Jesus intervenes into a sinner's worldly affairs, there is no salvific figure in "Obeah Woman" besides Simone herself, with no higher power above her: "I'm the Obeah Woman from beneath the sea / To get to Satan, you gotta pass through me."[105] Though this song would undoubtedly be considered demonic in her mother's worldview, it incorporates the worldview of many across the diaspora who believe that human will can shift spiritual energies from entity to entity and that Satan is not a demonic figure. In this song, Simone externalizes the diasporic continuity she feels between the Christian musical forms of her youth and the African cosmologies she became interested in later in life.

It was not until her adulthood that Simone discovered Africa like a missing puzzle piece to her spiritual wellness. When she first visited Nigeria briefly in 1961, she "felt for the first time the spiritual relaxation any Afro-American feels on reaching Africa."[106] When she moved to Liberia in the mid-1970s, Simone reveled in the feeling that "in Africa spirituality isn't separated from everyday life like it is in the west."[107] Her live albums and filmed performances hold particular traces of an everyday Afro-diasporic spirituality that we do not entirely see in her studio-recorded albums. It is clear that her performances are a practice of spirituality in everyday life. In the live album *Black Gold* (1970), for instance, Simone's performance is suffused with a reverence for Lorraine Hansberry and Langston Hughes, her departed friends, that surpasses a mere expression of grief. The Appalachian folk song "Black Is the Color (of My True Love's Hair)," for instance, despite being a part of Simone's repertoire before Hansberry's death, bears her palimpsest in this performance, where she adds verses of her own writing: "Her picture is painted in my memory / Without the color of despair / And everywhere I go / She is always there."[108] *Black Gold* is a search for a mourning ritual that will scale the barriers between past and present, that will incorporate the dead as part of the daily lived experience of the living. In her spoken introduction to the song "Who Knows Where the Time Goes," she introduces that concept of time as an entity with business of its own. "Where does it go? What does it do? Most of all, is it alive? Is it a thing we cannot touch and is it alive?"[109] The implications of time being alive puts the humans who live (in it like water? on it like fleas on the back of a living thing? through it like a catastrophe survived?) in a limbo between living and dead.

Simone's music is always relentlessly community driven and community building, but it is important to consider the dead as part of the community she seeks to build. In *Black Gold*, the song "Westwind," taught to Hansberry by Miriam Makeba and originally written by the South African musician Caiphus Semenya, is described by Simone as a prayer. It begins, "Westwind blow ye gentle / Over the shores of yesterday / My sun is brown and over / Here within my heart they lay, they lay."[110] These are the original lyrics as they are written, where the west wind is a force that blows over the shores of yesterday and can thus sweep up the souls of the dead and of "the young" alike. Her addition to the original—a repeated supplication of "Unify us, don't divide us"—makes the objective of the prayer an all-encompassing Pan-Africanism that includes the souls of the dead as well as living people across the diaspora. "Westwind" is cathartically reprised in her last song of the set, a rendition of "To Be Young, Gifted and Black." The songs are very different in tone, the plodding, martial pace of "To Be Young, Gifted and Black" and the sinuous, hypnotic drumbeats of "Westwind," which break through the shell of "To Be Young Gifted and Black" like a sky clearing of clouds. Simone combines the themes of the two songs—living Black excellence and Black ancestral aid—into one prayer: "Westwind with your wisdom gather all of your young for me . . . Make us free from exploitation and strife / Because nothing is more precious than black / Westwind with your splendor, take my people by the hand." "Don't divide us no more, we don't need it," she improvises; "Let us not fight over trivial things / Let us learn how to love ourselves first." Then she enlists the help of the dead: "Lorraine hear me, Langston hear me. Help me."[111] When the two songs collide—the prayer for the living and the memorial for the dead—it is a powerful renegotiation of time, a drawing of the past into the future.

Famously, Nina wrote the song "To Be Young, Gifted and Black" in remembrance of Hansberry, in conjunction with the posthumously produced play and biography of Hansberry of the same title. As she introduces the song, Simone explains that Hansberry is "A friend I miss more and more every day. . . . In this month's *Esquire*, you will find two articles about her, because you know who she *is* [emphasis mine]." The slight tension between Hansberry as someone Simone misses and Hansberry as someone who "is" in the world highlights the goals of Simone's onstage ritual making: to make sure the dead are never lost, and to reincorporate their power into living community at every turn. In fact, Simone's performance seems like a consummation of Hansberry's unfinished operatic elements in *Toussaint*. In one unpublished draft of the play, Toussaint's mother, Pelagia, "begins a sound; song: tribute [sic] to Legba, af ri [sic] first a capella as a few begin to start the rythms [sic] with only their hands then the drums arrive with an dn [sic] enormous sound join the music; other drums are cumulative and then the rattles and then all sing the responses and the dancing starts first with the women."[112] Hansberry's unperformed invocations of Legba are an opening for Simone's performances. Through Simone's invocations of Hansberry, the two women finally reach a cumulative vision of revolution: Hansberry's politics and Simone's spirituality, united at last.

Ultimately, Simone sees herself as an obeah woman (as magic workers and folk healers are often called in the Anglophone West Indies) in the original sense of the title: someone with the power and responsibility to shape the physical world, including by enlisting the still-vital power of the dead. It is a heavy responsibility, one she views ambivalently: "I didn't put the name on myself / And I don't like it sometimes / The weight is too heavy / The weight is too heavy / Let's finish it." The only way for the weight to be lifted and for her duties to be finished would be for her lifelong spell to work: for the dead to walk with her people, for slavers to know what it was like to be a slave, for the Black freighter to come with its cleansing violence. It is important to note that even the title of the album, *It Is Finished*, is a biblical allusion to Jesus's last words to his disciples before he died.[113] Simone's simultaneous invocation of Afro-diasporic and Christian messianic imagery implies a sacrifice and a return, a death and an eternal life. For Nina Simone, belief was Blackness was revolution. In order to shepherd her people toward the revolution that was destined to be, she made herself into the spiritual leader she thought they needed: "I'm the Obeah Woman, above the pain / I can eat the thunder and drink the rain / I kiss the moon and hug the sun / And call the spirits and make 'em run / You hear me? / You hear me?"[114] Though she positions herself in a leadership role, Simone refutes a neoliberal dream in which Black people hold leadership roles, because "anyone who has power only has it at the expense of someone else. . . . I realized that what we were fighting for was the creation of a new society."[115] In this new society, there would be no need for obeah women because balance would have been restored to the physical universe.

The seeds of revolution were always in Simone, from the moment she gave a piano recital at eight years old and saw her parents ejected from their front-row seats so that a white couple could sit there instead. In her autobiography, she muses, "The day after the recital I walked around feeling as if I had been flayed and every slight, real or imagined, cut me raw. But the skin grew back again a little tougher, a little less innocent, and a little more black."[116] Simone and Hansberry wrote of the global, transhistorical accrual of injustice that made them more Black, more deadly, and made revolution not a possibility but a destiny. "This is a showtune but the show hasn't been written for it yet," said Nina Simone, famously, in the midst of her Carnegie Hall debut of "Mississippi Goddam." She and Lorraine were writing the show.

CHAPTER THREE

Uneasy Blackness
Warrior Goddesses in the Age of Black Power

It has become a bit of a cliché to indict the Black nationalist ideologies of the 1960s and 1970s for their masculinism. As various scholars have noted, the rampant misogyny and homophobia that have come to be associated with Black nationalism of the 1960s and 1970s were only one particularly vocal discourse amid a multitude of others. To overemphasize this discourse is to ignore the way Black nationalist groups changed over time and to discredit the many Black women who were instrumental in shaping and changing their rhetoric.[1] However, even women who were instrumental to Black cultural nationalist formations tended to fall back upon a reified definition of womanhood that was both heterosexist and biologically determinist. As historian Ashley D. Farmer notes, women activists within Black nationalist organizations often "placed emphasis on gender-specific roles in the family, at work, and in political organizing endorsed an implicit heteronormative framework that denied the possibility of other sexual and gender identifications."[2] Though complicated by women's complicity, the rigid gender roles of the era did real violence to women, queer people, and gender-nonconforming people, and as such cannot and must not be swept under the rug. For instance, in Jayne Cortez's poem "Race," from her first published collection of poetry, she exhorts Black men to "slaughter" their "Faggot Queer Punk Sissy" sons for the crime of being "unable to grasp the fact / and responsibility / of manhood black."[3] Lest we forget, in a desire to reclaim the Black Arts movement from accusations of misogyny and homophobia, some of its most prominent members voiced such a toxic calcification of gender roles that a number of Black women writers willfully disavowed or distanced themselves from it. This chapter explores the work of two poets who sought to define themselves outside of and beyond the strictures on Black womanhood of the day, through a reworking of a feminized spiritual terrain left untouched by Black nationalist ideologies. Because of their distance from these ideologies, the Black nationalist themes of their work have often gone unnoticed.

Audre Lorde and Lucille Clifton are two Black poets who are seldom scripted into Black power ideologies of the 1970s and 1980s.[4] Especially in Clifton's case, this has resulted in an elision of the political importance of their poetic visions of Black liberation. While, according to literary historian James Smethurst, "the poetics and basic ideology of the Black Arts Movement were far from unified," the circles of literary influence comprising Amiri Baraka, Sonia Sanchez, Ishmael Reed, Nikki Giovanni, and Jayne Cortez, among others, did not include these two women.[5] Though Clifton and Lorde were by no means the only Black woman poets of the 1970s to express their uneasiness with the rigid identity categories of the Black Arts movement, the spiritual bent of their intervention into the politics of the 1970s is quite unique. As Cheryl Clarke notes in her study of the women poets of the Black Arts movement, many of its most central women writers, notably Nikki Giovanni and Gwendolyn Brooks, issued searing critiques of both the authenticity politics and the sexism of the movement, as "they critiqued and paid homage to the dictates, the orthodoxies, and the enunciated desires of their black brothers and comrades."[6]

For Lorde and Clifton, Afro-diasporic spirituality becomes both escape and antidote to a restrictive Blackness from which they were always already excluded. The virulent authenticity politics of the era and the dominion they held over memories of Africa shunted both women onto spiritual paths deemed outside the movement. Lorde turned to African and diasporic pantheons of spirits for a version of revolution in which Black lesbians are the vanguard rather than the outliers. Clifton turned to an active practice of spirit communication that allowed her to emphasize the primacy and specificity of the Black woman's body as a site of spiritual encounter, even as she complicates the notion of Black feminist embodiment by presenting the Black woman's body as one transitory incarnation among many. By reinscribing both of these poets into the dominant liberation discourses of their era, I hope to illustrate that their spirituality offered a vision of Black power beyond gender roles.

Africa Unbound: The Uses of Goddesses in the Works of Audre Lorde

Though deeply invested in redefining Black American life through the deployment of an "African" worldview, many Black nationalist organizations used Africa as a blind for patriarchal desires, as in the case of Kawaidaism, the cultural nationalist philosophy that produced the holiday of Kwanzaa. Amiri Baraka, who enjoyed a short-lived but enthusiastic adherence to the doctrine, wrote in his treatise on Kawaida, "We do not believe in 'equality' of men and women. We cannot understand what devils and the devilishly influenced mean when they say equality for women. We could never be equals . . . nature has not provided thus. The brother says, 'Let a woman be a wo-man . . . and let a man be a ma-an. . . .' But this means that we will complement each other, that you, who I call my house, because there is no house without a man and his wife, are the single element in the universe that perfectly completes my essence."[7] Kawaidaism was developed by Maulana Karenga in 1965, and given that the founder was convicted of a brutal assault on two of his female followers in 1971, it is perhaps unsurprising that this philosophy was responsible for one of the most gender-restrictive doctrines of the era. According to historian Ashley D. Farmer, Kawaidaists "based their doctrine and social practices on an inaccurate and ahistorical model of Africa that collapsed the cultural, economic, and social differences among past and present African societies, countries, and cultures."[8] The "healthy African identities" of which Baraka speaks indeed have no referent to any culturally or historically specific example. Here, we see Baraka under a guise of traditional "African" values, parroting Karenga's unsubstantiated claim that the historical and present role of the "African woman" was to "inspire her man, educate her children, and to participate in social development."[9] What, I wonder, would Oyá, a machete-wielding female spirit of change and death and thunder, have to say about this vision of the African woman? Kawaidaism leaves this unanswered, because it ignores the countless spiritual and cultural examples of African womanhood outside of the service to a man.

For all of the Afrocentrism of the 1970s, certain hallmarks of African spiritualities across the diaspora—namely, powerful female spirits and ancestral communication—are found to be incompatible with a patriarchal American vision, and are conveniently excised from Black nationalist rhetoric of the 1970s. See, for example, the rise in popularity of orisha worship as early as 1960 with Oseijeman Adefunmi's foundation of the Yoruba Temple in Harlem.[10] His conception of Africa "grew firmly out of the context of 1960s expressions of black nationalism, which required at that time no mass exodus to the continent, but instead the mining of its cultural, religious, and psychical resources in order to rehumanize and rehistoricize blackness in North America."[11] While Adefunmi's conception of Yoruba cosmology was shaped by American patriarchalism, featuring a largely male aristocratic leadership and male-centered polygamy, today this spiritual tradition boasts thousands of adherents in the United States, many of whom are women, many of whom occupy leadership or priestess roles. Three of this tradition's most powerful and popular spirits—Yemayá, Oyá, and Ochún—are woman-identified spirits governing principles as diverse as fertility, death, caretaking, storms, eroticism, and bodies of water; the creator of the universe, Obatalá, is a gender-less spirit whose pronouns vary depending on context and translation. Among all New World cosmologies stemming from religions of the African continent, Yoruba has particular traction in America precisely because of the characters of its female and gender-fluid spirits. Yet despite the fact that its development in the United States was coterminous with the civil rights movement and the Black nationalism of the 1970s, and despite the fact that key public figures like Malcolm X and Amiri Baraka frequented the Harlem Yoruba Temple for ceremonies and spiritual consultation, Yoruba cosmologies are rarely considered to be Black power ideologies.[12] This has everything to do with the masculinism at the heart of mid-twentieth-century iterations of Afrocentrism. The perceived divide between the spiritual and the political of the 1970s was really a divide between an essentialized conception of masculine and feminine, with woman-centered spiritualities relegated to a feminized space of frivolity—just one more thing women were asked to put aside until after the revolution.[13]

Together, Clifton and Lorde outline a feminist religious imaginary that had its own conception of Black power. At times specifically interpolating spirits of the African diaspora, at times dealing in metaphors and imagination, Lorde and Clifton lay claim to diasporic principles that are pervasive throughout theologies of the African diaspora. Many African diaspora religions readily incorporated women into the work of revolution. And not just by laying claim to a traditionally masculine symbology of weaponry, fire, and destruction. These religions also incorporated what Clifton might deem "ordinary womanhood" into the revolutionary matrix.[14] Taking up arms is not the only way that spirits aid Black liberation. They also appreciate the beauty of a nice dress, a spoonful of honey, cradling a baby, and all the other elements of Black life that elevate existence beyond a knee-jerk reaction to oppression. Clifton and Lorde seek to heal the fractures between the spiritual and the political by using their own bodies as proof that women are at the vanguard of the spiritual work of revolution.

Audre Lorde's interest in African and Afro-diasporic culture is well documented and self-avowed. When asked, in an interview with Adrienne Rich, to account for the historical and ethnographic research behind her conceptions of the Black mother, the Amazon, and African warrior goddess figures, Lorde replied, "I'm a poet, not a historian. I've shared my knowledge, I hope. Now you go document it, if you wish."[15] Within a context of contemporary Black feminist theory, the inventive nature of Lorde's African goddesses and mythological Black mothers may seem slightly dated at best and biologically determinist at worst, relics of a bygone 1970s fetishization of a fictive African motherland. But what if, rather than viewing these themes as instances of quaint essentialism, we viewed them as act by which Lorde creates diasporic kinship between women?

Lorde's 1978 collection of poems, *The Black Unicorn*, is the apotheosis of her interest in African-derived cosmologies. Written in the wake of her first journey to West Africa in 1974, it is so suffused with West African spirituality that the text includes a glossary of African names and a bibliography that cites, among others, Harold Courlander's and Melville Herskovits's classic ethnographic works. In this way, Lorde deploys the kinds of strategic essentialisms typical of the time period and of the Black Arts movement, to which Audre Lorde was only marginal but with which she shared a common goal of Black liberation.[16] Lorde was often caught in the crosshairs of debates between Black liberation and gay and women's liberation movements, unable to find easy identifications within any, yet she was still invested in unifying them through the imagery of the warrior woman. As James Smethurst notes, "The Black Arts warrior is both implicitly and explicitly male—though some black women writers in the post–Black Arts era, notably Audre Lorde, pointedly introduce figures of the woman warrior and the Amazon (with its lesbian subtext) into their work—both invoking and critiquing the Black Arts movement."[17] Similarly, Cheryl Clarke argues, "In Lorde's cosmology, black women are going to have to come to terms with their Amazon (women-loving-women and warrior) past."[18] Both scholars note Lorde's queer intervention into a fundamentally heteronormative iconography.

Lorde's Afrocentricity in *The Black Unicorn* is a meditation on unbelonging, by which she works in and through her feelings of betrayal and rejection at the hands of other Black people. It is ironic that a figure who has been heralded as the Black poet par excellence actually spent much of her work critiquing and struggling against Blackness as a category. In the poem "Between Ourselves," Lorde writes,

> When you impale me
> upon your lances of narrow blackness
> before you hear my heart speak
> mourn your own borrowed blood
> your own borrowed visions.[19]

In this poem, Lorde addresses her peers who are responsible for the ossified categories of Black, revolutionary, and woman that will always exclude her. For Audre Lorde, true kinship between Black people is a thing that has been interrupted by white supremacy and has yet to come again.

Lorde, who embodied a public persona as an out Black lesbian for most of her career as a writer, is obviously precluded from Black power ideologies invested in establishing gender norms predicated on heterosexual Black partnership. Her primary affect toward these ideologies is one of betrayal and hurt. In "Between Ourselves," she compares her sense of betrayal at the hands of other Black people to the original sin of Africans' complicity in the transatlantic slave trade, rendered as a "brother" who sold her great-grandmother into slavery:

> and whenever I try to eat
> the words
> of easy blackness as salvation
> I taste the colour
> of my grandmother's first betrayal.[20]

This calls to mind the variety of "skinfolk ain't kinfolk" proverbs across the African diaspora, including Zora Neale Hurston's original formulation and the Haitian Creole proverb *"Depi nan Ginen, nèg rayi nèg"* (Since we were in Africa, Black men have hated Black men). But here, Lorde turns this affect of mistrust into an interrogation of the notion of an "easy blackness" that seeks to unify Black people under a narrow banner without accounting for the multiplicity of sins we have been driven to enact on one another. By framing the origin myth of her great-grandmother betrayed by a "brother" (implying both a biological kinship and a generic Black manhood), Lorde highlights the historic uneasiness of Blackness and charts the need for reparative justice to heal the wounds of a centuries-long history of gendered violence against Black women.

Like New World Blackness itself, Lorde's feminism is also haunted by the specter of a lost communality between women. Throughout her work, she speaks of an ancestral memory of Black women's communalism, of a mythic time in West Africa when "we enjoyed each other in a sisterhood of work and power and play."[21] In the world of Lorde's essays, sisterhood between Black women is not a thing that exists in the present, but a thing that must be written into being to be placed like balm upon the wounds Black women inflict upon one another. In her devastating essay "Eye to Eye: Black Women, Hatred, and Anger," Lorde frames the vexed relationships between Black women as a direct result of the absence of a Black woman–centered cosmology: "Do we reenact these crucifixions upon each other, the avoidance, the cruelty, the judgments, because we have not been allowed black goddesses, black heroines; because we have not been allowed to see our mothers and our selves in their/our own magnificence until that magnificence became part of our blood and bone?"²² In her prose, Lorde makes clear that the answer to her rhetorical question—essentially, do we need Black goddesses to love one another?—is emphatically yes. It is through the spirit of African diaspora religions that Lorde finds an antidote to "all the . . . endless ways in which we rob ourselves of ourselves and each other."²³ Lorde's most pressing goal in her invocation of warrior goddesses is a union between seemingly disparate elements of Black womanhood. The goddesses mentioned by Lorde in her "Open Letter to Mary Daly" earn their categorization as "warrior goddesses" because they reconcile two seemingly dissonant elements: a so-called feminine imagery of flowers, fertility, and perfume with the so-called masculine work of rage and resistance. Thereby revealing, of course, that these elements are the exclusive domain of neither gender.

Though Lorde is clearly more interested and well versed in the religions and social practices of the African continent, she also has an understated interest in spirits of the Americas. It is clear from her letter to Mary Daly, in which she famously accuses white feminist theologian Mary Daly of ignoring African goddesses in Daly's 1978 text *Gyn/Ecology*, that Lorde is aware of Vodou. Providing a litany of spirits and heroines, all of whom are native to Africa, Lorde asks Mary Daly, "Where are the warrior goddesses of the Vodoun [sic]?"²⁴ Interestingly enough, this passing reference is the only reference Lorde makes to a spirit that originates in the New World. But because Lorde herself is a child of the Caribbean diaspora, born to a Grenadian mother and Barbadian father in the United States, I argue that Haitian Vodou (a revolutionary theology that created a number of new spirits to address the slavery and racism in the Americas) shares with Lorde a methodology and a set of principles that address the specific social problems of New World Blackness through a cosmological lens. Lorde's citation of Vodou goddesses is an oblique reference to Ezili, the most prominent pantheon of female spirits in Haitian Vodou. Ezili is not so much one figure as she is a set of problematics organized under one name. There are many versions of Ezili, each representing a different version of femininity: Ezili Freda, a beautiful light-skinned woman with an implacable love for luxury. Ezili Dantò, a dark-skinned single mother with a scarred face, a defender of women wronged. Lasirèn, a mermaid who lives at the bottom of the sea and imparts sacred knowledge. Following the lead of Omise'eke Natasha Tinsley's iconoclastic scholarship in *Ezili's Mirrors: Imagining Black Queer Genders*, I view Ezili's multiple manifestations as Afro-diasporic archetypes that work through a specific facet of Black women's lived experiences.

There is a rich tradition of feminist academic work concerning Ezili Freda. Contemporary scholars like Omise'eke Natasha Tinsley, Colin Dayan, and Karen McCarthy Brown, as well as early ethnographers like Zora Neale Hurston and Maya Deren, have all theorized the reason behind Ezili Freda's demanding and luxurious femme persona. I prefer to draw from Maya Deren's version of Ezili Freda in her 1953 ethnography, *Divine Horsemen*, which to this day remains one of the most influential claims for Ezili Freda's philosophical importance. Deren argues that, in contrast to cosmologies that equate the feminine principle with maternity and motherhood, "Vodoun [sic] has given woman, in the figure of Erzulie [sic], exclusive title to that which distinguishes humans from all other forms: their capacity to conceive beyond reality, to desire beyond adequacy, to create beyond need."[25] In Deren's representation, Freda's demand for material beauty in the form of gauzy fabrics, dainty cakes, and Florida Water is not a marker of the individual spirit's selfishness, but a defining condition of humanity. In a society scarred by slavery's attempts to eradicate human emotions and aesthetics in order to reduce enslaved peoples' lives to mere survival, Freda's demand for material beauty, for things that are not necessary to survival, is a radical claim to humanity. There are striking similarities between Deren's conception of Freda and Lorde's reformulation, in "Poetry is Not a Luxury," of "I think, therefore I am" as "I feel, therefore I can be free."[26]

Deren is the first American scholar to describe what others have seen as Freda's caprices not as deficiencies or cruelties on the part of the spirit, but as philosophical tenants in themselves. Freda's sexual promiscuity, her love of perfumes and sumptuous fabrics, and her frequent bouts of uncontrollable sobbing have inevitably led to femme-phobic devaluations of her frivolity and capriciousness. But it is within these denigrated markers of femininity that Deren locates the driving force for social change. Deren describes Freda's embodied presence at ritual ceremonies as exacting. She demands of her devotees the most precise attention to detail, and inevitably bursts into tears when her exact wishes are not satisfied. These tears are not about individual details of the ceremony, but rather about her disappointment in a sordid world that will never satisfy her.[27] Her tears are a reminder to her devotees not to be complacent with the injustices of the world and to continue to dream, "to begin where reality ends and to spin it and send it forward in space, as the spider spins and sends forward its own thread."[28]

Like Ezili Freda, Lorde is a woman who cries too much, a woman whose denigrated femininity interrogates the world. In "Eye to Eye," Lorde explains that one of the ways that Black women have been damaged by patriarchy and racism is by internalizing the idea that softness and tears are a luxury we cannot afford: "Most of the black women I know think I cry too much, or that I'm too public about it. I've been told that crying makes me seem soft and therefore of little consequence. As if our softness has to be the price we pay for power, rather than simply the one that's paid most easily and most often."[29] In the same essay, Lorde says, "survival is the greatest gift of love. Sometimes, for Black mothers, it is the only gift possible, and tenderness gets lost."[30] Lorde depicts tenderness and softness not as impediments to survival, but as its apotheosis. When we dispense with tenderness, in Lorde's thinking, we mirror the very state of mere bodily survival that slavery sought to reduce us to. Lorde's goal is to make the world a space where survival is not the only gift possible, where Black women can live in and share their own tenderness. This is why she develops the concept of the erotic.

Lorde's concept of the erotic is capacious, nonhierarchical, and intuitive, a union of knowledge and feeling that can take many forms. As evident from her famous line, "For me, there is no difference between writing a good poem and moving into sunlight against the body of the woman I love," the erotic can encompass the sexual but also exceeds it.[31] The erotic is all that is luxurious, all that is in excess of survival. But for Lorde, the erotic is above all a call to action: "For once we begin to feel deeply all the aspects of our lives, we begin to demand from ourselves and from our life-pursuits that they feel in accordance with that joy which we know ourselves to be capable of. Our erotic knowledge empowers us, becomes a lens through which we scrutinize all aspects of our existence. . . . And this is a grave responsibility projected from within each of us, not to settle for the convenient, the shoddy, the conventionally expected, nor the merely safe."[32] Like Freda's tears, Lorde's emphasis on softness and joy are a demand for the world to be better. Just as Freda is, according to Deren "the loa [spirit] of things as they could be, not as they are," Lorde's erotic is a map of a world that does not yet exist but that can be fought for.[33] The battle is for our own softness in a world that seems to demand, and yet is being destroyed by, the need for dominance. The erotic, like Ezili, is a form of Black femme warfare. It is not a militancy that subsumes itself in a warlike masculinism. It is not a militancy that destroys bodies and poisons the earth. It is a militancy grounded in the antithesis of these things: beauty, pleasure, and sensuality. And the prize to be won is nothing less than our own selves and our own right to touch, feel, and commune with one another.

This is not to say that Lorde eschews more directly confrontational forms of social change. Like Ezili, she presents multiple manifestations and multiple emotional responses to conditions of oppression. Lorde's reclamation of bad affects under the auspices of the warrior goddess is nowhere more prominent than in her series of essays about anger: "Eye to Eye," "The Uses of Anger," and (less explicitly but, I argue, quite concerned with anger) "The Transformation of Silence into Language and Action." Much like "The Uses of the Erotic," Lorde's conception of anger seeks to realize a future-perfect community of Black women. In order to do this, Lorde must take a deep dive into the internecine gender struggles of the Black community of the 1970s to reclaim the denigrated figure of the angry Black woman.

A post-Moynihan reclaiming of the angry Black woman is no easy feat, but Lorde endeavors it. The Moynihan Report (*The Negro Family: The Case for National Action*), that infamous 1965 document arguing that African American "matriarchal structure" of the "Negro family" was responsible for a "tangle of pathologies," had unparalleled repercussions within the Black community as Black women scrambled to show they were not castrators and Black men scrambled to show they were not castrated. Prominent Black women artists, writers, and activists, notably Alice Walker, Michele Wallace, and Ntozake Shange, became embroiled in controversy over their depiction of Black men in their work; in one article, Askia Toure compared Shange and Wallace to COINTELPRO (the Counterintelligence Program) in the harm they did to the Black community.[34] Ishmael Reed even went to the trouble of publishing an entire novel, *Reckless Eyeballing*, that was essentially a thinly veiled attack on Walker and Shange. This debate is crystallized in the controversy surrounding Robert Staples's 1979 essay "The Myth of the Black Macho: A Response to Angry Black Feminists," which prompted such an outcry when it was published in *The Black Scholar* that the journal devoted a subsequent issue to a reader's forum on "The Black Sexism Debate."[35] I will not devote much time to Staples's essay, which is poorly researched and speciously argued, but I will call attention to one statement from Staples: "At the end of the play [*for colored girls*], what I find especially unsettling, is Shange's invitation to black women to love themselves. This seems, to me, to be no less than an extension of the culture of Narcissism. She does not mention compassion for misguided black men or love of child family or community. . . . A black woman who loves only herself is incapable of loving others. What greater way to insure [sic] being alone the rest of your life than the self-centered posture so eloquently expressed in Ntozake Shange's play?"[36] There are a number of strands needing unpacking in Staples's paradoxical statement. That Black women's self-love should be so unsettling that Staples must resort to a facile bad faith reading (for in the same way that no one ever said *only* Black lives matter, Shange never said Black women should love *only* themselves, as Staples surely realizes) only speaks to the potential energy of Black women's self-love. What would the world look like if Black women redirected their steadfast and martyred love from their men and their children to themselves? What if Black women redirected their prodigious anger away from one another and toward the structures of the world that have caused their anger?

Lorde's response to Staples's article depicts a community in crisis, fractured by patriarchal notions of gender and family structures. Lorde's response to the essay, which was first published in *The Black Scholar* and later collected in "Sister Outsider," emphasizes the way American gender roles are rooted in white supremacy: "It is not the destiny of black america to repeat white america's mistakes. But we will, if we mistake the trappings of success in a sick society for the signs of a meaningful life. If black men continue to define 'femininity' instead of their own desires, and to do it in archaic european terms, they restrict our access to each other's energies. Freedom and future for blacks does not mean absorbing the dominant white male disease of sexism."[37]

In this essay, Lorde responds to discourses from both Black and white men that paint Black women's demands for accountability as part of a pathological unfemininity. Anger becomes an accusation by which supposed proponents of Black power ungender Black women. In Staples's original essay, he suggests that "some women do make the decisions and desertion is [the Black man's] form of masculine protest."[38] In Lorde's description of Staples, she argues that because of her anger, her decidedness, and her competency, the Black woman fails to conform to "the model of 'femininity' as set forth in this country," and that Staples, like the rest of society, views loneliness, abuse, and abandonment as her just punishment.[39] Here, Lorde's scare quotes around "femininity" bespeak an unwillingness to use the master's tools to destroy the master's house; Lorde will not make an appeal to "the model of femininity set forth in this country" if it means buying into a pseudo-Victorian ideal of bourgeois womanhood resting upon the laurels of white supremacy. Anger is the force by which Lorde seeks gender roles beyond white capitalist definitions of masculine and feminine, the innovative force that teaches us not to "accept only the designs already known, deadly and safely familiar."[40]

There is ample precedent within diasporic religions for the figure of the angry Black woman. Oyá, of Yoruba cosmologies, who dances with a horsewhip and destroys life to make it anew. Her sister spirits, Yemayá and Ochún, also have wrathful incarnations that use water to purify and destroy.

And Ezili Dantò, the patroness of single mothers and women wronged in Haitian Vodou, who represents "the maternal anger that is called into play when a mother must defend her children," which "turned Dantò into a woman warrior during the slave revolution."[41] None of these spirits are wanton destructresses, however: in Afro-diasporic cosmologies, as in Lorde's own cosmology—"I speak hear as a woman of Color who is not bent upon destruction, but upon survival"—the spirits of death are often simultaneously the spirits of rebirth and purification.[42] I will focus on the principles represented by Ezili Dantò as the animating force behind Lorde's writing on anger and silence. Here, I draw from Karen McCarthy Brown's depiction of Dantò in *Mama Lola: A Vodou Priestess in Brooklyn*, which offers a window into the potentially feminist valences of the spirit.

Often represented as a symbol of Haiti itself (abused and racialized, yet powerful), Dantò's image as an advocate for women wronged is full of contradictions, the first among them being that she cannot speak. As Brown notes, when Dantò possesses people, the only words she can produce are a stuttering "dey-dey-dey" sound.[43] Given Lorde's virulent opposition to silence as expressed in "The Transformation of Silence into Language and Action," I am aware of the irony in viewing a spirit who cannot speak as the patron saint of Lorde's uses of anger. However, Dantò's speechlessness brings up important themes of nonverbal communication, and occasions a loving act of interpretation by all worshippers present as they come together to interpret her wants and needs: "Dantò's inarticulate sounds gain meaning in a Vodou ceremony only through her body language and the interpretive efforts of the gathered community."[44] These same powers of Black women's collective interpretation are what Lorde calls for to allow women to process their anger and transform it into revolutionary sentiment. Dantò's iconic refrain in one of her praise songs—"Seven stabs of the knife, seven stabs of the sword. / Hand me that basin, I'm going to vomit blood"—speaks to the corrosive elements of unexpressed rage and to the physical manifestations of Black women's betrayals by society.[45] No one knows why she is vomiting blood, or who has stabbed her. No one knows if she has been injured or poisoned or if she suffers from some mysterious illness. What is clear is that she is being attacked from the inside and that she must rid herself of toxicity in order to keep fighting. When Dantò is vomiting blood, she is purging herself of the fears behind the silences; she is, insofar as she is capable, speaking. And it is her community of worshippers who are inspired to write a song that expresses the depth of that love and that betrayal that compels her to continue fighting for them even as she is vomiting blood. Interpreting the bodily language of Ezili, listening to her anger, is an example of the ways Black women can realize the collective nature of their seemingly individual angers, a collectivity that Lorde describes:

> Women of Color in America have grown up within a symphony of anger, at being silenced, at being unchosen, at knowing that when we survive, it is in spite of a world that takes for granted our lack of humanness, and which hates our very existence outside of its service. And I say *symphony* rather than *cacophony* because we have had to learn to orchestrate those furies so that they do not tear us apart [emphasis in original]. We have had to learn to move through them and use them for strength and force insight within our daily lives. Those of us who did not learn this difficult lesson did not survive. And part of my anger is always libation for my fallen sisters.[46]

The idea that Black women form a symphony is, at first glance, at odds with the despair of Lorde's anger essays. If Black women form a symphony, then why are we so at odds with one another, so discordant in our jealousy and despair? In Lorde's thought, the expression of anger reveals the symphony. "Anger is loaded with information and energy," says Lorde.[47] The songs that we have been playing, wrathfully, bitterly, in the dark, are revealed to be harmonies of our sister's songs. And those fallen sisters, the ones who could not express their anger, are those same sisters who in "The Transformation of Silence into Language and Action" eventually died of their inexpressible anger: "What are the tyrannies you swallow day by day and attempt to make your own, until you will sicken and die of them, still in silence?"[48] Lorde's project is above all to encourage Black women to express their anger, to play anger like an instrument, in order to redeem that community of Black women who have fallen into the abyss between anger and language. Perhaps this symphony of anger is the foundation of a community yet to come.

In order for this community to be built, some of the anger that dispels silence must, inevitably, be used among Black women. Like Audre Lorde's essays, Ezili Dantò's backstory is filled with troubling stories of the violence Black people enact on one another. One version of Dantò's mythology holds that her face is scarred because she and Freda got in a fight over a man.[49] Another maintains that she cannot speak because her own people tore out her tongue to keep her from divulging their revolutionary secrets.[50] Some also say that her beloved child Anais, with whom she is usually depicted in visual representations, was killed during the Haitian Revolution. What do we make of these stories in which some of the trying circumstances that prompted the need for Dantò's heroism were precipitated by her own people rather than her enemies? What do we do when we are cast not just as the victims but as the perpetrators? According to Lorde, these inconsistencies are useful in themselves: "Often we give lip service to the idea of mutual support and connection between black women because we have not yet crossed the barriers to these possibilities. . . . And to acknowledge our dreams is to sometimes acknowledge the distance between those dreams and our present situation."[51] Part of caring for Dantò involves reckoning with a legacy of betrayal so that we can bridge the gap between our dreams of connection and our reality of violence. Dantò is a divinity, but she is also a Black woman, crucified on a cross of broken promises and intimate betrayals, spouting blood and willing to spout more blood—what is more diasporic, more heroic, than that? Despite these rumblings of betrayal, Dantò continues to fight for her serviteurs, and in so doing represents Black women's incredible capacity for loyalty and forgiveness even and especially when we have wronged one another. Those are the true uses of anger—not as an interpersonal violence, but as a way of making tangible our aspirations for redress and reconciliation.

Some Damn Body: Spirit and Embodiment in the Writings of Lucille Clifton

Like Audre Lorde, Lucille Clifton was coterminous with, but not part of, the Black Arts movement. Like Lorde, Clifton was deeply ambivalent about the authenticity politics of the era. Lucille Clifton's protest of Black power gender roles is perhaps more understated than Lorde's, but ever present throughout her poetry. Clifton's poem "apology (to the panthers)," for instance, is at first glance a confession of her failure to be properly radical. She addresses the Panthers as men exclusively: "brothers i thank you for these mannish days." Odd, as Clifton must know of women Panthers, and as the label of the era as "mannish" seems to preclude her own participation. But then she tells her brothers, "i grieve my whiteful ways." This word choice of "grieve" does not carry the idea of repentance that a word like "regret" might. There is a slight indictment of the Panthers for creating the conditions of her grief, for condemning her whiteful ways to death. "Whiteful," when placed in opposition to "mannish," becomes a tenuous analogue to the unspoken "womanish." To be a revolutionary, the poem implies, is to be a man; all else is whitefulness.[52] Where do Black women fit into this 1970s dichotomy between whiteful and mannish? Painstakingly, exuberantly, Clifton's spiritual practice carves out a space beyond the unspoken impossibility of a revolutionary Black woman.

Interviewers and critics are often fixated on asking Clifton to account for her place in the Black activism of the 1960s and 1970s, an impulse she thwarts magnificently.[53] When asked point blank what she was doing in the 1960s, with the implication being that she was absent from the freedom struggles of the decade, Clifton responds, "Well, during the 1960s I was pretty much pregnant. I have six kids, and they're six and a half years apart in age, from the oldest to the youngest."[54] In emphasizing the biological constraints preventing her from participating in visible forms of Black activism, Clifton subtly shifts the definition of radicalism beyond masculinist modes of charismatic leadership. In a cryptic poem titled "the 70s," Clifton says,

> will be the days
> i go unchildrened
> strange women will walk
> out my door and in
> hiding my daughters
> holding my sons
> leaving me nursing on myself
> again
> having lost some
> begun much[55]

The strange women, yet to come, are the Black nationalist ideal of womanhood. The women demanded by the ideologies of the 1970s, who will uplift and inspire sons, and hide the desires of daughters out of sight. Those strange women supplanting Clifton in her insufficient Blackness and womanness to be the perfect embodiment of the African Woman. Queenly and inspirational as a statue, and just as loving. But Clifton ultimately forgives what this rhetoric of ideal Black womanhood has cost her ("lost some"), because of the things it has set in motion ("begun much."). She acknowledges that the 1970s were a time of similar longings and divergent methodologies between Black men and women.

All this is really a question of memory. Of who gets to remember, and how. The Black cultural nationalism of Clifton's youth is so concerned with resurrecting Africa that it has forgotten the muscle memory of difference already encoded in its warring soul. In the popular poem "why some people be mad at me sometimes," Clifton says,

> they ask me to remember
> but they want me to remember
> their memories
> and i keep on remembering
> mine.[56]

This poem was Clifton's quiet but biting response to a prompt she found problematic: as poet laureate of Maryland, she was asked to write a poem to commemorating the state's 350-year colonial history.[57] While the easy interpretation of the poem would be to label these "some people" as white, I think Clifton said "some people" and not "white people" for a reason. These people who place prohibitions on her memory can also be those whose memory of Africa is an excuse to impose uniformity on the living Black community. Clifton's own memories—the words of her ancestors, reminding her of where she came from and where she is going—are lost under authenticity politics labeling Blackness as synonymous with its vociferous self-proclamation. As Kevin Quashie compellingly argues, considering the interiority of the everyday lives of Black people beyond a demand for Black people's compulsory "resistance" is a way "to restore humanity without being apolitical."[58] Similarly, Clifton's insistence upon her Blackness outside of a visible political framework seeks to counter the fact that "people have a tendency, I think, to believe that if you don't say 'black' in every other line, you must be somehow not wishing to be part of Black."[59]

Clifton's poem "africa" reads,

> home
> oh
> home
> the soul of your
> variety
> all of my bones
> remember.[60]

She feels, in a deeply embodied way, that there is more "variety" in the African cultural reality than the Afrocentric game of telephone has conveyed to her. Rather than the knowing of unrecoverable historical details, the embodied experience of her "bones" tells her that there is something more in her history than the skeletal offering of motherhood and wifehood. Africa is often connected with memory throughout Clifton's work. It stands in for a kind of muscle memory and for all that is forgotten. In the lines "i long for the rains of wydah / [. . .] not just this springtime and / these wheatfields / white poets call the past," Clifton gestures toward the tropical seasonal rhythms of rainy and dry seasons rather than the winter-spring-summer-fall of temperate regions.[61] By linking her Black American body to the memory of a different climate, Clifton argues that a sense of historical dysphoria imposed by white conceptions of history is felt deeply in the Black body, even when its contours are not fully known by the mind.

In "ca'line's prayer," Clifton writes from the perspective of her great-grandmother, who was born in West Africa, possibly Benin, in 1822. This woman, Mammy Ca'line, figured prominently in Clifton's family lore as a "Dahomey woman," meant to convey a lineage of warrior-like strength and endurance running through Clifton herself. Clifton describes her father describing his grandmother: "she used to always say 'Get what you want, you from Dahomey women.' And she used to tell us about how they had a whole army of nothing but women back there and how they was the best soldiers in the world."[62] However, in "ca'line's prayer," the speaker is no Amazon taking stock of her conquests. In the poem, she is an old and thirsty woman who has spent her years "in a desert country." The first stanza is a confession of her current state ("i am dry / and black as drought"), but the second stanza forms a prayer:

> remember me from wydah
> remember the child
> running across dahomey
> black as ripe papaya
> juicy as sweet berries
> and set me in rivers of your glory
>
> Ye Ma Jah.[63]

Some might recognize here, chopped and disjointed, the name of the Yoruba spirit of the ocean, Yemayá. Syllables detached from meaning. The goddess dismembered, but dredged from the deep. Though she asks Yemayá to remember her, through this act of prayer, Ca'line is also remembering the distinct cosmology of her African youth. Ca'line's prayer is as much a prayer for water as it is for memory, because in Clifton's theology, the two are synonymous. All of her poems that speak of water's revenge are really a call to the body to remember.

Clifton's poetry of the 1970s has an eschatological framework in which water brings judgment and memory. This calls to mind Toni Morrison's assertion that when a river floods "it is not flooding; it is remembering. Remembering where it used to be. All water has a perfect memory and is forever trying to get back to where it was."[64] Humans being 60 percent water, Clifton's linkages between water and flesh memory hold a profound and bodily sense of rightness. As M. Jacqui Alexander puts it, "the body's water composition seals our aquatic affinity with the divine."[65] Clifton taps into an Afro-diasporic imaginary of water as both womb and tomb, as a force that baptizes and heals as well as drowns and destroys. In a poem called "jonah," for example,

> what i remember
> is green
> in the trees
> and the leaves
> and the smell of mango
> and yams
> and if i had a drum
> I would send to the brothers
> —Be care full of the ocean—[66]

Jonah is reimagined as a victim of the Middle Passage, remembering Africa from the bottom of the ocean. Beginning in one of the few capitalizations of Clifton's oeuvre, Jonah's twofold message to "the brothers" back in Africa is both warning and instruction. Beware the ocean. Care for the ocean. Jonah's sojourn at the end of the sea is not a death, however; if he follows the same trajectory as the biblical Jonah, he will someday survive to impart what he has learned to his brothers. As, indeed, the ancestors of Clifton's spirit writing did.

Similarly to Lorde, Clifton drew from a combination of mythological imagery to write a more capacious Blackness into being. Clifton, however, has a more global imaginary: she has more poems about Kali than any African-derived spirit, and at the pivotal moment in 1976 when she receives a spirit visitation from her ancestors, she chooses to narrate the visitation through Catholic imagery invoking the Virgin Mary and Joan of Arc. Clifton likes earth-churning goddesses. Spirits that rise from the sea—that are the sea, in fact—to enact revenge. Though her turn to spirit communication beginning in 1976 might have come as a surprise to her, her visitation as described in *Two-Headed Woman* was perhaps not sudden but conjured over time by the themes of her earlier poetry. Clifton's brand of Afrocentricity, unlike Lorde's, is based less in an invocation of African cosmology than a state of humility before all the details of that cosmology that have been forgotten. In Clifton's poetry, you will find no glossaries of African terms, no African warrior goddesses, no myths of matriarchal society. Instead, there are the gentle but persistent calls to an Africa remembered in shadows.

Clifton's poems written throughout the 1960s and 1970s are libations poured to ancestors remembered and unremembered, but midway through the 1970s, the ancestors answered back. In May of 1976, while sitting in her living room with two of her daughters, Lucille Clifton thought to herself, "Why not get out the Ouija board?" Or rather, "something told" her to get out the Ouija board.[67] What began as a casual evening with her daughters in which the Ouija board told one of them she would marry John Travolta quickly turned into an announcement that unsettled all who were present: that Clifton's mother, who had been dead for eighteen years, was speaking to them.[68] Clifton's mother, Thelma, died when Clifton was twenty-two years old, and Clifton had already resigned herself to the reality of her untimely passing, remarking, "It is the tradition of my race, my sex, and my family to continue with our lives. We have borne enormous deaths before. We go on."[69] However, notions around the inevitability of Black women's suffering and death were completely reversed by her mother's dramatic spiritual contact. By 1978, the spirit of Clifton's mother was a household presence spoken to almost daily by Clifton and her six children, once even saving her oldest daughter, Sidney, from falling down the stairs.[70]

Lucille Clifton is part of a long and storied tradition of clairvoyant Black American women. The trope of clairvoyant Black women, known as rootworkers, two-headed women, and hoodoo women, has existed as long as Black women have been in the Americas but saw a renaissance in the last decades of the twentieth century. This trend is glimpsed through characters like Minnie Ransom in Toni Cade Bambara's *The Salt Eaters* (1980) and Miranda Day in Gloria Naylor's *Mama Day* (1988), as well as in popular iterations like Whoopi Goldberg's character Oda Mae Brown in the 1990 film *Ghost*. Alice Walker, at the end of *The Color Purple* (1982), even signs off as "A.W. author and medium." However, Clifton literalizes this writerly trope and thus both diverges from and complicates the traditionally conceived definition of the Black medium, or, as she calls it, the two-headed woman. In Clifton's theory of spirit, Blackness and the Black body are decentered by the concept of reincarnation. When she asks her spirit interlocutors about her previous incarnations, she is surprised to learn that in many of them, she was not a woman at all.[71] The spirit of her mother, Thelma, who apparently having found her last incarnation as a Black woman painful, prefers to go by the name Greta, which belonged to one of her prior incarnations.[72] The transcendental nature of Clifton's cosmology might seem at odds with a Black feminist worldview that positions race and gender as defining factors of a person's lived experience. What is Black feminism when the Black woman's body is just one of many costumes a soul can wear, and then discard? What happens to those specificities of race and gender when a person's soul is not bound by them?

This is the first published study to make use of her vast unpublished archive of spirit writing, which is currently housed at Emory University's Stuart A. Rose Manuscript, Archives, and Rare Book Library.[73] Lucille Clifton's spirit writing, while ostensibly fitting into a race- and gender-blind New Age tradition, is actually an important contribution to Black feminist theories of embodiment. The specificity of Clifton's body—fat, brown-skinned, mother—is the sweet stuff upon which spirits alight like butterflies, carrying messages for the salvation of humanity. Although the spirits admonish Clifton for her fixation on earthly matters of race and gender—"you wish to speak of / black and white . . . have we not talked of human"—she maintains a delicate balance between the idea of a raceless soul and her incarnation as a Black woman.[74] Far from being an esoteric post-racialism, Clifton's theory of spirit is made possible by her Black womanhood. It is no accident that her body and its specificities that could serve as a channel for the spirits. As the departed spirit of her own mother said to her, "*You are a natural channel.*"[75] Here, the Black woman medium is a meeting place, a body already accustomed to being shared—with children, through labor, in history—without losing itself. Clifton describes her clairvoyance as a balancing act between selfhood and self-sharing in which she tries "not to abuse it, or be abused by it."[76] Alice Walker, similarly, is quick to clarify about her clairvoyance that "what I'm working on meets in me and merges with me, and that is what happens, rather than people just coming through totally as themselves with none of me in them."[77] In other words, the work of the Black woman medium is not as a tool for the spirits, but as a partner. I argue that in Clifton's writing, Black womanhood is represented as particularly fruitful ground for this kind of spiritual partnership. It is to be a lightning rod for everyone else's electrified narratives and desires, yet to remain discrete, unburned, and incandescent.

In her study *Soul Talk*, Akasha Gloria Hull identifies a trend in New Age spirituality among African American women like Clifton, arising around 1980. Unlike the often raceless ideology of mainstream New Age–isms, Hull argues that Black women's engagements with it are "socially embedded [and] can be used in a socially responsive way to fight societal ills."[78] This involves a melding of New Age beliefs around astrology and reincarnation with African diasporic spiritual traditions, as exemplified by Lucille Clifton's self-identification as a "two-headed woman." As Hull explains, "throughout diasporic African cultures, people such as healers, savants, and rootworkers who possess innate, intuitive insight into the invisible world are termed *two-headed*, which is to signify that they have a command of that world as well as the everyday, external one that is considered by most people to be real."[79] In an eclectic style typical of the era, Clifton's beliefs range from serious reflections on the fate of the universe to zany meditations on Black astrology (in her incomplete manuscript "Soul Signs: An Astrology for Black People," for example, she includes lists of all the astrological signs as Black movies or as soul food; for instance, Taurus: Candied Yams). Even at her most whimsical, however, Clifton recognizes that Black spirituality, including astrology, "is a product of one's history and one's circumstance and the history and circumstance of Black people is unique, especially in America."[80]

Greta/Thelma's initial spirit communications began a lifelong family practice for the Cliftons, most heavily documented throughout the late 1970s and early 1980s, of communications with the spirit world. It was an endeavor that enlisted Clifton's six children to varying degrees, sometimes as automatic writers, sometimes as interpreters for non-English-speaking spirits, and sometimes even channeling the voices of spirits through their own bodies. Even Clifton's husband Fred, who is never described by her as participating in her organized efforts to talk to the spirits, had a robust meditative practice in which he was visited by a variety of spirits stemming from Eastern spiritual traditions.[81] There was a time when Clifton herself sought to publish the results of her family's endeavors, but she encountered some resistance about publishing them; an agent wanted her to write the work under a pseudonym, and publishers she approached didn't like it because it wasn't "sensationalistic" enough, ignoring Clifton's assertion that "nothing was like *The Amityville Horror*. That kind of Hollywood ghost stuff doesn't happen, that's not real."[82] In contrast, Clifton insists upon the ordinariness of her family ("We are not unusual people") and refuses to indulge in any claim of exceptionalism regarding whatever skill or circumstance might contribute to their clairvoyance.[83] Instead, Clifton tries to shift society's perception of reality by emphasizing the commonplace nature of spirits: "Our house, our home is not haunted of course, not by robe-wearing ghosts springing from dark corners and booing us during the night, it is not that. It is simply that we are able to perceive and to receive communications from the spirits of the dead. And it is not that there are ghosts in our house, it is simply that there are spirits in the world."[84] An ordinary family, an ordinary woman, talking with ordinary spirits. But her goals are anything but ordinary: to acknowledge the presence of spirits in the world is to acknowledge the veracity of their messages to Clifton and her family, some of which prescribe radical changes in the way that humans live their earthly lives. By making the experience of one black family universal and transcendental, Clifton seeks to change what the spirits call "the world of the Americas."

Although some of the spirits that communicated with the Clifton's family were the spirits of ordinary people whose lives were largely forgotten by the living, in 1977, Clifton put out an open call to the spirit world for celebrity spirits who would like to take part in an anthology of sorts. Twenty spirits volunteered, though some of the volunteers never made it to the interview stage.[85] She devised a questionnaire that she posed to each spirit, including questions such as "What was the experience of death like for you?" and "Would you like to clarify anything about your life for our world?" The resulting interviews were a strange, rollicking, and deeply moving compilation of voices as diverse as Lizzie Borden, Beethoven, Emily Dickinson, Bessie Smith, and Jesus of Nazareth. Clifton proves to be a sensitive and reassuring interviewer, soothing spirits who are troubled or agitated. Clyde Barrow (of *Bonnie and Clyde* fame), for example, proves to be particularly nervous and morose, so upon hearing from him that he loved to draw when he was alive, Clifton asks him to draw a picture in order to calm him down.[86] She also planned an anthology of poems by the spirits of deceased poets, but it appears to be unfinished, comprising a handful of poems by ee cummings, Emily Dickinson, and Langston Hughes. Perhaps the spirits did not see the utility in composing poetry; for, as ee cummings told her when he returned to compose a few poems, "Poetry is unnecessary here; here all is understood."[87]

These spirits, having shed their gendered and racialized bodies, have an interesting and world-weary perspective on the prejudices of humanity. Jesus of Nazareth, when asked what he looked like, replies somewhat dismissively, "Shall we deal in statistics?" but concedes to say that he had brown hair, brown eyes, and medium height. Some spirits still seem deeply traumatized by the tragic events of their lives and deaths, while others find these past sadnesses to be irrelevant. "Some spirits are reluctant to deal with our world, others a bit eager to do so," says Clifton. Clyde Barrow and Bessie Smith both confess their same-sex desires in response to the question of "Would you like to clarify anything about your life for our world?" while Billie Holiday emphatically denies her putative queerness. Beethoven, when asked whether it was true that he was of African descent, replies, "Yes. Yes, Grandfather, yes. Of course in the old days in my country we would never admit it. Silly." Emily Dickinson reveals that she became a recluse as the result of a traumatic rape, but will not reveal the perpetrator because "it is of no consequence." Two spirits, Isadora Duncan and Jack Cassidy, express the desire to be reincarnated as the opposite gender, while Billie Holiday does not want to be reincarnated, "Not for awhile, till things get better. I want to come back when I can go anywhere and be a Negro and nobody notices." All of these answers strip back the seemingly all important aspects of class, race, gender, and sexuality to reveal them as the changing weather of a soul's journey, not the journey in itself, and certainly not the most valued aspects of the spirits' incarnations on earth. When asked what things still attract them to our world, the spirits' answers are quite lovely: trees, autumn, children, happy families, laughter, singing, running around.[88]

However, it cannot be ignored or denied that these spirits are speaking through Black women's hands and mouths in the embodied forms of Clifton and her daughters. According to the spirits, though "all humans have the capacity to communicate," they particularly enjoy speaking to Clifton and her daughter Sidney because they are "positive, harmless people" by whom "all is done with a spirit of humility and love."[89] Echoing the Black feminist idea that Black women's unique perspective on liberation comes from the fact that they are at the bottom of the social hierarchy and thus cannot oppress others, one spirit says to Clifton, "You have no exploitive tendencies."[90] And so the spirits, identifying the household's openness to viewing bodies as something to be shared rather than controlled, enlist the bodies of the Clifton women. Beethoven, for instance, at first "attempted to speak through Sidney" but resorted to automatic writing when he proved hard to understand. Like in traditions of spirit possession across African diasporic religions, two entities temporarily share the same body, as evidenced by Clifton's description of "placing her/his hand on my lips." The "her" here represents Sidney's body; otherwise the words are attributed to "he," Beethoven.[91] This illustrates what Roberto Strongman deems as "the distinctly Afro-diasporic cultural representation of the human psyche as multiple, removable, and external to the body that functions as its receptacle."[92] In other words, the Clifton family's opening of their own bodies and psyches to the spirits without fear of loss or reprisal denotes an Afro-diasporic sensibility, even if they do not label it as such.

Sometimes, this diasporic belief in the transportability of psyches led to complicated situations within individual bodies. According to Clifton's theory of reincarnation, not all spirits of the formerly living were available for conversation because some of them were currently living through their next lives. Gillian, one of Clifton's daughters, "was regressed" at fourteen years old, meaning that she was brought to a state of unconsciousness in which she could experience her past lives, including one as a Nazi-era policeman named Karl who surprised the family by speaking German, a language Gillian did not speak. Her daughter Sidney's past life regression revealed Katy, a soft-spoken enslaved woman born in Nashville in 1800. In her notes on her family's past lives, Clifton reminds herself of the importance of remembering "that we are dealing with two different kinds of entities. Greta et al are dead. Karl, Katy et al are now alive again as Gillian, Sidney et al."[93] The eeriness of the voice of a former Nazi emanating from the body of a young African American girl is not included in Clifton's notes, but his inclusion in the written archive speaks to the scope of Clifton's vision. Throughout her spirit writing, Clifton takes it upon herself as a Black American woman living in the 1970s and 1980s to reckon with global atrocities and to take on the work of spiritual healing on a transnational and transhistorical scale.

Mediumistic traditions among African Americans, though indebted to theories of nineteenth-century Spiritualism first devised by white Europeans and Americans, are never divorced from the racialization of the bodies channeling the spirits. As Emily Suzanne Clark argues in her study of the Cercle Harmonique, a group of Afro-Creole spiritualists in nineteenth-century New Orleans, the spirit world can model a social harmony absent from the disequilibriums of the material world, with the spirits typically taking a progressive stance on social issues of the day. However, in Clark's example of a largely educated and affluent group of men of color, these mediums were able to use the language of the Euro-American and Christian tradition of Spiritualism to mask or elide the African influences of their practices, while their woman contemporaries, among them Marie Laveau, were the targets of repressive laws against "voodooism."[94] For women especially, the idea of a post-racial spirit world—as "the Cercle Harmonique believed death was an event that released the spirit and left the raced body on earth"—was particularly at odds with their lived experiences and their spiritual practices.[95] The New Orleans priestess Marie Laveau, a lifelong devoted Catholic and priestess of Afro-diasporic syncretic religion, is a particularly good example of the complex set of influences on Black spiritual practice.[96] Figures like Laveau are a testament to Lucille Clifton's idea that "either/or is not an African tradition. Both/and is tradition."[97] Clifton herself is a practitioner of the both/and, as Rachel Elizabeth Harding argues that she "pushes 'Christian' stories into territory more deeply aligned with indigenous/

Afro-Atlantic meanings of religion than with Western Christian doctrine and practice."[98]

Indeed, it is impossible to talk about a Black woman's ancestral communication and embodied spirituality without considering Afro-diasporic traditions of possession. Following M. Jacqui Alexander in her characterization of "spiritual work as a kind of body praxis," a consideration of Clifton's spiritual practice as a form of Black feminism requires an attentiveness to the Black woman's body and its specificities.[99] However, incorporating the sacred into feminism requires an acknowledgment that "bodies continue to participate in the social but their raison d'être does not belong there, for ultimately we are not our bodies."[100] Clifton never called herself a Black feminist, and she adopted a very ethereal take on the human body: "The soul survives bodily death, has survived numerous bodily deaths, will survive more. There is some One in each of us greater than the personality we manifest in any life. The soul does not merely select her own society, the soul is her own society. And love is eternal, is God. Is."[101] But the fact that, following Clifton's own theory, her soul has selected this particular era in which to exist is indicative of the particular lessons that being a Black woman can teach. As Toni Cade Bambara, a contemporary of Clifton's and a fellow mystic Black writer, puts it, "This soul is having an adventure in this woman, this body, and we're hanging out, and it's being fun."[102] If a Black woman's soul is her own society, it follows that a soul, not beholden to contingent social constructs like race and gender, has the capacity to change them.

Clifton's 1980 poetry collection, *Two-Headed Woman*, is her first collection to narrate her clairvoyance.[103] It begins, however, not with the story of Clifton's spirit visitations, but with a series of oft-quoted homages to various aspects of her body: "homage to my hair," "homage to my hips," and "what the mirror said," which ends with the exhortation,

listen,
woman,
you not a noplace
anonymous
girl;
mister with his hands on you
he got his hands on
some
damn
body![104]

This poem both reveals and interrupts the interchangeability of the Black woman's body, as evidenced by the anonymity of "somebody" and the emphatic imposition of an admonitory "damn." Clifton's emphasis on her body in a poetry collection that describes the demands of the spirits is not accidental. In addition to the "mister" of the poem, Clifton asserts the preciousness and integrity of her body in the draining work of spirit communication, although the spirits inform her "your tongue / is useful / not unique."[105] After all, it is her Black woman's body, which has struggled and strained and been found wanting in a variety of times and ways, through which these spirits choose to speak. Even when the spirits speak from a realm in which bodies do not matter, Clifton insists upon the importance of her own embodied experience in the world. Clifton does not disagree with the spirits but supplements their messages with her own body. When read together, Clifton's poetry and her spirit writing represent a woman possessed of the knowledge that race is an imaginary concept with material consequences. And the message borne by the spirits are shaped by the instrument of her body, though the message does not change, just as the same melody can be conveyed by a piano, or a trumpet, or a voice. Race may be earthly, profane, and temporary, but her raced body matters in this realm.[106]

A consideration of Clifton's spirit writing brings new life to readings of her most canonical poems. For example, one of Clifton's most famous poems, *won't you celebrate with me*, takes on special significance in light of her spirit writing. Its famous conclusion—"come celebrate / with me that everyday / something has tried to kill me / and has failed"—takes on a whole new meaning in light of her belief in the deathlessness of spirits in Black bodies.[107] On some of these days, for some Black people, the forces of death appear to prevail. But the energy that was these Black women's truncated lives continues, in Clifton's belief system: "That energy is real, just like this table. Any physicist will tell you that. We don't have to deal with metaphysics about that. So energy doesn't dissolve. Science knows that. So the energy that is those who have left their flesh is still around."[108] When one considers the trials of Clifton's mother's life—afflicted with epilepsy and a philandering husband, dead at forty-four years old—this notion of energy provides some comfort. Thelma Moore's spiritual return as Greta presents a Black woman's soul unbound by the structural misfortunes of her life, which becomes one negative experience among ample possibilities for joy and pleasure.

Though Clifton evinces a kind of optimism about the arc of history swinging toward justice for Black women as they travel on to more fortuitous incarnations, she is also realistic about the spiritual perils of living as a Black woman in the Americas. In an untitled poem in *Two Headed Woman*, Clifton describes how the women of her maternal line are polydactyl, born with an extra finger on each hand that is cut off in infancy, because "somebody was afraid we would learn to cast spells / and our wonders were cut off." But those doctors who chose to sever the babies' extra fingers "didn't understand / the powerful memory of ghosts."[109] In an interview, Clifton expresses sadness that her eldest daughter's fingers were severed by the doctor without consent at the time of her birth—"they had hers off by the time I came to. Isn't that awful?"[110] The ghost fingers represent the nonconsensual amputations, physical and spiritual, that Black women are subjected to as a result of being born in this society, a legacy that proves to be intergenerational: "we connect / my dead mother / my live daughter and me / through our terrible shadowy hands."[111] The magical link between mother, daughter, and Clifton does not imply an easy connection. The ghost fingers, which began as "wonders" before they were cut, have in their nonmaterial form become terrible. The ghostly memory has been marred by mutilations to the flesh, and though they are still able to cast a spell of connection between living and dead, that connection becomes a shared memory of severed possibility rather than a shared repertoire of wonders.

Because of the themes of self-possession and body positivity that run throughout her poems, Clifton has a healthy sense of ambivalence about the things the spirits ask her to do with her Black woman's body. In fact, one could say that her ambivalence is produced by her embodied presence as a Black woman. As she points out in *won't you celebrate with me*, the fact that she was "born in babylon / both nonwhite and woman" has fundamentally shaped the kind of life she has led.[112] And yet here are the spirits speaking of a life beyond and devoid of race, and she cannot help but feel the pangs in her own Black woman's body:

> father
> i am not equal to the faith required.
> i doubt.
> i have a woman's certainties;
> bodies pulled from me,
> pushed into me.
> bone flesh is what i know.[113]

Her "woman's certainties" are certainties of the body, certainties about the social roles that being a Black heterosexual mother of six have confined her to. The crisis of faith she experiences is not merely whether the spirits exist or that she must share her body with them, but that they do not have bodies in the gendered way she has previously experienced the sharing and opening of her own body. The spirits completely disrupt this insufficient but familiar certainty of penetration and childbirth as the definitive ways a woman can use her body.

Connecting the sexual with the spiritual, Clifton constructs the Virgin Mary as a kind of two-headed woman, negotiating her own ambivalence through this potent metaphor. The figure of the Virgin Mary is a woman holding contradiction in perfect balance, mother and virgin, Black and white, colonizing and colonized. Mary is a spiritual figure who has long since been woven into the fabric of African diaspora religions. In Haiti she is Ezili Freda/Our Lady of Sorrows and Ezili Dantò/the Madonna of Częstochowa; in Cuba she is Ochún/La Virgen del Cobre and Yemayá/La Virgen de Regla. Syncretism is the simplistic term for what is happening here. Mary and her African diasporic twin spirits walk together, conjoined like branches at the same trunk. Clifton uses the figure of the Virgin Mary to express her own ambivalence about her spirit visitation and the both/and nature of her spiritual practice. The Marian cycle of poetry detailing Clifton's visitation was originally published in *Two-Headed Woman*. These poems make up the bulk of the eponymous section of the collection, "Two-Headed Woman," bringing to the Virgin Mary connotations of both duality and spiritual power. Clifton's Mary is "shook by the / awe full affection of the saints"—the double valence of awe full/awful fully operative throughout the Marian cycle.[114] In "island mary," for instance, Clifton depicts an aged Mary perplexed by her own lack of agency:

> could i have walked away when voices
> singing in my sleep? i one old woman.
> always i seem to worrying now for
> another young girl asleep
> in the plain evening.
> what song around her ear?
> what star still choosing?[115]

Mary's conception is written as a violent imposition on a young girl, something that is not unique to Mary but happening even now, to other young women, in different ways. The social burden of proof of Mary's veracity and sanity following her immaculate conception is something Clifton relates to in her own struggle to explain her spiritual practice to others. In the poem "friends come," she describes the way her friends thought she was crazy: "explaining to me that my mind / is the obvious assassin."[116] Even the spirits are conscious of the social ostracism that their communications may cause her; as in the case of Langston Hughes, who initially does not want to communicate with her because, as he told her, "Lucille, I do not want your friends to think you are crazy."[117] All to say that the call of the spirits is a burden as well as a gift, constituting a false choice no mortal girl could have walked away from.

The burdens of spiritual communications included a sense of responsibility for the coming catastrophes of the human world, of which Clifton is warned by a group of ethereal spirits she calls "The Ones." Unlike many of the spirits with whom Clifton is in communication, The Ones do not assume the personality of a departed human, and do not weigh in on day-to-day affairs. They speak of things of cosmic importance: the deep past of human civilization (for instance, the origins of Atlantis and demystifications of ancient Egyptian civilization) and its tenuous future. They "return to remind human beings that they are more than flesh."[118] In August and September of 1978, for instance, The Ones imparted to Clifton a series of dire warnings about the fate of the human world:

> If the world continues on its way without the *possibility* [emphasis in original] of God which is the same as saying without Light Love Truth then what does this mean? It means that perhaps a thousand years of mans life on this planet will be without Light Love Truth It is what we were saying indeed that there will be on Earth that place which human beings describe to the world of the spirits Hell Now there is yet time but not very much your generation Lucille is the beginning of the possibility and your girls generation is the middle etc.[119]

Characterized by their mythic tone and liberal use of a royal "we," the refrain of the message from The Ones was, "There are so many confusions so many potential dangers in the world of the Americas." An interesting formulation, given that the fate of the entire world, not just the Americas, seems to be in the balance. Though these spirits may seem to espouse a kind of post-racial universalism, their distinction of "the Americas" as the source of the world's dangers and confusions signals the intertwined histories of slavery, genocide, and environmental degradation that have defined the Americas since 1492. As they tell her, "America is not a country where things sounding right are taken as right," and it is this American resistance to the truth that is destroying the world. Eerily, by the spirits' generational clock, the generation born at the end of the twentieth century marks the end of the possibility of avoiding an earth turned to Hell. But in the loneliness of clairvoyance, the burden of saving the world falls disproportionately on Black women. The Ones emphasize their message as a bid for global salvation, exhorting Clifton that "it is also very important that ones who understand the truth not keep the truth to themselves" (August and September 1978). Despite the heaviness and impossibility of this task, Clifton still regards it as a privilege of her incarnation as a Black woman. An untitled poem in *Two-Headed Woman* reads,

> the once and future dead
> who learn they will be white men
> weep for their history. we call it
> rain.[120]

Here Clifton's theory of reincarnation collides with the limitations of the racially stratified "world of the Americas." To be born a white man, despite its material benefits, is here represented as a kind of cosmic misfortune, a sullying of the soul with all the dirty deeds of white men's history. If a soul's incarnation as a white man is cause for weeping, then it follows that a soul's incarnation as a Black woman is cause for something akin to celebration.

In the poem "if something should happen," Clifton describes the revenge water takes when its humanity and life-force are disregarded by the world of the Americas:

> if the seas of cities
> should crash against each other
> and break the chains
> and break the walls holding down the cargo
> and break the sides of the seas
> and all the waters of the earth wash together
> in a rush of breaking
> where will the captains run and
> to what harbor?[121]

In this poem, the living denizens of the city are a sea, connected with the "waters of the earth" in a unified act of purification. Clifton's apocalyptic vision and its prescient connection with rising sea levels predicts early twenty-first-century concerns with climate change, as well as the image of Black women in a world after the collapse of racial capitalism as envisioned by Afrofuturist feminists like Octavia Butler, Adrienne Maree Brown, and Alexis Pauline Gumbs. Perhaps this catastrophe is what was meant by The

Ones who warned Clifton about the demise of the world. But as in the works of later Afrofuturists, in this poem only the "captains"—those accustomed to floating above the storms while their cargo lies below in chains—will have nowhere to run. In Clifton's eschatology, the human cargo is—miraculously— water-logged and free. The advantage to Clifton's theory of spirit is that it does not succumb to fatalism by assuming that the future is both bleak and unchangeable for the most oppressed of this world. It is "not the end of the world / of a world," and the principles represented by Black womanhood are given the possibility of reincarnation in a different world, on "a star / more distant / than eden."[122]

When women like Clifton and Lorde are excluded from patriarchal definitions of Afrocentricity or included in only ancillary or subordinate roles, they are doubly disenfranchised, deprived of both the past of Blackness and the building of its future. In the words of Oseijeman Adefunmi, the 1970s sought to address the fact that "there is no tragedy which has caused deeper personal conflict in the mind and spirit of the black American than the question of his pre-American origins. Nothing fills the average American born black with more discomfort and embarrassment than discussion about Africa. . . . Briefly stated, 'it is impossible to know where you have been.'"[123] Clifton and Lorde had their own alternative narratives of where we have been that laid the groundwork for a future where Blackness rights, rather than replicates, the wrongs of this violent world of the Americas.

CHAPTER FOUR
Weird Sisters
Spiritual Bridges to the Third World

Since its first publication in 1981, *This Bridge Called My Back* is largely considered to be a masterpiece of solidarity. It contains the voices of an astonishing cross-section of racialized and queer American women, all in the service of, as Toni Cade Bambara writes in her foreword to the first edition, realizing the dream. "The dream is real, my friends," writes Bambara, quoting a character from her 1980 novel, *The Salt Eaters*; "the failure to make it work is the only unreality."[1] Bambara's language of the nonspecific "dream" and the unspecified something that would make it work is necessitated by the broadness of the congregation she is speaking to and for, by the diversity of dreams huddled under the umbrella of Third World feminism. It is clear that, in the historical intersection between Third World organizing and alternative spiritualities, women were the primary drivers of interracial coalition building. Women were the ones who set about the hard work of realizing the impossible dream. However, it is evident even from within the interlocking texts of *This Bridge* that the dream was fractured. Barbara Cameron, a Native contributor to *This Bridge Called My Back*, critiqued "the narrow definition held by some people that third world means black people only."[2] Meanwhile, Cherríe Moraga, a Chicana feminist and editor of the anthology, acknowledged the "painful, painful ignorance" that keeps her separated from women of other identity categories.[3] *This Bridge Called My Back* reveals many of the struggles and fault lines in Third World feminist thought of the 1970s and 1980s, revealing that the Third Word was not an easy coalition.

Third World feminism enjoyed its heyday in the 1970s and 1980s when racialized peoples in the United States and national liberation struggles in Latin America, Asia, Africa, and the Arab world threw grand bridges at one another across the void of Western imperialism. Later, it fell out of vogue in the United States in favor of terms like "transnational feminism" that decentered the concept of the nation-state and thus stigmatized national liberation as parochial.[4] Third World feminism in the United States included not just literary projects like *This Bridge* but also activist and advocacy groups like the Third World Women's Alliance, which was founded in 1970 when several Puerto Rican women asked to be part of the all-Black Black Women's

Alliance, an organization founded by former members of the Student Nonviolent Coordinating Committee (SNCC).[5] It is no accident that this uniquely multiracial women's organization counted Black, Asian American, and Latinx women among its members. In her study of women in Black power movements, historian Ashley D. Farmer identifies the category of the Third World Woman "as a freedom fighter and revolutionary in her own right. She was also part of an activist collective and a cooperative reordering of race, gender and nation-state that resulted from black women's identification and collaboration with other women of color." However, Farmer argues that the organization relied on "an idealized conception of the Third World that 'first world minorities' created" and "collapsed the very real differences between being a black woman in America and being a colonial or neocolonial subject abroad."[6] This chapter is a tale of these differences and their collapse, told through the work of two understudied Third World Black feminists: Luisah Teish and Toni Cade Bambara. Both of these women wielded a feminist spirituality as a coalition-building tool, seeking a universal religious grammar that might unify the oppressed of the world against the impending catastrophes of late capitalism. While the category of Third World Women has largely been abandoned today due to its flattening of difference and its essentializing of complex global issues, I argue that there is utility in honoring the labor of Black Third World feminists. They knew the Sisyphean nature of their unifying work and chose to undertake it anyway, proving that even their missteps can be seen as a relevant call to ongoing struggle rather than as a dated experiment.

The Spiritual Is Political: Feminist Spiritualities

Feminist spiritual organizations of the 1970s and 1980s struggled, sometimes unsuccessfully, to provide an antidote to cultural alienation by creating a zany patchwork of cultures and traditions, in keeping with the anthologizing impulse of the time.[7] One 1978 anthology, *Womanspirit Rising*, somehow managed to compile an anthology of feminist spirituality composed entirely of works by cisgender straight white women.[8] In the preface to a second edition in 1992, the editors offered the tepid excuse, "Our choice of essays for this book was originally determined in large measure by the work available when it was edited."[9] This was quantitively untrue, as most of the woman of color contributors to the anthology's apologetic sequel, *Weaving the Vision* (1989), had published works of feminist spirituality throughout the 1970s. Only after the success of *This Bridge Called My Back* did the white woman editors of *Womanspirit Rising* come to the shocking realization that "sisterhood is not a reality when it is predicated on the experience of only a small group of women," and *Weaving the Vision* included excerpts from works by Audre Lorde, Alice Walker, Gloria Anzaldúa, and Luisah Teish—all of whom contributed to *This Bridge*.[10]

Feminism in the 1970s and 1980s was coterminous with a rise in interest in non-Abrahamic belief systems from a variety of different angles. From New Age modalities to neo-paganism to people of color's reclamations of their ancestral religious traditions, what all these spiritualities had in common was a turn to previously denigrated and feminized spiritualities as an antidote to colonialism, patriarchy, and other forms of injustice. Among the adherents of these belief systems, there was a sense that no matter which road you took to arrive at it, alternative spiritualities led to unity, cohesion, and wholeness. Many of these new or reborn spiritualties, whether implicitly or explicitly, engaged in coalition building based on their belief in the equal validity of multiple belief systems. However (perhaps the predictably), the coalition building of white-led movements engaged actively in the tokenization or exotification of non-Western religions. According to Margot Adler, a Wicca priestess and scholar, a desire for cultural wholeness animated a variety of New Age religious forms in the 1970s and 1980s, including the rise of Wicca and neo-paganism: "Many Neo-Pagans are drawn to the Native American traditions, to Voodoo [sic] and Santería. . . . These traditions are often more vital than the groups we have been discussing, simply because they too form within whole cultures and communities. But most white North Americans lack a culture that is still tied to the earth and its seasons. The neo-pagans are attempting to build a whole culture from a pile of old and new fragments. When they are honest with themselves, they admit their impoverishment, for even if their groves and covens succeed, it will take generations to create successful ritual forms."[11] It is wrong, however, for Adler to assume that white people are the only ones who mourn a loss of culture, who crave wholeness and authenticity and attempt to construct it from "old and new fragments." All Third World "sisters" existed in a larger capitalist rubric that robbed everyone of each other and themselves. This universal longing for a more "vital" feminist spirituality, in fact, led to the sometimes uninformed experiments in coalition building between disparate religious traditions in the 1970s.

Between people of color, religious tensions were no less pronounced as they also struggled to build interracial coalitions. As I discussed briefly in chapter 3, Yoruba religious traditions in the United States were popularized by Oseijeman Adefunmi. Initially, he was introduced to orisha worship by his friend Christopher Oliana, a Cuban immigrant. After being initiated into Santería together in Cuba in 1959, the two men initially began a temple together in Harlem in honor of the spirit Shango, but Adefunmi rejected Oliana's use of Santa Barbara, the Catholic saint with whom Shango is syncretized in Santería. "That is not an African god," Adefunmi objected. "That is a white woman."[12] A year later Adefunmi founded the Yoruba Temple of Harlem, which ministered primarily to African Americans. The Latinx–African American alliance of the Shango Temple was short-lived, and within a decade "the Cuban community no longer recognized the religion of their Caribbean home as its black North American practitioners paraded through the streets of Harlem, transformed the iconography, adorned themselves in African clothing, married polygamously, and communicated in black nationalist rhetoric."[13] The groups sometimes operated at cross purposes, with the Cuban immigrants sometimes needing to practice their religion in secrecy to avoid deportation and the African Americans desiring to ride the wave of Black power by publicly instilling pride in Black Americans. Between these two camps of orisha worshippers, a rift developed—on one side stood the Spanish-speaking wearers of white with their candles and saint statues in hand, and on the other side stood dashiki-clad African Americans eager to liberate themselves through African names and practices.[14]

This history of the rift in American orisha worship in some ways obscures the unifying efforts of women of color. As early as the 1950s, Cuban and Puerto Rican *santeras* led "thriving multiethnic and multiracial spiritual houses in New York that served both Hispanic and African American communities."[15] Marta Moreno Vega, a Nuyorican *santera* who came to the faith in the 1970s, was and continues to be someone whose goal is "to promote and link communities of African descent."[16] This goal implicitly signals that these communities were not already linked, as indeed she points out in her description of the infighting between Cuban and Puerto Rican Santería practitioners, as well as between African Americans and Latinx practitioners, in the 1970s.[17] In 1976, she founded the Caribbean Cultural Center African Diaspora Institute (CCCADI), and in 1981 she organized the First International Conference of Orisha Tradition and Culture in Ile Ife, Nigeria, the sacred birthplace of the orishas. For this gathering, she traveled throughout the diaspora to recruit participants, and even she was surprised by the sheer heterogeneity of the practice. In Trinidad, she "witnessed Amit, an East Indian Yoruba priest, include his Indian gods beside the Yoruba gods on his altar."[18] In Cuba, she was told by Ma Mina, an elderly *santera* whose Chinese-Cuban husband was a child of the orisha Oyá, "The divinities of the Chinese community are very similar to the *orishas*. People like to argue about the differences between the *orishas*, the Catholic saints, and the Chinese divinities. For me, they are different roads to the same destination."[19] In other words, people of color in the Americas have long built bridges between their religious traditions and reconciled difference in the name of a shared history of resistance, long before the 1980s.

Another architect of an intentionally interracial spiritual community is Yoruba priestess Luisah Teish, who formed a Bay Area altar circle in the 1970s that included practitioners of African, neo-pagan, Latinx, Native, and Arab traditions, and though they worked together as a family in their rituals of ancestor reverence and self-care, she acknowledged that "we sometimes have problems with terminology and the conflicting meaning of symbols."[20] This is evident from the introduction to Teish's 1985 book *Jambalaya*, provided by her altar sister Starhawk, a white neo-pagan woman, who makes troubling comparisons between the Salem Witch trials and the transatlantic slave trade, lamenting the fact that "both European witchcraft and the Afro-Caribbean traditions that Teish writes of have suffered centuries of patriarchal propaganda."[21] This statement, while grounded in truth, ignores the scale and pervasiveness of the intergenerational trauma that resulted from European attempts to eradicate African diaspora religions, in contrast to the historically distant persecution of European paganism. Much has been written to debunk the idea that European and American witch trials persecuted actual practitioners of paganism, in direct contrast to the well-documented genocidal assault of enslavers and colonizers upon traditional African religions. Starhawk's persecution narrative runs counter to the consensus of many scholars of neo-paganism that there was no unified pagan religion in Europe after the eleventh century, and that for today's neo-pagans the "universal Old Religion [functioned] more as a metaphorical truth than a literal reality—a spiritual truth more than a geographic one."[22] Starhawk also claims that *Jambalaya* is important because "racism has diminished our lives by cutting us off from the richness of other traditions."[23] Who is this we, and what exactly do "we" stand to gain from the knowledge of other traditions? Starhawk's well-intentioned introduction ultimately still falls into a capitalist language of enrichment and utility to white readers. As Teish notes, there is indeed a conflict in the meaning of symbols within religiously diverse women's organizations; but it is not just a matter of owls being inauspicious in one culture and sacred in another; it is a matter of the organizations' members becoming symbols to one another, standing in for the mystery and allure of secrets unknown.

Black women are not absent from the nexus of longing, appropriation, and misunderstanding that characterized feminist spirituality. Like Christianity, alternative spiritualities have a long history within the Black American community, to such an extent that there are independent Black New Age traditions. As was the case for Lucille Clifton in chapter 3, the 1980s were a particularly fruitful time for the definition and redefinition of non-Black mysticisms. However, in the words of the Black feminist scholar Akasha Gloria Hull, "New Age wisdom is not really new—only our enlarged capacity to accept, explain, appreciate, and benefit from it is fresh."[24] Black astrology is present in the works of Lucille Clifton, Luisah Teish, and Toni Cade Bambara, as well as in popular work like Thelma Balfour's *Black Sun Signs*. As early as the 1970s, Oseijeman Adefunmi even developed astrological correspondences for the orishas and offered astrological readings for his followers.[25] Baba Ife Karade also derived chakra correspondences for all of the orishas in his influential *Handbook of Yoruba Religious Concepts*. Though Akasha Gloria Hull admits that much of New Age spirituality is both whitewashed and apolitical, she argues that it is transformed by the practice of Black women in the 1980s: "We read the usual New Age books and journals, sat before altars and meditated, rejected materialistic modes of existence, embraced yoga and tai chi and Buddhism. . . . However, we simultaneously applied our new learning to black subject matter, found spiritual transcendence in black revolutionary struggle, and sought metaphysical origins in Africa."[26] The uncomfortable eclecticism of "yoga, tai chi, and Buddhism," all anthologized together without cultural context or historical specificity, might suggest a key blind spot in Black women's engagement with other religious traditions of the Third World.

In addition to its questionable politics of appropriation, alternative spirituality was consistently called into question by the political concerns of the day as the spiritual and the material came into a constant gridlock among Black activists. Ruby, a veteran organizer and one of the more cynical characters of Toni Cade Bambara's novel *The Salt Eaters*, even says, "Don't nobody talk political anymore, talk Black anymore? If it ain't degree degree, it's job job, boogie boogie, or some esoteric off-the-wall sun/moon shit."[27] This character more explicitly diagnoses New Age spirituality as a self-indulgent follow-up to the civil rights movement: "Malcolm gone, King gone, Fanni Lou [sic] gone, Angela quiet, the movement splintered, enclaves unconnected.

Everybody off into the Maharaji This and the Right Reverend That. If it isn't some far-off religious nuttery, it's some otherworldly stuff."[28] This was part of a larger debate within the Black community after the civil rights movement about whether or not the spiritual was political. Luisah Teish, for instance, originally rejected Eastern religion because in "the late 1960s and early 1970s, when many black people embraced the religions of the East," she "watched community activists don white or saffron robes and chant that the struggle was merely an illusion."[29] Teish was involved in the tumultuous Black organizing and activism of the 1960s and 1970s, when anti-spiritualist trends morphed into pretexts for controlling women's bodies. Just like the Black women of Bambara's novels, she encountered the misogyny and anti-spiritualism of Black male revolutionaries. She was told by the "brothers" that her "most important job was to have babies and teach those babies African culture."[30] She was told that "it was counterrevolutionary to *praise* ancestors who had allowed us to fall into slavery."[31] Like Lorde and Clifton, whom I discussed in the previous chapter, Teish would eventually find solace in a woman-centered theology. Facetiously, she foreshadows her spiritual awakening even in those alienated days before she discovered her own blend of feminism, revolution, and spirituality, in this clever parenthetical statement: "(But the sisters were busy paying homage to a Goddess. I and several other women I knew constructed small altars in our bedrooms consecrated to the worship of the birth control pill.)"[32] Teish's joke highlights an important point: that the rejection of the spiritual was a masculinist enterprise, and that its reclamation must be a feminist one.

Damballah; or, the Dream

Toni Cade Bambara is widely known for her compelling blend of art and activism, as evidenced by her oft-quoted maxim "The role of the artist is to make revolution irresistible," but few scholars have discussed the spiritual dimension of her efforts.[33] Bambara, influenced by both the Harlem of her youth and the New Age awakenings of her adulthood, incorporated alternative religion into much of her writing. *The Salt Eaters* in particular is at the spiritual crossroads of 1970s America, bearing down on the question, "Here we are in the last quarter and how we gonna pull it all together and claim the new age in our name?"[34] Doc Serge, an uncomfortable character who oscillates between sophistry and wisdom, phrases the dilemma as this: "The man thought the new age and the new order began with his arrival on these shores. Ha! They convinced us they knew about this country's manifest destiny.

Clearly, they were ignorant of its latent destiny, its occult destiny. Understand? Now, its latent destiny is a Neptunian thing, a Black thing, an us thing."[35] Far from viewing New Age spirituality as white or anti-revolutionary, Bambara views it is as "a Black thing, an us thing": a historically Black tradition with the ability to make or unmake the world. It is impossible to understand the world of *The Salt Eaters* without discussing Third World feminist spirituality, According to Akasha Gloria Hull, starting around 1980, the new spirituality of African American women "brings together three interlocking dimensions: 1) the heightened political and social awareness of the civil rights movement and feminist movement, 2) a spiritual consciousness that melds black American traditions such as Christian prayer and ancestor reverence with New Age modalities such as crystal work and self-help metaphysics, and 3) enhanced creativity."[36] Each of these modalities is present in *The Salt Eaters*, with the characters struggling to dismantle the supposed mutual exclusivity of Black radical politics and spiritual self-care. In order to lay claim to the "occult destiny" of the Americas, Bambara incorporates preexisting forms of Black occultism into the New Age vocabulary of *The Salt Eaters*.

Bambara has acknowledged the influence of "[growing] up in Harlem in the late thirties, forties, and fifties," and the way "this period was also characterized by people's consciousness that Harlem was, indeed, a wealthy community where African genius was very much in evidence in individuals, organizations, and forums," notably the importance of Speaker's Corner as a model for the type of dialogue she would like her work to foster.[37] However, Bambara was also influenced by a long intercultural tradition of Harlem spiritual workers. Born in Harlem in 1939, Bambara herself is part of a syncretic tradition of Harlem spiritual workers. Scholarship on the Harlem Renaissance and the interwar period has revealed the extent to which magic and alternative spirituality were a pervasive and normalized part of the Harlem landscape. Historian Shane White goes so far as to say, "Few, if any, societies can ever have expended so much time and energy on the recollection, analysis, and discussion of the details of dreams. Sigmund Freud would have had a field day in interwar Harlem."[38] As LaShawn Harris notes in her study of the informal economy of Harlem in the interwar period, spiritual workers in Harlem were often closely aligned with crime and illegal activity. Not only were many spiritual workers themselves criminalized for fraud and larceny, but they also contributed to the illegal numbers game, Harlem's storied community lottery, by interpreting their clients' dreams for signs of the winning number of the day. Dream interpretation was a key part of finding the right two- or three-digit number to play, and a cottage industry sprang up around it selling everything from "dream books" that gave every dream topic a numerical analogue to "dream pills" to give the wishful numbers player more vivid dreams.

The Harlem that Bambara was born into was not just a space of African American spirituality but a deeply heterogeneous mix of African, Asian, and American traditions. The spiritual economy of interwar Harlem was stoked by both real and imagined Caribbean immigration, in which foreign Blackness and brownness were crucial sources of credibility and cachet. As Lara Putnam puts it, "islanders' supernatural expertise was familiar enough to be meaningful, exotic enough to be valued."[39] Of the sixty-seven spiritual workers advertising their services in the *New York Amsterdam News* from 1922 to 1926, fourteen had stage names that gestured toward foreignness, for example, Professor Alpha Roktabija and Professor S. Indoo.[40] Philip Deslippe argues that the Eastern elements of Harlem spiritual work are a modernizing effect of the Great Migration: "An Orientalized repackaging of Hoodoo in the urban North could have also allowed many people in places like Harlem and Chicago to engage in a familiar system of magic and divination, while avoiding the connotations of the practice of Hoodoo being Southern, old, or country."[41] Indeed, Harlem's Black press, notably the *New York Amsterdam News*, repeatedly painted belief in the efficacy of magical remedies as backward and anti-modern, as in Ken Jessamy's sarcastic 1927 article, in which he painted magic as " a throwback to the days when their foreparents believed in voodoo gods and the magic to be found in the application of roots and herbs."[42] Under an illustration representing a Black man wearing a turban and a long robe with a mandarin collar, the article describes a Harlem where "on every avenue in this community there are men, some with their heads wrapped in turbans, others wearing snakes around their shoulders, who can give you the lucky number for the morrow."[43]

The Harlem spiritual workers were described universally as charlatans and "fakers" (meant as a double entendre with the term "fakir" which some of the turbaned savants adopted), and numerous incidents of fraud and swindling among them were loudly and splashily reported.[44] There were some gender divisions within this economy of healers: the grand titles of "Professor" or "Master of Science" were exclusively used by male healers, while women healers preferred to go by "Ms." or "Madame."[45] Madame Fu Futtam, the professional alias of Dorothy Matthews, an Afro-Chinese woman from Jamaica, ran her own spiritual supply store, and published a bestselling dream book in 1939. Despite the accusations of quackery and fraud that surrounded spiritual workers in the interwar period, and skepticism about the cultural authenticity of practitioners claiming to come from abroad, Matthews seemed to be an immigrant of Chinese descent, complicating the idea that her blend of different spiritual traditions was a ruse for economic gain rather than a complex negotiation of her own multiraciality.[46] Matthews's place within Harlem society highlights a dimension Bambara found to be missing in Black organizing of the 1960s but which was very present in Bambara's own life experience: a multiculturalism that does not center or even include whiteness. "When people talked about multicultural or multiethnic organizing, a lot of us translated that to mean white folks and backed off," Bambara explains. "I think that was an error. We should have known what was meant by multicultural. Namely, people of color. Afro-American, Afro-Hispanic, Indo-Hispanic, Asian-Hispanic, and so forth. Not that those errors necessarily doom us. Errors may result in lessons learned. I think we have the opportunity again in this last quarter of the twentieth century to begin forging those critical ties with other communities. It will be done. That is a certainty."[47]

The Salt Eaters is itself a dream book in that time-honored Harlem tradition, blending horoscope, Orientalized mysticism, and dream interpretation, but instead of helping her readers find auguries of the numbers game, Bambara helps them find the winning number for revolution. The cultural appropriation, gentle charlatanry, and zany pulpit-pounding of Bambara's characters is a direct descendent from the spiritual workers of her hometown. Bambara seeks to integrate the increasingly globalized imagery of twentieth-century Black spiritual work with the roots of healing work performed by enslaved people, without stigmatizing either. Bambara's vision is almost messianic in its belief in the last quarter of the twentieth century as a pivotal moment in world history, and in a single Black woman's capacity to save the world. *The Salt Eaters* presents a world both our own and not our own, its uncanny resemblance sometimes giving way to disorienting differences. In the world of the novel, for instance, the character of Minnie Ransom is a flamboyant local healer whose showstopping healing rites draw crowds of tourists and medical students. Minnie's spirit healing is a fact acknowledged by believers in folk healing as well as visiting doctors forced to acknowledge "something more powerful than Western science."[48] This undoes a binary between medicine and healing, between faith and skepticism, that was institutionalized in the nineteenth century by white Southern doctors to discredit the work of enslaved woman healers who were running them out of business.[49] It also removes the criminal and legislative barriers to the practice of Black folk healing, such as the 1922 Medical Practice Bill by the New York State Assembly, which criminalized spiritual workers for practicing medicine without a license and thus "effectively wrested individuals' autonomy in making health decisions."[50] Other states and cities, most notably New Orleans, also instituted laws against fortune telling or practicing medicine without a license that specifically targeted Black healers.[51] These were paternalistic attempts to supposedly prevent gullible Black people from being duped by charlatans, ignoring centuries of Black healing traditions by presenting them as antithetical to institutionalized medicine rather than as forms of medicine in themselves. In Bambara's idealized world of unstigmatized Black healing, there is a message "chiseled over the archway of the Infirmary: health is your right."[52] In this world, spiritual health is deeply connected to physical health, and Black spiritual health is unimpeded by white skepticism. This allows Bambara to explore the full potentiality of Black healing without the looming threat of criminality to interrupt it.

In *The Salt Eaters*, Velma Henry, an overworked activist who was deeply involved in the civil rights movement, suffers a mental and spiritual break that can only be cured by Minnie Ransom. This is a universe where supernatural healing is possible, where Black women's spiritual power has tangible and acknowledged effects on the physical world. In Claybourne, Georgia, the fictional setting of the novel, the spirits of Haitian Vodou exist alongside a coterie of civil rights activists, artists, dance instructors, Mardi Gras revelers, and hospital patients, all living under the shadow of a chemical plant that is slowly poisoning them. Bambara collapses geographical boundaries in Claybourne order to showcase the interconnectedness of global justice movements. This metonymic leveling of cultural barriers, however, raises as many questions of appropriation as it does ties of solidarity, shuttling between the consciousness of the African American residents of Claybourne and that of a women of color performance troupe known as the Seven Sisters, composed of caricatural Third World women of different backgrounds. In *The Salt Eaters*, Toni Cade Bambara simultaneously critiques cultural eclecticism and falls prey to some of its most glaring blind spots. Velma, the heroine of the novel, critiques another character "whose so-called solutions to the so-called problem always lay in somebody else's culture: Tai Chi, TM, Reichian therapy, yoga. She argued that the truth was in one's own people and the key was to be centered in the best of one's own traditions."[53] However, what counts as "one's own tradition" is a slippery category in this novel. Bambara's primary religious framework seems to come from Haitian Vodou, which she represents as part of the Black American heritage of the fictional town of Claybourne. Because this dreamed-of direct lineage from Haiti is in the real world neither simple nor direct, Bambara deliberately elides the difference between African American and Haitian religious practice in the service of her spiritual vision.

The character of Campbell, a journalist-turned-waiter whom Akasha Gloria Hull identifies as Bambara's "alter ego or psychic double" in the novel, views Vodou as part of an almost mathematical set of principles that govern the rules of the universe.[54] Campbell "knew in a glowing moment that all the systems were the same at base—voodoo, thermodynamic, I Ching, astrology, numerology, alchemy, metaphysics, everybody's ancient myths—they were interchangeable, not at all separate much less conflicting."[55] Bambara's messianic and apocalyptic language lends a menacing air to the scene, as if to say that we don't have time for specificity or nuance when regarding different religious traditions. In the same coffee shop where Campbell comes to this epiphany, a thunderstorm sounds like "death running in the streets to overtake the café. Or an explosion at the [chemical] plant."[56] In the shadow of nuclear apocalypse, environmental disaster, and white supremacy, it seems it is our duty to find each other before the bomb that brings us together. Bambara's desire for wholeness and unity stems from the cultural fractures of the Middle Passage, sparking her interest in a religious system that might reconstitute broken structures of kinship and sisterhood. This explains her interest throughout the text in the Haitian snake spirit Danbala. Unlike most *lwa*, Danbala is not an anthropomorphic spirit, and when he possesses people he behaves as a snake, slithering on the ground and eating raw eggs. But his nonhumanity signifies a depth of understanding that is beyond humanity, which Bambara seizes upon to say, "Damballah is the first law of thermodynamics and is the Biblical wisdom and is the law of time and is . . . everything that is now has been before and will be again in a new way, in a changed form, in a timeless time."[57] Like the first law of thermodynamics, which holds that energy can be neither created nor destroyed, Danbala is the idea that no thing—not souls, not culture, not ritual—is ever destroyed. It simply exists elsewhere in a different form. This is an incredibly powerful idea in a diasporic culture that must constantly reckon with loss as its raison-d'être. Bambara's interest in Danbala is not a New Age essentialism, but a way of doing justice to a lost and impossible unity by acknowledging its possibility in another realm.

In her archives, Bambara has a series of loose scraps of paper which she has labeled her "LOA Notebooks" in honor of the Haitian spirits and the principles they represent. Despite the fact that she has admitted, "I am not a good researcher" because she looks for her predetermined conclusions rather than facts, these notebooks provide insight into Bambara's search for a universal cosmology in her research on world religions.[58] Before they dissolve into meeting notes and musings on other topics, the LOA notebooks contain fragmentary information on a variety of spirits from different traditions: Yemaya's predilection for blue and white, Isis mother of Horus with wheat in her mouth, and Seboulisa, a Fon creator goddess also known as Mawulisa. Hera, Venus, and Aphrodite. Written tentatively in pencil, with a small question mark beside it: Erzulie Frieda [sic] under the category of feminine spirits represented by Oshun.[59] Some pages are attempts to make sense of universal spiritual principles. For instance, under the title of the ancient Egyptian spirit Sebek, she includes the characteristics "messenger/ trickster / god of the crossroads / live by wits / intermediary to the gods." She also lists Elegba, Eshu, Mercury, Odin, Puck, Anansi, Set, and Satan. On other pages, she lists Tibetan, Incan, and Malagasy spirits. These archives offer key insight into Bambara's meaning-making as she ambitiously seeks "to break words open and get at the bones, deal symbols as though they were atoms."[60] In Bambara's spiritual vision, everything is everything, as in *The Salt Eaters* when Bambara creates an oneiric sequence that breaks from the narrative, projecting a future in which "one" could hypothetically be found:

> Stumbling through the thorns and briars, following the rada rada big booming of the drums or the weh weh wedo riff of reed flutes, running toward a clearing, toward a likely sanctuary of the saints, the loa, the dinns, the devas. And found, would open up and welcome one in before the end, welcome one in in time to wrench time from its track so another script could play itself out. One would tap the brain for any knowledge of initiation rites lying dormant there, recognizing that life depended on it, that initiation was the beginning of transformation and that the ecology of the self, the tribe, the species, the earth depended on just that.[61]

Bambara's inclusion of the djinns and devas [sic] of Islamic and Hindu traditions and her emphasis on a need for global salvation speak to the capaciousness of her vision. Here, Bambara presents linear time as a force that must be stopped in favor of a circular time, a return to the "dormant" principles that lay at the heart of every spiritual tradition. Like some neo-pagans, Bambara identifies "the legacy of the West" in the past 500 years: a "time when wise folks were put to the rack was also a time when books were burned, temples razed to the ground, and certain types of language 'mysteries'—for lack a better word—were suppressed."[62] Rather than seeking solidarity with white people, however, Bambara reaches out to the cosmologies of people of color, those who have been most damaged by this "legacy of the West." In an interview with her friend and poet Kalamu ya Salaam, Bambara discusses prior moments of Third World collaboration—Seminoles harboring Black maroons, collaborations between the Young Lords and the Black Panthers, Asian student unions working with Black student unions—to advance the notion that "we are not asking people to do something new." She emphasizes that Third World collaboration is "not only a call to unite to wrath or to unite to vision, but there's also an awful lot in our own cosmology that is so similar it's really striking."[63] In other words, Bambara calls for unity based on not just common oppression, but what she perceives to be a more fruitful, lasting form of unity, based in a mutual spirituality.

The character of Campbell, like Bambara, believes in universal principles that different cultures have named as different spirits, but which remain constant across human experience.[64] In *The Salt Eaters*, Bambara draws on these principles rather than on elements unique to the African diaspora. All people of color's cultures and religions are aired at her fictional café in Claybourne, where people gather to "trade stories, sifting and sorting among the tales as if at a rummage sale, taking on those pieces still wearable to get them through passage, rejecting those pieces too threadbare, too contaminated too cumbersome."[65] We can apply the same logic to the many different ideas, philosophies, and personalities represented in *The Salt Eaters*; in fact, Bambara has structured the novel as a series of provocations to encourage the reader to do so. Bambara herself was provoked by global events and encounters "to identify internationally. . . . The African family is worldwide. And to that extent I tend to have an international perspective because I'm concerned about everything that happens in the family."[66] Her visits to Cuba in 1973 and to Vietnam in 1975 solidified her development as a revolutionary writer and made her realize that art and activism were not incompatible. In Bambara's life and work, the Third World is a pedagogical space, a space that imagines the alter-destiny of a world dominated by capitalism, oppression, and anti-spirituality.

The Salt Eaters sits at the intersection between Third World feminism and New Age religious movements of the 1970s and 1980s, in which the desire for wholeness is a vector shooting from white to Black Americans to Caribbean people to people in Africa, circling the globe only to arrive, exhausted, at oneself once again. It circles the globe much like Danbala himself, without beginning or end. Danbala is the dream of an elusive unity that is only possible in the realm of spirits. This dream and its work are children of the 1970s and 1980s, and they are only dated in the sense that Cherríe Moraga discusses in the fourth edition of *This Bridge Called My Back*: "*dated*; marked by the hour and place of these writers' and artists' births, our geographies of dislocation and homecoming, the ancestral memory that comes with us, and the politics of the period that shaped us."[67] In Bambara's particular case, it is marked by the divisions between people of color in the heyday of Third World feminism but also by the unprecedented hope that true solidarity was somewhere on the horizon.

It is helpful here to turn back to the example of Luisah Teish's life as a young revolutionary. From her involvement with a Khemetic temple in Saint Louis, she, like Bambara, reached the conclusion that "all the religions of the world are *essentially* the same and that the highest principles were born from the fertile waters of Africa."[68] Teish moved to Saint Louis when she received a scholarship to attend Katherine Dunham's Performing Arts Training Center (PATC), which Dunham founded in 1967 as part of her community engagement efforts in East Saint Louis. There, Teish "had access to trustworthy reading material [and] to people born in the culture." Thanks to Dunham's choreography, she too learned of unity from the Haitian spirit Danbala, whose dance became a universal ordering system for her: "Undulating chest, hip rotations, quick-stepping feet, revolutions of the head, and delicate hand gestures. The drum became my breath, my blood; it told my muscles what to do. I heard the drums when they were playing, and I heard them when they were not playing. Everything sounded like the drum—human voices, car brakes, the movement of the Mississippi."[69] The dance she describes is in fact the *yanvalou*, a praise dance for the snake spirit Danbala, to whom Dunham was initiated while she was in Haiti. Danbala is a pre-linguistic yet wise spirit, so it makes sense that he would be the foundation upon which global unity rests. If Third World feminism relies on the unification of disparate peoples through a search for communalities in struggle, Third World feminist spirituality seeks unification through a universal religious grammar of the oppressed that is beyond, and underneath, language. However, even within the unifying work represented by *This Bridge Called my Back*, Gloria Anzaldúa cautions its readers against "the danger [of] being too universal and humanitarian and invoking the eternal to the sacrifice of the particular and feminine and the specific historical moment."[70] The consequences of being "too universal," while not specifically outlined by Anzaldúa, were deeply and ambivalently explored in the work of Teish and Bambara.

New Orleans; or, the Failure to Make It Work

Luisah Teish was born in the iconic New Orleans French Quarter and raised on the West Bank across the Mississippi River. The New Orleans of her childhood was a space of cultural hybridity, in which "African ancestor reverence, Native American earth worship, and European Christian occultism" coexisted and mutually influenced one another.[71] She left New Orleans as a teenager and lived for many years on the West Coast, in California and Oregon, with a stint in Saint Louis. Along the way she had a spiritual awakening, became an orisha priestess of Oshun, and picked up knowledge of her hometown's importance in the history of African diaspora religions. Returning to New Orleans before the 1984 World's Fair, however, she declared it "a wreck!"[72] The traffic in the French Quarter was terrible, she had "seen nothing Haitian," and shops sold voodoo doll pencils instead of real hoodoo paraphernalia. The Black residents of her hometown cussed one another out and spouted racist observations about the recent influx of Vietnamese refugees. It was not the return of the native daughter she had anticipated, now that she has been away from home and come back wanting to "meet the true practitioners, to know their number and nationality . . . to salute their altars and attend their ceremonies."[73] Even her own mother disappoints her when she attempts to mine her mother's ancestral spiritual knowledge and her mother tells her, "I ain't much on working the spirits."[74] Her conclusion, whispered to her by her spirit guide, is *"you* can't get there from here."[75] There being spiritual enlightenment, here being New Orleans.

Flying back to the Bay Area, which is now her home more than New Orleans, she thinks of "Our Lady of Perpetual Help," her spirit guide. "She allowed me to live among the trees and warm people long enough to instill ancestral values in my being; and She got me out of that place and into the world just before the trees fell and those values began to decline. Blessed be the strategy of the Mother!" New Orleans, and her own mother, are supplanted by more universal concepts. There is the sense that she has moved on from New Orleans' false multiraciality in favor of a more authentic Third World community. However, New Orleans' perceived failures of solidarity are not unique to the city, but indicative of global barriers to coalition building between people of color, and which Teish encountered in different forms in her Oakland-based altar circle.

Still based today in the Bay Area, Teish has identified as a part of the womanspirit community, which she describes as "women who seek to create a tradition other than the patriarchal religions."[76] The womanspirit movement was first developed in the 1970s as adjacent to the Goddess movement and feminist neo-paganism. It published a magazine of feminist spirituality from 1974 to 1984, and its editors were part of a lesbian separatist community in southern Oregon. Much like New Age communities, whose hierarchical structure it rejected, the womanspirit movement was largely white in its membership.[77] But unlike the New Age movement, in which predominantly white adherents worshipped the image if not the reality of people of color's spiritual traditions, adherents of womanspirit usually worshipped white goddesses. Teish remains the only person of color among its best-known writers and adherents.

Presumably to maintain the harmony of her altar circle and the feminist spirituality circles of which she is part, Teish takes a diplomatic and conciliatory view of spiritual difference. Differences in custom and ritual food can all be overcome with a little knowledge, humor, and understanding. In her spiritual memoir, *Jambalaya*, big differences like race, class, and sexuality are equalized with statements like "Blacks have a corresponding set of stereotypes of white," "Each class has its 'cross to bear'" and "The heterophobe assumes that every 'straight' woman is a weak, whimpering, male-dominated slave."[78] Her altar circle's commitment to "an evolution that transcends the boundaries of racism, classism, erosphobia, and political dogma" is complicated and undermined by the effort to present straight, white, and class-privileged members' hurt feelings on an equal playing field with centuries of systemic oppression. This bridge building was a peculiar experiment of the era, a far cry from the divisive Trump era in which I write these words, in which terms like "Karen" and "white fragility" have precluded any self-respecting multiracial organization from considering the tears of someone who has been offended by stereotypes of whiteness or "heterophobia." We have things to learn from this bridge building, however. Teish was not uncritical of her altar sisters, but chose to do the work of educating, listening to them, and growing in community with them. Teish tread carefully though the ground moved beneath her feet.

Take, for instance, the issue of music. According to Teish, "Music and dance are big problems" in interfaith altar circles because of the historic importance of dance and rhythmicality in African diaspora religions, in contrast to the use of music as a pleasant backdrop in goddess tradition.[79] Writing in the 1980s, Teish reflects on a phenomenon where "recently a number of feminist spiritualists have created a thing called 'Goddess music,' played on the dulcimer. Although it is generally sweet and serene, it scratches my eardrums to no end. At women's spirituality conferences, where Goddess music is often featured, the Black, Latin, and Native American women try to enjoy it out of consideration for the artists but we invariably find ourselves drifting to the bathroom and tripping out the back door."[80] Humorous though this anecdote is, conjuring images of linen-clad white women plucking earnestly and inharmoniously at their obscure instruments, the mere fact that white women would take up space in this way with so little regard to the desires of women of color in attendance is telling. And the sinister image of women of color fleeing through "the back door"—historically the only door of a white residence through which they could enter as servants and domestics—is difficult to laugh off.

Perhaps to bolster the minority of womanspirit members in opposition to the dulcimer-wielding machinations of her white altar sisters, Teish's overtures to other women of color in the preface to *Jambalaya* are earnest but slightly overblown: "Native American women will find long lost relatives waiting for them at the river. Las Latinas, vengan a rumbear con las Negras! Asian women will see the Black Tao."[81] This invitation is belied by the fact that, despite her promises of a Black Tao, Asian women did not join her altar circle. As of the 1980s, "My altar circle, the House of the Mother, is a rainbow. We are of African, European, Middle Eastern, Latin, and Native American traditions. I await the arrival of my sisters from the East."[82] No Asian members, in an area of the country with no shortage of Asian Americans. Their loud absence speaks to all of the ways in which they might not have been welcomed or understood even within a supposedly multiracial, interfaith organization. The problems that Teish had fled New Orleans to escape—cultural appropriation, historical amnesia, and failures of solidarity—all plagued her newfound progressive community. New Orleans was not an anomaly; it was the urtext.

Toni Cade Bambara similarly sought to escape New Orleans' overdetermined legacy by setting *The Salt Eaters* in an ideal and idealized world of unadulterated Africanisms, in a town that resembled New Orleans yet was deliberately not. Bambara describes Claybourne as "a cross between a little Atlanta, a big Mount [sic] Bayou and Trenton, New Jersey, in winter."[83] Due to this fictional town's busloads of white tourists, Mardi Gras tradition, and its history of engagement with the Haitian spirits, or *lwa*, I would also like to add the geographic and cultural parallel of New Orleans to this curious list. Kalamu ya Salaam, himself a native of New Orleans, describes how he "used to see [Bambara] 'round Mardi Gras time in New Orleans, sitting on a stoop waiting for the Indians, once (maybe it was twice) the other Toni was with her, Toni Morrison; the two Toni's hung out in our city from time to time."[84] This fantastic image of the two Tonis waiting for the Mardi Gras

Indians to emerge along their spectral parade route is a thing of beauty in itself. But it also betrays the unspoken influence of New Orleans upon Bambara's creation of the Mardi Gras–celebrating, *lwa*-worshipping town of Claybourne. Even the name "Claybourne" seems to be a reference to the major New Orleans thoroughfare of Claiborne Avenue, where a vibrant corridor of live oak trees and Black-owned businesses was bulldozed during the construction of the I-10 overpass through the Treme in 1969.[85] What was the harm in acknowledging the city that very clearly served as the template for the setting of *The Salt Eaters*?

Indeed, the absence of New Orleans feels concerted, as Bambara has admitted in multiple interviews that, in her initial draft of *The Salt Eaters*, it was set in "someplace like New Orleans" and then shifted to Palmares, Brazil (complete with Portuguese-speaking characters), and then presumably shifted again, since there are no traces of Portuguese speakers in the published novel.[86] Bambara's description of her early drafting of the novel is chaotic, reflecting the call of many geographies and cultures that did not make it into the final draft: "It seems to be South. It seems to be everywhere. . . . It seems to be vaguely Louisiana and there's a character who's obviously from New York and there's somebody else who's obviously from the Coast and I have a couple of West Indian folk and I have an Arapaho in there as well as an Aleutian and two people from the Philippines. So I'm not sure what the setting of the novel is. But it's driving me crazy."[87] Although the setting ended up being definitively "South," little of the other cultural elements survived publication—no Arapaho, no Aleutian, no Filipinos. The lived reality of New Orleans could not hold Bambara's polyphonic imaginary in which the idea of different cultures, rather than those cultures themselves, were represented.

New Orleans is an interesting case study in the sensationalization and fetishization of a Haitian spiritual practice that no longer exists in its original form, and I think it is a helpful referent in explaining Bambara's desire to situate Claybourne as a site of undiluted Haitian spiritual practice. In Claybourne, the *lwa*, or Haitian spirits, are an ever-present, if under-utilized, part of Black people's lives: "Called upon so seldom, they were beginning to believe their calling in life was to keep a lover from straying, make a neighbor's hair fall out in fistfuls, swat a horse into a run just so and guarantee the number for the day. They were weary with so little to perform."[88] This tension between the restless Haitian spirits and the mundane desires of the American humans of Claybourne is illustrative of one of the fundamental differences between American hoodoo and Haitian Vodou. While many scholars argue that hoodoo is a set of magical practices aimed at manipulating the physical and spiritual worlds (and thus distinct from formalized practices of African diaspora religions more concerned with service to a pantheon of spirits), Katrina Hazzard-Donald argues, innovatively, that hoodoo may have been a religion in the early antebellum period.[89] Bambara creates a world not unlike eighteenth- and nineteenth-century plantation society in its rapid waning, shifting, and transforming of African religious systems in their new, American context. Like the nineteenth-century New Orleans priestess Marie Laveau, the character of Minnie Ransom blends elements of hoodoo with the worship of Haitian spirits. But unlike Marie Laveau, who lived in nineteenth-century New Orleans at a critical historical juncture in which the influx of Haitian refugees to Louisiana in the aftermath of the Haitian Revolution infused local magical practices with the worship of Haitian *lwa*, Minnie Ransom does not exist in a world that shows any direct linkage to Haiti. The world Bambara has created for her healer is one in which Haitian history and cultural specificity, not to mention Haitian people, simply do not exist. No wonder the spirits are weary—various tenants of Vodou theology posit that without the Haitian ceremonies and prayers to serve them, the spirits weaken, lash out, or withdraw.[90] As Bambara writes, the spirits of Vodou are made for loftier projects than influencing human affairs of love and money, but the people of Claybourne seem not to know it. Only Bambara's omniscient gaze sees the possibilities of the *lwa* as the unifying principles that will save a self-destructing world. The Haitian Creole word for the Vodou spirits, *lwa*, is also the word for law, something Bambara brings up in her extensive engagement with the Haitian spirits throughout the text. "They are the laws alive," says Minnie Ransom, positioning the lwa as an invisible ordering system undergirding the psychic life of all Black people, not just Haitians.[91]

In Claybourne, the *lwa* live in the "Old tree the free coloreds of Claybourne planted in the spring of 1871" and kept feeding through "exacting ceremonies."[92] Even in New Orleans, as I will discuss in the following chapter, African American relationships with the *lwa* are neither simple nor direct as Bambara represents them in *The Salt Eaters*. Coming with the influx of Haitian migrants to New Orleans in 1809, Haitian religious practice melded with preexisting spiritual practice that did not necessarily center on a worship of the *lwa*. As documented by Zora Neale Hurston in *Mules and Men*, by the early twentieth century New Orleans spiritual practices had largely moved away from a service to *lwa* that would be recognized in Haiti. Rather, *lwa* worship in contemporary New Orleans is sustained today by a heady combination of Haitian immigrants, white converts, and educated African Americans rather than an unbroken lineage of Creole Vodou practitioners dating back to the early nineteenth century. This dynamic would certainly be evident to a visitor as perceptive as Bambara, a possible disappointment in her hopes for the false historicity that New Orleans mythology offers. In Claybourne, Bambara creates an idealized version of New Orleans unburdened by the real city's pesky inauthenticities. As noted in the groundbreaking collection *Remaking New Orleans: Beyond Exceptionalism and Authenticity*, "manufacturing authenticity for notoriety and profit has been a time-honored occupation for generations of New Orleanians and its many suitors."[93] As one of its suitors, Bambara is perhaps cognizant of the representational violence that is sometimes created by New Orleans' overdetermined image, and absents herself from a sensationalizing economy of New Orleans spiritual exceptionalism. This same rhetoric, after all, has led to persecution and hostility against Black New Orleanians for centuries, from a crackdown on Black public assembly in the antebellum period, to the city ordinances against "fortune-telling" in the early twentieth century which were specifically used to jail Black hoodoo practitioners, and media accounts of the immediate aftermath of Hurricane Katrina that borrowed directly from racist accounts of African diaspora religions that emphasized bloodlust, unfettered impulse, and snake worship.[94] Bambara attempts to avoid a history of exoticizing New Orleans' proximity to the religion and culture of the Caribbean but does not entirely avoid fetishizing global spiritualities.

Despite the fact that *The Salt Eaters* takes place solidly on American soil, Bambara still diagnoses and replicates some of the essentializing desire characteristic of other African American engagements with Caribbean cultural elements. In a humorous exchange between Minnie and her ancestral spirit guide, a no-nonsense spirit called Old Wife, it appears that tensions exist between African American and Caribbean religious practice even in the afterlife. Old Wife, in life an eccentric African American woman, in death is no less prone to her prejudices against the foreign, powerful spirits of Haitian Vodou and Yoruba cosmologies, though she must work with them in order to perform the miracles of healing that Minnie is famous for. In comparison with the folksy, quotidian nature of Old Wife's wisdom, she portrays the *lwa* and the orishas as haughty and bourgeois, like celebrities whose egos are too inflated to be concerned with provincial life in Clayborne. Old Wife complains that the two female orishas "Oshun and Oye [sic] prettyin up to hop a bus to New Orleans. Carnival in this town ain't fancy enough for them."[95] She also distrusts the ritual drumming that calls these spirits to the world, saying, "I can't stand all the commotion them haints calling music." When Minnie points out that Old Wife is a haint too, being dead, Old Wife chastises her: "There is no death in spirit, Min."[96] In this lighthearted exchange, Old Wife reveals the tensions between African American magical practices like hoodoo, which are not beholden to a cosmology of spirits, and the glittering allure of foreign spirits as a taunt to African Americans who have only their own ancestors, rather than gods and goddesses, to speak to.

This idea of African American cultural homelessness is part of a decades-long search for sisterhood that Bambara recycles from *The Salt Eaters*, as well as in short stories written as early as the 1950s and as late as the 1990s in which she invokes a coalition of Third World women called the Seven Sisters. The Seven Sisters are "transplants all. Chezia from the Tupercuin hills, Nilda from the contested Black Hills, Mai from the hills of San Francisco, they liked to joke, or the paddy fields of Berkeley, Cecile from a maroon community in the hills of Jamaica. Only Palma was at home, and not even, she said to herself."[97] Palma, as an African American woman, is the only one without a "hill," meaning a perceived privileged cultural vantage point that allows these women to be rooted while adrift, secure in the knowledge of their cultural purity. This representative, clichéd smattering of women from storied sites of oppression and resistance rings false because it promotes the idea that they exist in perfect, unalienated harmony with their own cultures, unlike the culturally orphaned African American women struggling to find healing and wholeness throughout the text.

The cultural cacophony of *The Salt Eaters* is both an ethical move toward Third World coalition building and a glaring failure of understanding on Bambara's part. In her forward to the first edition of *This Bridge Called My Back*, she makes an overture to "Blackfoot amiga Nisei hermana Down Home Up Souf Sistuh sister El Barrio suburbia Korean The Bronx Lakota Menominee Cubana Chinese Puertoriqueña reservation Chicana campañera and letters testimonials poems interviews essays journal entries sharing Sisters of the yam Sisters of the rice Sisters of the corn Sisters of the plantain putting in telecalls to each other. And we're all on the line."[98] In *The Salt Eaters*, Velma's sister Palma is part of the Seven Sisters, who descend upon Claybourne calling one another sisters, sisters of the various starches that sustain their respective ethnic cuisines. Unto some supposed sisters, however, Bambara layers stereotypes and caricatures without giving these sisters a distinctive speaking voice. Mai, the Asian "sister of the rice," writes calligraphy in a coffee shop and somehow manages to be Chinese, Japanese, Vietnamese, and Filipina all at once. Equally inscrutable is Nilda, a Native woman who spends most of her time thinking about peyote and medicine dances and staring off into space, wearing a hat with a feather in it. Mirroring the anthologizing impulse of the 1970s and 1980s, Bambara promotes the idea that intercultural proximity can foster understanding. That people can be stitched together like squares of a quilt. The idea that wholeness exists, somewhere, in some culture, or beneath all cultures, and that all it takes is a little sisterhood to reconstruct it.

The Native character, Nilda, and the Asian character Mai (as well as two cringe-inducing male Asian characters, the masseur Ahiro and the scientist Rising Sun) are particularly exoticized nodes in Bambara's imaginary. The limits of her cultural knowledge are transparent enough for her to acknowledge them yet not important enough for her to attempt to resolve them. Nilda does not speak and seems to be in a perpetual state of spacey rapture because she "was in the hills with the *peyotero*, listening to the tongue of the sacred cactus where Our Elder Brother, the Deer of the Sun, resides."[99] Mai has a somewhat nonsensical backstory that involves Chinese child brides, Filipino cannery workers, and Japanese internment camps, "keeping separate, even there [in the internment camps], the threads of the Japanese, Chinese, Filipino elders."[100] The brief glimpses into the histories of these characters match the frenetic trauma of those of the Black characters but lack their specificity. In an attempt to speak to all the diverse issues and oppressions under the umbrella of Asian American, for instance, Bambara's Asian sister becomes an amalgam of stereotypes.

Humor plays an important role in Bambara's depiction of the Seven Sisters and other non-Black characters in the novel. She is not entirely unaware of her cultural blind spots, and her overblown essentialisms are in part a gesture toward the work that needs to be done. Third World feminism remained on her mind before and after the publication of *The Salt Eaters*, with the Seven Sisters standing in for all the work that had yet to be done:

> What alliances make sense in this quarter? Where are the links of resistance to be forged, the links of vulnerability to be strengthened? Once again, I'm exploring ways to link our warriors and our medicine people, hoping some readers fling the book down, sneer at my ineptitude, and go on out there and show how it's supposed to be done. Too, I'm staying with a group of women from my novel, the Seven Sisters—a group of performing artists from the African American, Asian American, Chicano, "Puertoriquena," and Native American communities—also in hopes that sisters of the yam, the rice, the corn, the plantain, might find the work to be too thin a soup and get out there and cook it right.[101]

This reveals that she does see that her depiction of the Seven Sisters is indeed a "thin soup" and that she perhaps exaggerated her own "ineptitude" in regard to cross-cultural understanding to showcase how long the road toward true sisterhood was and how far left to travel. Bambara puts her own reputation on the line by ridiculing her own ignorance, a "medicine person" (artist) provoking the "warriors" (activists) to fill in the gaping holes of understanding that she has made bigger so that they would be clearly visible. Perhaps part of making revolution irresistible was this antagonizing humor, this galvanizing self-deprecation.

An even more stark example of this is Bambara's narration of a local dance class in *The Salt Eaters*. The dance group provides its own ironic rejoinder to the chaotic stereotypes of the Seven Sisters, and serves as proof that Bambara is well aware of her own cultural limitations. The dance teacher, "Miss Geula Khufu, formerly Tina Mason, the seamstress' daughter," struggles with what to call the motley assemblage of Third World women who are her students: "She'd started out with 'bitches,' then 'witches,' which was just too much, too much. Sometimes to puff them up on a rainy day she'd say 'goddesses' or 'queens.' . . . The women finally sat Miss Geula down and exercised their democratic rights. There were eight votes for 'ladies' and six for 'goddesses.' Five held out for 'sisters' and were lobbying all the time."[102] This passage strikes on a very problem of the disunity of a group of women of color who cannot even find the language to unify themselves. What about the symbols beneath language, however? As Miss Geula walks among the dancers, she asks them to "remember" their ancestral rhythms: Lebanese and Pakistani and Greek women and "the one little Chinese woman who was, welllll there'd been no strong African presence in China, just a visit long ago in a golden boat with giraffes and gold and spices, a quick hello." Mirroring Bambara's particular authorial stumbling block regarding Asian characters, Miss Geula also seems a bit confused yet eager to incorporate her Asian student. Though she posits that "their roots in the sacred, their roots in the pelvic movements were different that's all," her lukewarm gesture at equality is underlined by the fact that, regarding the non-Black women "she [did not] expect much from them, they were not ancient women after all." Miss Geula's folly lies in her failure to recognize that all women are equally ancient, and Bambara's poking fun only serves to highlight where Bambara stands on the issue herself: though she may not know the roots or specificities of every woman's sacred traditions, Bambara truly believes that they exist. In her book *Black Feminism Reimagined*, Jennifer Nash advances a "despecified intersectionality" "as an opportunity for black feminists to imagine a kind of intimacy with both transnationalism and the broader category 'women of color.'"¹⁰³ Bambara was an early adopter of this methodology. In fact, though Nash does not consider Third World feminism in her analysis, perhaps because of its associations with dated essentialisms, Third World feminism was the condition of possibility for what Nash describes. Bambara remained relentless in her pursuit of sisterhood with women of color both within the United States and abroad, and even at the time of her death she was still conscious of how much work remained for the Third World to exist in practice and not just in name.

Again, the disappointment and potentiality of New Orleans as a model for an unbroken lineage between Black people in the United States and their estranged cousins in the Third World continued to haunt Bambara until her death. In the 1990s, Bambara was writing a manuscript called "Goddess Sightings," which remained unfinished when Bambara passed away in 1995. In this story, she continues her oblique explorations of New Orleans as a spiritual crossroads. It centers around the character of Shirley Fenster, an alcoholic, neurodivergent woman (in her handwritten notes, Bambara writes, presumably describing Shirley: "possessed by uncons. imagery = insane") driven by visions of Afro-diasporic spirits, most often a mermaid spirit who stands in for the Yoruba spirit Yemaya and the Haitian spirit Lasirèn. Shirley is the kind of woman who stands and preaches on a soapbox on a rainy Philadelphia night, who accosts men at a pool hall, the kind of woman who pours rum straight onto the table as libation to the ancestors in the middle of a nice family dinner. Her family tolerates her eccentricities, but they are always "hoping she won't come to the wedding, the christening, funeral, reunion, and show out. but she always does."¹⁰⁴

Bambara's notes reveal her plan for an extensive frame narrative that hearkens back to the Haitian Revolution and a story of nineteenth-century migration from Haiti to New Orleans that was meant to feature as a historical flashback or as the genealogical background from one of the story's characters. She died, however, without ever being able to flesh out this plot point. All that is written in "Goddess Sightings" that betrays the haunting of this backstory is the final sequence of the story, in which Shirley drives to New Orleans with her niece and stops on the north shore of Lake Pontchartrain before she enters the city, thinking of an imminent arrival that never comes as she looks out at the waters of the estuary:

> There'd be the tourist traps to get past. The deliberate misdirections. Then the testing. Even if she found somebody in the bizniz, as they

say, they'd put her through some phoney stuff first. But she would find the place—the house with the yard where the drummers and dancers were Everyone in white with a red scarf at the throat a goat tethered to a post maybe a hen And inside, an altar Someone twirling shaking ecstatic A bowl of cornmeal someone would pinch up to draw the veves. The gods would enter the place. Smoke filled rum soaked. The gods would enter the dancers. The gods would come of the mouths.[105]

Again, Bambara's longing for an unbroken diasporic lineage causes her to imagine New Orleans differently, a hidden New Orleans under the "phoney stuff." Her references to animal sacrifice, an altar, and the Haitian ritual symbols known as *vèvè* all point, once again, to visitors' desire to find an unadulterated Haitian spiritual practice in New Orleans. This fantastical montage, written in a conditional mood rife with the word "would," exists in a tense apart from the past, present, and future of the text. When would this happen? What would it take for this to happen? This is never answered. Bambara remains deliberately utopian to the last, invested in a divine future in which the gods of the past would speak through the bodies of our fractured present. Ultimately, even her most exalted spiritual explorations were always in the service of the material, of the present, and in interviews with Akasha Gloria Hull, she insisted, "I'm not a spiritual being. I'm very much grounded and mundane and political and historical. . . . Some people call it spirit, spiritual. . . . But I'm looking for another word for it."[106] We are still looking for words, dear Toni.

CHAPTER FIVE

Looking for Marie

Hoodoo Histories and the Making of a Black Feminist Genealogy

The Silence of the Initiated

Flora Café sits at the confluence of Franklin, Royal, and St. Roch streets in New Orleans. A narrow heart of land pierced by three different streets. Under banana-leaf bowers, tarot card dreams are spun, armchair philosophies are laid out, and backgammon tiles are set down with a click-clack. For a brief but well-timed number of years, my summer afternoons at Flora's coincided with Ramadan. During Ramadan, the owner Ali spent each of his thirsty, cigarette-less afternoons preparing for dinner. As soon as the sun had dimmed and the bars across the street began to yawn and stretch their limbs, we were all invited to dinner. Whether you were a Persian immigrant or a local drag queen, whether you were a former follower of Elijah Mohammed or a gutterpunk, a social worker or a self-proclaimed artist, you were invited. There was plenty of room for an overcurious, ethnically indeterminate girl in her early twenties, so I melted in with the crowd. At Flora's, no one ever asked me where I was "really" from or compared my skin to any food products—caramel, honey, coffee-with-a-cloud-of-cream, each time as though I've never heard it before, each time as though all the ways in which I can be consumed are supposed to be a kind of compliment. No, not at Flora's. Flora's was generous, Flora's asked no awkward questions, made no overtures thinking she was cute. Flora's existed the way a lake existed—queenly, needing to convince no one that her waters were good enough to drink.

One Ramadan afternoon, I sat outside Flora's with Don Edwards, Omar, and Iam Bennu. Don, gray-bearded, moved to tears of laughter, sometimes, before the punchline of his own jokes. Omar, who owns a warehouse in the Bywater full of unhomed doors, one-eyed dolls, and chandeliers, among whose mazes film crews and antiquarians quarry for treasure. Iam Bennu, who auditioned for the part of the evil hoodoo doctor in Princess and the Frog, who cuts his grass by ripping it up with his bare hands. As usual, we were fending off mosquitoes and downing endless iced coffees, sometimes speaking, sometimes not. Huffing and puffing, a large white woman walking with the help of a cane sat at our table. I did not know her, but the others seemed to, because they nodded and inquired after her health. She made the obligatory comments about the heat, fanning her neck and chest with a real, flower-patterned fan she had conjured from somewhere in the depths of her bra. Then, pulling her skirt up to her hips, she beckoned the four of us closer to her thigh. There on the skin, haloed in the puffy redness of a fresh tattoo, was the head of a woman wearing a headscarf. The woman's body, a line with four stick limbs, had been sketched on in pen.

"It's Marie Laveau," she explained, before we could ask. "Hurt like a bitch, though, so I'm going back tomorrow to get the rest of her body done. I just had my friend draw it on so Marie Laveau's ghost won't juju me out."

I got right up close to the thigh of this woman I did not know. Her tattoo looked nothing like the hoodoo priestess as I had imagined her. To me, the tattoo looked like the head of a white woman floating disembodied in a galaxy of mosquito bites. Marie Laveau's fabled and fetishized mixed-raceness — her skin undoubtedly caramel, honey, coffee-with-a-cloud-of-cream — had been lost in the translation of this image. Black lines on white skin. The whiteness of this Marie Laveau irritated me, and I had to hold my tongue to keep from saying that I hoped Marie Laveau's ghost did juju her out.

My friends, who had been going to Flora's for decades and for whom there was surely nothing new under the sun, delivered a few laconic compliments on the tattoo and changed the subject to Bobby Jindal. By comparison, my response seemed childish, spiteful. After all, this woman, who could not even shift positions in her rickety chair without wincing in pain, had not committed the greatest of all crimes against Marie Laveau's memory. What about all those shops with names like "Voodoo Exotica," who for the low price of $149.99, would permit the curious to witness their secret, savage rituals? What about Chicken Man, who in the 90s had made his living off "voodoo" tours for tourists, famous for the spectacular finale in which he would bite the head off a live chicken as a sacrifice to unnamed "voodoo" gods? What about all the generations of thrill-seekers, journalists, and born-again pagans who looked to the Black population of New Orleans as gatekeepers to a demonic orgy to which they longed to be invited? This woman and her tattoo could not be blamed for all that. Nor could she be blamed for the fact that, in all my years in New Orleans, I had yet to meet a single Black person whose spiritual practice formed an unbroken chain back to Haiti. Never once had I met someone's eyes in recognition of our mutual mystical leanings, never once had anyone offered me the keys to the sacred African lineage I so hoped existed. This was before I watched a Black woman with green eyes balance the chakras of an ailing tuxedo kitten, before I heard Luisah Teish speak in a house in the Seventh Ward, before I sat in anticipation of a ceremony for the spirit Gede and a Haitian mambo sang, with infinite kindness, "Janbe lanmè, janbe lanmè, nou kite lafrik o." We crossed the sea, we crossed the sea, we left Africa. We were here but I did not yet know the signs.

That afternoon, I wondered what hoodoo was if white people could tattoo themselves with our sacred signs and remain unsmitten by our gods. And was I, Black though I was, any closer to hoodoo than this woman with the tattoo? In the echoing silence surrounding Marie Laveau and her heirs, I did not know. I did not know the difference between my own attachment to Marie Laveau and the tattooed woman's connection to her. I did not know.

Once Bobby Jindal had been soundly skewered, the woman with the tattoo got up with the help of her cane, and as a parting gift, told us, "If you're craving figs, there's this tree on the corner of Port and Royal, and it's got the best figs I've ever tasted."

"Who does it belong to?" I asked.

"No one. Everyone."

DESPITE THE MYTHOLOGY AROUND MARIE LAVEAU, and her reputation as one of the most famous female spiritual leaders in American history, very few historical details of Marie Laveau's life are certain. It is widely acknowledged that there were two Marie Laveaus in nineteenth-century New Orleans. The elder one's death in 1881 is well documented by a number of obituaries, but the site of her grave is contested. It is known that the first Marie Laveau was a free person of color living in New Orleans from her birth in 1801 to her death in 1881. It is known that she lived, for a time, in a house on St. Ann Street in the French Quarter. It is known that she was in two long-term partnerships, first a marriage to another free person of color of Haitian origin called Jacques Paris, then a common-law marriage with a former military officer called Christophe Glapion. This is what can be gathered from newspapers and parish registries documenting births, marriages, and deaths. As for the exorcisms and love spells, the dances in Congo Square and the rituals on St. John's Eve, the curing of yellow fever victims during the Civil War—there are no official documents to memorialize these actions, and the only written traces left by Laveau herself are the Xs that stood in for her name.[1] Yet they are said to have happened.

Marie Laveau is a cipher of New Orleans exceptionalism, a symbol of the spiritual power that comes with the city's long and, as the city likes to tell itself, especially close relationship with Haiti and a larger context of Afro-diasporic spiritual practice. Though the Haitian Revolution brought thousands of migrants from the former colony of Saint Domingue to the city in 1809, bringing with them the spirits and practices of a nascent Haitian Vodou, most scholars agree that "by the end of the nineteenth century, organized Voodoo [in New Orleans] had been virtually eradicated due to police harassment and religious intolerance."² Today many Haitians have never heard of New Orleans, and most New Orleanians, even those descended from Haitians, have never been to Haiti, do not speak Creole, and do not have an ancestrally derived practice of Haitian Vodou.³ Today, New Orleans fixes a gaze of diasporic longing across the Gulf toward Haiti, like sailors toward a decommissioned lighthouse that once guided them. Marie Laveau, who was born in New Orleans but lived through the radical demographic changes of the city after 1809, seemed to have incorporated elements of Vodou into her religious practice—namely, the worship of specific spirits through altars, ritual dance, and drumming—but her legend presents only a photo negative of a cultural moment on the verge of disappearance.⁴ Historian Kodi A. Roberts stresses the fallacy of drawing an easy link between New Orleans religious and magical practices directly back to Haiti or Africa in the era after Marie Laveau died: "Rather than being essentially African as scholars to date have claimed, New Orleans Voodoo as practiced [from 1881 to 1940] was a dynamic set of historically contingent spiritual and religious practices whose practitioners drew overwhelmingly on the immediate social and economic contexts of the early twentieth-century United States and of New Orleans specifically."⁵ In other words, New Orleans of the 1920s—where Hurston went looking for Marie Laveau—was no bastion of authenticity, no missing link between Africa and the Americas.

Historian Carolyn Morrow Long refers to the colorful narratives surrounding Marie Laveau's life as the Laveau Legend. It is not my intention to undertake an uncovering of Marie Laveau's truth, at least not in an archival sense. Rather, it is to dwell in the Laveau Legend, and to speculate about the motives of its authors rather than the elusive truth of its subject. The archive is skeletal, and the authors of the Laveau Legend clothe it in fear and aspirations. Zora Neale Hurston, as well as white writers like Lafcadio Hearn and Robert Tallant, had access to archives and interviews detailing Laveau's life but chose instead to ignore, elide, or embellish the details therein. None of these authors, for instance, mention some of the messiness and uncomfortable facts of her historical being: that she owned slaves, that she was the domestic partner of a white man, and that some of her descendants crossed the color line in the wake of *Plessy v. Ferguson* in 1896.⁶ Everyone, it seems, has his or her own Marie Laveau. To her detractors, she was a charlatan, a glorified madame who exploited the superstitions of Black and white people alike to make a profit.⁷ To her supporters, she was a feminist trickster, a champion of the oppressed, and a subverter of race and gender hierarchies.⁸ But whether she is feared or discredited, desired or harnessed, her silence feeds and propels the narratives swirling around her. As is the case for many other nonliterate Black women of the nineteenth century, historical reclamations of Laveau's life must proceed in the absence of any written testimony in her own voice. However, unlike many of her contemporaries—Black women who, in Saidiya Hartman's now canonical phrasing, "are visible only in the moment of their disappearance"—Marie Laveau's legacy is one of power. The way that Marie Laveau's silence and her power have become intertwined has profound implications for Black feminism as a project, which so often rests upon the search for ancestral Black women whose lives we will never fully hear.

In Zora Neale Hurston's account of New Orleans hoodoo in the 1920s, grave dust is an important ingredient in many protective spells.[9] I argue that the construction of Black feminist genealogies is akin to hoodoo in its use of ancestors to shore up power in the present. The Black feminist quest for ancestors in a lacunar archive is often marked by a desire on the part of contemporary Black feminists to reconstruct a visible lineage of survival, passed from dead Black women to living ones. This is why Black feminists from Zora Neale Hurston to Alice Walker have gone looking for ancestors in the historical archive, so that the grave dust of Black women past may allow them to strengthen the living in their personal, professional, and romantic pursuits. According to Henry Louis Gates, this view of intergenerational legacy is particular to Black women: "while black male writers have ardently denied a connection to those who came before them, Hurston's daughters [Alice Walker, Toni Morrison, Gayl Jones, Toni Cade Bambara] acknowledge her influence."[10] The recovery work of Black feminism is fundamentally a spiritual project, not unlike the supplications of countless practitioners of African diaspora religions throughout the centuries, who have derived their power from their place in an unbroken chain of ancestors.

In writing about New Orleans hoodoo, women spiritual leaders are often referred to as "queens" or "mothers."[11] In contrast to the male title of "doctor," which is often deployed parodically by critics of hoodoo, the term "queen" connotes an innate leadership role rather than a trade.[12] The title of "queen" or "mother" implies a power that is in the blood. But unlike the idea of genealogical inheritance implied by these words, the queens and mothers of New Orleans hoodoo are unrelated by blood but linked by complex networks of apprenticeship. Marie Laveau, for instance, was probably seceded not by one of her own daughters, but by an apprentice who adopted her name and continued her ministry in the last two decades of the nineteenth century.[13] The question of this second Marie—the fact that her power is earned, not passed down in the blood—opens up the possibility of Marie's successors as myriad and unpredictable. Unlike a blood lineage, Marie Laveau's power cannot be stamped out by the genocidal machinations of a white supremacist state, nor can it be denied by generations of passing. The meaning of the second Marie is that Black power is not the result of inborn qualities but is, rather, a craft. This broadens the scope and accessibility of Marie Laveau's brand of magic, and perhaps explains her appeal in contemporary New Orleans to those unaffiliated with her by culture and ancestry. Even in the 1920s, Marie Laveau's legacy was already open to the filial claims of those who are ideologically (but not genealogically) related to her. As Hurston notes, "There is a general belief that power can be transmitted, and for this reason most of the older doctors in New Orleans claim kinship with Marie Laveau."[14] The benefit of the capacious filial claim is that it allows Black people to access the spiritual validation of ancestry, even when their biological ancestors are unknown. The filial claim is a strategy often deployed by Black people against a voyeuristic white gaze that seeks to either undermine or appropriate Black culture. The language of kinship lays irrefutable claim to the work of Black ancestors. But it also brings up thorny ethical issues within the Black community about victimization, appropriation, and who can speak for the dead.

Zora Neale Hurston's 1935 ethnography *Mules and Men* is an expedition to New Orleans in search of power, but it is not a rescue mission. Her goal was not to give voice to a silenced archive or to unveil any kind of historical "truth" about Marie Laveau. When she first traveled to New Orleans in 1928, Hurston encountered a tradition of hoodoo already shrouded in mystery, already embroidering Marie Laveau's exploits with fictions. Hurston stitches together the scattered iconography of Marie Laveau's legacy to create an archive of silences. Instead of viewing the gaps in the historical archive in the places where Black women's voices should be as moments of irretrievable loss, Hurston meditates on the spaces of power that these gaps open up. Hurston asks us to think about the powers of those who might be considered as victims of the process of silencing that occurs when sources, archives, narratives, and history are made.[15] In her ethnographic and historical philosophy, Hurston makes clear the ways in which historical actors can use silence both strategically and deliberately.

Sallie Ann Glassman, a contemporary Vodou priestess in New Orleans, suggests that Marie Laveau created the legend around herself even before her death—because her livelihood depended on her reputation as a priestess, she was "terrific at marketing and PR." The spookiness and embroidery of her legend, according to Glassman, is what has "kept Vodou alive in the world today."[16] Marie Laveau's silence on the true nature of her identity and practices sparked the curiosity and admiration of nonpractitioners, while shielding her religious rites from desecration or imitation by those nonpractitioners. Of course, Marie Laveau's nineteenth-century PR campaign, if that is indeed what it is, has had its consequences, as it leaves room for a number of appropriations and misinterpretations by critics who have too much to say.[17]

One such appropriation is Robert Tallant's popular 1946 pseudoethnography, *Voodoo in New Orleans*, in which he describes a so-called voodoo dance: "The dance grew faster now. They spun and gyrated and leaped high into the air. They fell to their hands and knees, imitating the postures of animals, some chewing at the grass, shaking their posteriors violently. They bit and clawed at each other. Their scanty garments fell upon the hot earth, still panting and gyrating. Some fell unconscious and were dragged away, into the deep darkness of the trees that edged the clearing."[18] As is evident from this selection, in Tallant's imaginary, hoodoo is little more than an excuse for an orgy.[19] In a scornful review of Tallant's book in *Journal of American Folklore*, Zora Neale Hurston argues that his work is not an ethnography: "It is rather a collection of the popular beliefs about hoodoo from the outside. The snake-worship sex-orgies, Greek Pythonesses, and goat-sacrifices, proceeding from false premises, and governed by hasty generalizations."[20] However, rather than laying bare the falsehoods of Tallant's text and speaking the "truth" of hoodoo on behalf of its practitioners, Hurston does not disturb the silence around the ceremonies she herself witnessed only ten years earlier. In fact, as Daphne Lamothe and Cynthia Ward have argued, Hurston herself was a proponent of the very opacity she identified in her informants, as evidenced by the slippage in her language away from the third-person when she discusses the "feather-bed resistance" that "we" Black people provide to the questions of researchers.[21] In the words of Daphne Lamothe, Black modernist ethnography like Hurston's carved "open spaces from which Black people's experiences and desires seep out, refusing the social scientist and the larger society's attempts at cultural acquisition, mastery, and containment."[22]

Hurston's ethnographic starting point is the inevitability, and even desirability, of silence. Not only the silence of historical writing surrounding Marie Laveau, but the silence of hoodoo practitioners themselves regarding their practices: "That is why these voodoo ritualistic orgies of Broadway and popular fiction are so laughable. The profound silence of the initiated remains what it is. Hoodoo is not drum beating and dancing."[23] For those initiated into hoodoo, silence is a form of protection from the hostile and voyeuristic gaze of those who would interpret it as spectacle rather than religion. But the silence of the initiated is more than a defense mechanism. It is also a spiritual practice ingrained in the initiation ritual itself. As part of her participant observation of New Orleans hoodoo doctors, Hurston undergoes a separate initiation ritual with each one. Each initiation is different, but each entails a period of fasting and silence. In one particularly memorable initiation, Hurston lies naked on a snake skin with only a glass of water at her side: "Three days my body must lie silent and fasting while my spirit went wherever spirits must go that seek answers never given to men as men."[24] Silence in this context becomes an ethical way of interacting with spirits whose voices may not necessarily be heard or remembered. Rather than speaking for them, the initiate is silent until the spirit chooses to speak to them. In this way, initiates give the spirits the respect someone like Tallant does not—when one is silent, one leaves room for another to speak, one *listens*. Once assured of the initiate's sincerity and respect by the initiate's willingness to listen, the spirits confer their power upon the initiate. According to Hurston, "no one may approach the Altar without the crown, and none may wear the crown of power without preparation. *It must be earned.*"[25] Hurston eschews the language of filiation in favor of one of apprenticeship, representing her engagements with hoodoo as a process of learning rather than as the reclamation of a birthright. In so doing, Hurston emphasizes her own vocational skill as an ethnographer, without undermining Marie Laveau's vocational skill as a priestess. She is not saving an obscure dead relative, but learning from a powerful mentor whose influence extends beyond the grave. While Hurston's representation of Marie Laveau is as much an invention as anyone else's, the character of Hurston's Laveau marks an innovatively symbiotic relationship between dead mentor and living initiate, whereby both women are represented as masters of their respective trades. Hurston's egalitarian approach is by no means typical of historical writing or historical reclamation projects in general. In fact, the asymmetries of power between the living and the dead are often the foundation upon which a Black feminist constructs the validity and imperative of her project, namely, in the claim that the living writer has the power rewrite the forgotten dead in her own image.

The Crown of Power

Her eyes make you hesitate. Her eyes are an inexorable "yes" to your perfunctory "no." I've seen it happen dozens of times, and it happened to me first, at Fair Grinds on Ponce de Leon Street. I was reading a book, and I looked up to find a luminous little Black woman who had set up a display of what looked to me like bent copper wire and rocks on one of the coffee shop's primary colored tables. "Want to take a look?" she asked, catching my eyes with her sage green ones. Not really — I wanted to keep reading. But she smiled, and she was about my mother's age, and her coloring was so unusual, so much green and gold. Seeing an opening, she gave me the litany I would come to know so well: "I'm Cora, also known as the Sage Gem, and I'm just here to raise the vibration of the universe one soul at a time." Into my listening ear she poured her ambitions to start her own healing center, where she would balance chakras, cure insomnia, and otherwise coach and cajole the troubled people of the world out of their ailments. All she was lacking was the money. I left bemused and weighed down by copper and crystals, under the agreement that I was to be her assistant. After all, she was personable and charismatic and her pieces had a certain charm — it might be nice to see her beat the gentrifiers at their own game. Over time, I came to know that like the crystals Cora wrapped and sold, each with their own tasks of healing and protecting and grounding, she held her own medicine. She even smelled like the copper she had grown wiry from handling: sour and vital, like a nutrient you didn't know you were lacking.

It was a sorceress apprenticeship, although not of the kind I had imagined. We smoked rolled-up sage with the fruit vendors in the little concrete shotgun temple on Bayou Road. Clutching tourmaline, she warned me about the effects fluoride can have on the Third Eye, and made me crystal prescriptions for money and menstrual cramps. Once I waited in the foyer of a pet shop while she balanced a sickly kitten's chakras in the back (when I asked her what she did, she said, "Have you ever seen The Green Mile? It's like that."). I drove her to the French Quarter to the one crystal shop in the city whose energetic vibrations were acceptable to her, and picked up the tab at bars where we discussed her past life as a Lemurian. To this day I am listed in her phone as "Marina My Assistant."

Was she the one I had been waiting for all those times that, in some vague and New Agey sense, I had gone looking for Marie Laveau? All those aimless nights of my twenties, biking through the liquid blackness of the French Quarter, past the corner of St. Ann and Rampart where the priestess once lived. As I turned toward the river, the muted unholy noises of Bourbon Street reached me. Toward the lake, the lights of Armstrong Park mocked the demise of that space formerly known as Congo Square. I was hemmed in by music to the south and silence to the north, in a city cradled in the crook of a river's arm. You would think I would find comfort, encased in so many unseen pasts. It was almost like an embrace. But still I was looking for something, looking for someone, looking for Marie Laveau to put her arm around my shoulders and say, "Oh my daughter, I have heard your woes and your pains and tribulations, and in the depths of the wisdom of the gods I will help you find peace and happiness."²⁶ *I had wanted to knock at her door and ask her the recipe for power. I had wanted her to tell me exactly what combination of lemon and gunpowder, what sacred root, what written plea, what black cat boiled and then eaten, would hold the key. The key to being something more than a Black girl wrenching scraps of freedom from the closed fist of the world.*

"This life isn't for everyone," Cora told me once, years later, as she opened the door of her van to show me where she slept each night on a fleece leopard print blanket folded neatly on a yoga mat. "But it's for me." And she stood proudly, sharpening her oyster knife, preparing to slide into another day where no one could tell her where to be or what to do. Except the universe. But that was the beauty of working for the universe, she told me once at a bar on Broad Street, tears rolling freely down her face: "It gives you jobs, but you have the freedom to turn them down." Sometimes—there's power—so quickly. I was looking for Marie and I found Cora. I was looking for the past and I found the universe.

WHAT WOULD ZORA NEALE HURSTON's legacy be without Alice Walker's famous quest to find her? Or Nella Larsen's without the biographical and editing work of Thadious Davis and Deborah McDowell? Or Audre Lorde's without the tender ministrations of Alexis De Veaux? And surely, Black women's literature would not be the vaunted and eminently soundbyte-able field it is today without the literary criticism and anthologizing of Mary Helen Washington, Cheryl Wall, Cheryl Clarke, Barbara Christian, Akasha Gloria Hull, and countless others. This generation of literary critics defined a Black feminist literary tradition long before it held cultural or monetary capital. Amid the shifting buzzwords and theoretical trends of the American academy, these foundational thinkers have yet to be given their full due within the academy. In addition to the usual suspects of racism and sexism, I also speculate that early Black women literary critics are underappreciated because the nature of their work tends to be seen as informational rather than theoretical, and thus their contributions remain obscured and feminized—a kind of intellectual care work.

In 1994, Black feminist scholar Ann duCille diagnosed the way that Black women do not reap financial or institutional rewards when our ancestral care is enshrined as an academic subject of study: "What for many began as a search for mother's gardens, to appropriate Alice Walker's metaphor (1974), has become for some a Random House harvest worth millions in book sales and prestigious university professorships."²⁷ Since then, the problem has only been exacerbated by the ongoing instrumentalization of diversity by the corporate university and the current vogue for "anti-racist" literature. DuCille was specifically critiquing non-Black women scholars capitalizing on Black feminist scholarship for professional gain, and she argues that this critique is *"not simply* about property rights."²⁸ The framing of this claim interests me, its implication being that Black women's literature is a kind of property and that her investment is not simply, but partly, about the rights to it. What does it mean for a Black woman scholar to have even partial property rights over the legacies of our ancestors? As Black women, we undoubtedly have some right to speak on behalf of the ancestors uplifted by our labor, in whose deaths we will eventually share—debatably a stronger claim than even the most well-intentioned and rigorous of our allies. However, Jennifer Nash has identified the weaknesses of the defensive posture that Black feminist scholars can adopt as "a form of agency that is seemingly exercised on behalf of black women's intellectual production, and on behalf of black women as subjects worthy of study, and one that does its work through an exertion of ownership."²⁹ What would it mean to participate in a Black feminist archival praxis outside of the framework of ownership and property rights?

One of the primary problems of the ownership model of archival praxis is that it markets the contemporary searcher as the subject and protagonist, without need for interrogation or negotiation. Hazel Carby alludes to this in her 1990 essay on Hurston, in which she argues, "Clearly, a womanist- and feminist-inspired desire to recover the neglected cultural presence of Zora Neale Hurston initiated an interest in her work, but it is also clear that this original motivation has been transformed. Hurston is not only a secured presence in the academy; she is a veritable industry, and an industry that is very profitable."³⁰ The transformation of the search for Zora from bespoke quest to moot point brings up the uncomfortable point that Hurston's victimization sells. As Carby points out, it has been half a century since Hurston's works were out of print, or since anyone doubted her importance in American letters. However, Hurston's canonization is still entirely bound up with—and perhaps produced by—the legend of her undeserved poverty and obscurity, which must be continuously redeemed by her latter-day saviors.

The seeds of Hurston's victimization were sown in 1973, when Alice Walker went looking for Hurston in Florida. A constant theme throughout Walker's work is the contemporary artist's need for historical models. Walker frames this need as both an act of respect for ancestors and an act of cultural nationalism in the present: "*We are a people. A people do not throw their geniuses away.* And if they are thrown away, it is our duty *as artists and as witnesses for the future* to collect them again for the sake of our children, and, if necessary, bone by bone."³¹ This sense of responsibility to the dead is a fundamental question throughout Black artistic production, especially when faced with archival gaps and elisions in the stories of the dead. While Walker's famous 1975 essay, "Looking for Zora," canonized Hurston as one of the greatest American authors of the twentieth century, it also popularized the view that Hurston died alone and penniless, victim to the twin evils of racism and misogyny. The central figure of this essay is not Hurston, but Walker herself. What one remembers from this essay is not Hurston's genius, but the heroic image of Walker hacking her way through a snake-infested field of waist-high grass to find Hurston's forgotten, unmarked grave.

Walker first came across Hurston's writing when she was researching the story "The Revenge of Hannah Kemhuff," about an impoverished Black woman who uses hoodoo to curse a white woman who played a key role in her misfortunes.[32] After reading collections of African American folklore by racist ethnographers, Walker wonders,

> How was I supposed to believe anything they wrote, since at least one of them, Puckett, was capable of wondering, in his book, if "The Negro" had a large enough brain? Well, I thought, where are the *black* collectors of folklore? Where is the *black* anthropologist? Where is the *black* person who took the time to travel the back roads of the South and collect the information I need: how to cure heart trouble, treat dropsy, hex somebody to death, lock bowels, cause joints to swell, eyes to fall out, and so on. Where was this black person?[33]

The repetition of the word "black" belies the fact that Walker is not looking for just any Black person, but a Black *woman*.[34] When she finds Hurston's ethnographic work in *Mules and Men*, Walker finds more than the historical background for her story. Walker's discovery seems to prompt a kind of magic for her, whereby Hurston's existence endows Walker with a literary power equivalent to a conjure woman's powers of death and healing.

Alice Walker's purported mission, in her search for Zora Neale Hurston's unmarked grave, was to rescue a forgotten genius from obscurity. However, Walker's mission had as much to do with ancestral respect as with contemporary struggles of Black writers in general, and Black women writers in particular. If, as Robert Hemenway says in his biography of Zora Neale Hurston, Hurston's burial in an unmarked grave is "a resting place generally symbolic of the black writer's fate in America," exhuming Hurston's legacy is a symbolic act of particular importance for living writers.[35] Walker seeks to create a distinction between her own creative powers and the disempowerment of Black women of the past—"the agony of women who might have been Poets, Novelists, Essayists, and Short-Story Writers [. . .] who died with their real gifts stifled within them"—in order to claim for herself the artistic career they did not have access to (or, in Hurston's case, could not complete successfully).[36] This is why Walker considers the telling of Hurston's life to be a "cautionary tale" of unappreciated Black female genius.[37] Walker couches her representation of Hurston in a language of filial responsibility: the task of telling Hurston's story was "a duty I accepted as naturally mine—as a black person, a woman, and a writer—because Zora was dead and I, for the time being, was alive."[38] In saving Zora, however, Walker is also saving herself, because if Zora fades into oblivion, Walker wonders, "what chance would someone else—for example, myself—have?"[39]

While looking for Hurston's grave in Florida in 1973, Walker pretends to be her niece. She says that "the lie comes with perfect naturalness to my lips" because "as far as I'm concerned, she *is* my aunt—and that of all black people as well."[40] The claim of matrilineage is poignant—unlike so many of us blocked from connecting with our ancestors by the silences of the archive, here is a Black woman who has found, rather than lost, her mother. However, Walker's embrace of matrilineage allows her to speak on Hurston's behalf while also smudging out some of the words Hurston wrote about herself. For unlike many Black women in the archive, Hurston has left the contemporary searcher a multiplicity of narratives like so many breadcrumbs, and some of those narratives are at odds with the cautionary tale of Walker's rendering. In Walker's case, her representation of Hurston's victimization is at more of a testament to Walker's resolve than it is to Zora's genius. In a certain sense, Zora must become the victim so that Alice may be the hero. When Walker cannot afford the nicest tombstone for Hurston's grave when she finds it in Fort Pierce, Florida, she shrugs it off with the flippant remark, "I realize I must honor the dead, but between the dead great and the living starving, there is no choice."[41] By framing it as a matter of the living's literal starvation if they are denied access to the resources of the dead, Walker justifies her symbolic consumption of Hurston's hard-won power.

It is clear from Walker's research files on Zora Neale Hurston that this image of Hurston as a victim is at odds with Hurston's self-representation—and more significantly, that Walker must have realized the disparity and still chose to represent Hurston as disempowered. Among Walker's research files, which include various photocopied articles by and about Hurston and requests for Hurston's WPA recordings, is one newspaper clipping from the *St. Louis Post-Dispatch* from April 24, 1950, titled "Successful Author Working as a Maid: Zora Neale Hurston, Who Has Written Seven Books, Took Job in Florida Home as Change of Pace—Likes the Work."[42] Hurston is quoted: "You can use your mind only so long. Then you have to use your hands. It's just the natural thing. I was born with a skillet in my hand. Why shouldn't I do it for somebody else awhile?" Here, we have a typical example of Hurston's storied capacity for blurring the line between tricksterly pragmatism and self-degradation. This tendency on Hurston's part has fueled critiques from Langston Hughes and Richard Wright. Hughes, for example, calls her "the perfect darkie" in the eyes of her white friends,[43] and Wright, in a review of *Their Eyes Were Watching God*, asserts that "Miss Hurston voluntarily continues in her novel the tradition that was forced upon the Negro in theatre, that is, the minstrel technique."[44] Her defenders, on the other hand, celebrate her ability to negotiate and manipulate complicated interracial dynamics in her own favor. In addition to the misogyny of Hughes and Wright's statements, they are deliberately misreading the anti-victimization thread that runs throughout Hurston's writing. Her oft-quoted declaration in "How It Feels to Be Colored Me," for instance, explicitly positions her as above the fray of racism and misogyny:

> But I am not tragically colored. There is no great sorrow dammed up in my soul, nor lurking behind my eyes. I do not mind at all. I do not belong to the sobbing school of Negrohood who hold that nature somehow has given them a lowdown dirty deal and whose feelings are all about it. Even in the helter-skelter skirmish that is my life, I have seen that the world is to the strong regardless of a little pigmentation more or less. No, I do not weep at the world—I am too busy sharpening my oyster knife.[45]

This is not to say that Hurston's bravado did not exist alongside significant financial and personal woes. Hurston's archives are riddled with past-due utility bills, and her papers are quite literally scarred by an attempt to dispose of them in a bonfire after she died in a care home in 1960. Fannie Hurst, a white Jewish author who employed Hurston as a secretary, describes being puzzled by Hurston's (in her eyes) unperturbed response to the racism she experienced when the two were traveling together. In a fit of white saviorism, Hurst pretends that Hurston is a foreign princess so that the two can eat together at a whites-only restaurant, and Hurston tells her, pointedly, "Who could think that a good meal could be so bitter?"[46] What is clear is that Hurston put considerable energy into seeking dignity in a world of white patronage and often humiliating bouts of financial dependence, in favor of a blithe and confident persona at odds with her financial constraints. Regardless of the "truth" of this persona, it is a tactic Hurston employed throughout her career, a tactic that Walker dismantles in her representation of Hurston. Walker appears to view Hurston's flippancy as a kind of false-consciousness that Walker must unveil, because "she did not complain. . . . She was not the type."[47] So Walker complains for her, without considering the variety of reasons that Hurston might not have been the complaining type. What is missing from Walker's representation of Hurston is the recognition that silence on certain topics is not universally disempowering. What is missing is an acknowledgment of the gap between the lived experience of our ancestors and the stories we tell about them.

The desire to create stories like these, according to Saidiya Hartman, is a natural symptom of the ruptures of the Black Atlantic, and such stories can be seen as "a form of compensation or even as reparations, perhaps the only kind we will ever receive." The mistake would lie in viewing them as an answer to what we cannot know: our ancestors obscured desires and interiority. Hartman calls these stories "a history of the present" and argues that their purpose is "to illuminate the intimacy of our experience with the lives of the dead, to write our now as it is interrupted by this past, and to imagine a free state, not as the time before captivity or slavery, but rather as the anticipated future of this writing."[48] Similarly, Michel-Rolph Trouillot asserts that "only in the present can we be true or false to the past we choose to acknowledge."[49] The question, then, is not so much about whether our narratives of the dead are true, but about what our treatment of the dead signifies for the world we are trying to build.

I argue that Hurston's version of Laveau, like Walker's version of Hurston, was a history of the present. Like Walker, Hurston was deeply committed to changing the lives of Black women in the present, but Hurston chose to embrace rather than elide the lacunae in Marie Laveau's iconography. Hurston entered a social scene in which Marie Laveau loomed large as a mythological figure, and in her discussions with hoodoo doctors she found that "they all claimed some knowledge and link with Marie Laveau. From so much of hearing the name I asked everywhere for this Leveau [sic] and everybody told me differently."[50] Though Hurston's historical vantage point fifty years after the death of the first Marie Laveau allowed her some access to people who may have known, remembered, or worshipped alongside the priestess, the fact remains that the persecution of many in the community and the absence of written documents by nineteenth-century practitioners and Marie Laveau's own illiteracy made this archive shadowy at best.[51] Hurston's narrative is also complicated by the fact that some of her descriptions of Marie

Laveau, attributed to the possibly fictional and/or composite character of Luke Turner, are apparently drawn from the now out-of-print spell pamphlet called *The Life and Works of Marie Laveau*, a popular item for sale at some of the biggest hoodoo drugstores on South Rampart Street.[52] One of the reasons for Hurston's murky citations may have been the dangers of exposing the true identities of her informants: at the time of her fieldwork, the city of New Orleans was enforcing ordinances against "fortune-telling" that targeted Black spiritual workers like her informants. Coupled with the long history of repression of Afro-diasporic spiritual practice in New Orleans, the truth of the past or present of hoodoo would have been difficult to convey, even in Hurston's time. The collaged, altar-like aesthetic of Hurston's borrowings—a citational politics in which authorship and authority never quite emerge—sidesteps the dialectic between truth and fiction, between silence and speech. Her curation organizes history, and her selection of events, stories, and voices can only be seen as her particular ordering of the world. The slippery, fabulist melding of different characters, voices, and sources creates a world in which the opacity of the past is preserved, a sullied archive of the unknowability of our ancestors.

The version of Marie Laveau that Hurston chooses to recount comes from the character of Luke Turner, Laveau's self-professed nephew, through whom Hurston presents Marie Laveau as a political and spiritual leader.[53] True power, in Hurston's estimation, is the power to make new social arrangements, not merely to change them. She cites Moses as the original and most powerful hoodoo doctor because "many a man thinks he is making something when he's only changing things around. But God let Moses make." However, Hurston reveals other people behind Moses: "But Moses never would have stood before the Burning Bush, if he had not married Jethro's daughter. Jethro was a great hoodoo man. . . . he took Moses and crowned him and taught him."[54] In her typically oblique fashion, Hurston also attributes King Solomon's mythical knowledge to the Queen of Sheba, who "was an Ethiopian just like Jethro" (185). Hurston establishes an even longer genealogy of silent but powerful Black women obscured by more vocal men. Marie Laveau seems to unite both traditions of hoodoo men and silent women.

The Marie Laveau of Hurston's account shares many qualities with the biblical Moses: the ability to part waters, to make a mockery of state power, and to lead an oppressed people. However, the gendered nature of Hurston's construction of power cannot be downplayed; the fact that Marie Laveau is a Black female leader factors significantly into addressing the power imbalance between black men and women that Hurston critiques in both *Mules and Men* and *Their Eyes Were Watching God*. In both texts, Hurston questions the uses of freedom, if even after emancipation, Black women continue to be subject to the kinds of unfreedoms they experienced in their relationships under slavery.

In *Mules and Men*, Hurston's search for Marie Laveau is motivated by Hurston's own commitment to restructuring a sexual and romantic economy in which Black women are systematically devalued. If, as a result of slavery, "de nigger woman is de mule uh de world," Hurston seeks to use Marie Laveau's legacy to turn mules back into women.[55] The shroud of mystery surrounding Marie Laveau's doings allows Hurston to construct her own narrative of Black women's power. In Hurston's account, most of her informants' clients are women seeking to keep or revenge themselves upon men who abuse and abandon them. A woman named Minnie, who comes back to the same hoodoo priestess every week in tears, mistreated by her man, feeling him slipping from her grasp, asks, "Miss Kitty, Gabriel done got to de place I can't tell him his eye is black. What can I do to rule de man I love?"[56] Miss Kitty gives the woman spells and rituals to perform, but they never change the character of Minnie's relationship. Similarly, the wife of a powerful hoodoo priest wants to leave him but cannot because he controls her with a piece of brain coral. Impatient, Hurston tells her, "But if that piece is so precious, and you're his wife, I'd take it and let *him* get another piece."[57] Still, she stays. Surely disheartened at the seeming inevitability of Black women's exploitation, Hurston turns to Marie Laveau for guidance on how not just to change the possibilities of Black love but to make it anew.

Despite the frequent narrations of Vodou ceremonies ending in orgies, and Marie Laveau's reputation as a "procuress" of mixed-race prostitutes for the enjoyment of wealthy white men, the Marie Laveau of legend does not participate in sexual transactions. In most nineteenth-century journalistic accounts, the queen is imperious, above sex, above the machinations of white men. One reporter for the *Daily Picayune* remembers her on April 11, 1886, five years after her death: "Gifted with beauty and intelligence, she ruled her own race, and made captives of many of the other." Even representations that do revel in Marie Laveau's supposedly magnetic sex appeal are mitigated by an obvious admiration for her intellectual gifts. For example, George Washington Cable represents Marie Laveau as the seductive yet clever mixed-race hairdresser/priestess Palmyre la Philosophe in *The Grandissimes*, who holds even her former enslaver under her thrall: "He tolerates her even though she does not present herself in a 'strictly menial capacity.' Reason why—*he's afraid of her.*"[58] Indeed, Hurston plays upon Marie Laveau's fearsome reputation in her selection of anecdotes attributed to Luke Turner:

> The police hear so much about Marie Leveau [sic] that they come to her house in St. Anne Street to put her in jail. First one come, she stretch out her left hand and he turn round and round and never stop until some one come lead him away. Then two come together—she put them to running and barking like dogs. Four come and she put them to beating each other with night sticks. The whole station force come. They knock at her door. She know who they are before she ever look. She did work at her altar and they all went to sleep on her steps.[59]

Marie Laveau's power is no small representational feat for a woman from a caste of women thought to exist for the pleasures of white men, performing the rites of a religion thought to be little more than an occasion for mass psychosexual satisfaction. Marie Laveau's sexuality is present but never obstructive, and her works are never relegated to it. In her evasion of the burdens of Black female sexuality and in her elevation to a status based on spiritual prowess alone, the question one might ask as a Black woman is, "How?" Or, perhaps more importantly, "How can I?"

Contrasting the power of Marie Laveau with the ailments of the female supplicants of hoodoo doctors, it would seem that power does not exist in the present; it is a strength we must draw from the silences of the past. Requesting power from Black female leaders of the past is a way for Black women of the present to reformulate their social relations with men.[60] Luke Turner describes Marie Laveau's unique prayer ritual on behalf of her supplicants: "She go to her great Altar and seek until she become the same as the spirit, then she come out into the room where she listens to them that come to ask. When they finish, she answer them as a god. . . . Marie Leveau is not a woman when she answer the one who ask. No. She is a god, yes."[61] According to Hurston, one of Marie Laveau's trademarks is "a ritual consisting of a series of formal petitions with answering questions from the god."[62] Though it is not named as such, the process here described is spirit possession, a practice not documented elsewhere in Hurston's descriptions of hoodoo in *Mules and Men* and "Hoodoo in America." Possession is a more common feature of the Haitian practices imported to New Orleans in the early nineteenth century, and to the African religious practices criminalized by slavery and colonialism.[63] The fact that Marie Laveau embodies this important hallmark of formalized African diaspora religion through listening is significant. Hurston's research on Black Christianity has held that "the great masses are still standing before their pagan altars and calling old gods by a new name."[64] Like many across the diaspora, Marie Laveau can still access unnamed gods presumed to be lost. The gods who speak through her are nothing less than her own ancestors, through a mode of spiritual communication developed before the slave trade. Marie Laveau derives her power from her receptivity to ancestral voices, as does Hurston, as does Walker, in one long, unbroken chain back to Africa. Just because there are moments of silence does not mean the chain is broken. In construing Marie Laveau as a palimpsestic voice, not as an individual voice lost to history, Hurston conjures a powerful corrective to the seeming inevitability of Black women's voicelessness in the tides of sociohistorical processes. Here, the Black female leaders of the past are not the silenced mules of history, upon whose unprotesting backs history was made. Rather, their voices interpenetrate like clashing ripples in a pond, strengthening one another even as they grow indistinguishable.

This is an important lens through which to view Turner's supposed recollections of Marie Laveau, not as historical facts but as parables compiled by Hurston herself. Turner describes Marie Laveau's dramatic entrance to the St. John's Day Festival over which she presided every year: "She would rise out of the waters of the lake with a great communion candle burning upon her head and another in each one of her hands. She walked upon the waters to the shore."[65] Marie Laveau's control over the seemingly inexorable and destructive forces of wind and water in New Orleans is equally at work in her acts of vengeance as in her acts of pleasure. This is evidenced by this spell of revenge—narrated by the character of Luke Turner but actually drawn from *The Life and Works of Marie Laveau*—which she launches on behalf of one of her petitioners: "That the South wind shall scorch their bodies and make them wither and shall not be tempered to them. That the North wind shall freeze their blood and numb their muscles and that it shall not be tempered to them. That the West wind shall blow away their life's breath and will not leave their hair grow, and that their finger nails shall fall off and their bones shall crumble. That the East wind shall make their minds grow dark, their sight shall fail and their seed dry up so that they shall not multiply."[66] By rewriting history to include this spell performed by hoodoo practitioners and supplicants across 1920s New Orleans, Hurston conjures a kind of historical continuity that is not always evident in the lacunar connections between New Orleans' past and present, between Vodou and hoodoo, between Marie Laveau and herself. These lines are used, in real time, as an antidote to loss and mistreatment, to degradation and abuse, to all the seemingly monolithic social formations that make black women the "mules of the world."

Part folktale and part incantation, it takes to task all that is seemingly "natural" about Black women's disempowerment and turns these forces of nature upon those who have used their unquestioned powers to enforce Black women's disenfranchisement. With this prayer, Hurston questions the inevitability of Black women's historical disempowerment. Hurston's Laveau is not a case study in the world's unfairness toward Black women, but its antidote. As such, Hurston and her version of Laveau are mutually empowering. The measure of Hurston's prestige as an ethnographer lies in Marie Laveau's stature as a spiritual mentor, and Laveau's reputation depends on Hurston's representation of her as powerful. This results in a sympathetic rendering of the dead priestess, a representation in sync with the leadership role Laveau occupied in life. This history of the present holds the future's hopes.

The Black Cat Bone

Don Edwards holds my trust in the palm of his hand, and he has never closed his fist. In all our rambles across the city—to impromptu brass band concerts at nursing homes, for a bag of the eponymous donut holes at The Buttermilk Drop, to a museum in someone's garage or living room, to catch a bit of coolness along the Mississippi at sunset, once to an Episcopalian church that loaded us into a plushy air-conditioned bus and whisked us away on a racial justice field trip to the Whitney Plantation—my trust has never wavered. I gave him my copy of Langston Hughes's The Big Sea, and he loved it so much he said he wished he could keep reading it forever. He gave me a picture of a young boy touching the forehead of the Louis Armstrong statue right before they put it up in Congo Square, and when I look at it now in my living room I think about how the boy is blessing the statue. Once, when I walked into Flora's in a headwrap and fur coat, he told me I looked like Zora Neale Hurston, and it remains to this day the highest compliment anyone ever gave me.

Don Edwards lost all of his records during Katrina, but he sometimes wakes up forgetting he has lost them, thinking he can just reach for them and the needle will find its groove and all will be well in the world. Memphis Minnie will sing "Hoodoo Magic Lady." Sonny Rollins will play the saxophone and it will be so sublime, so irresistible that the mockingbirds will gather outside his window to sing along, just like they used to. Billie Holiday will ask us if we know what it means to miss New Orleans. And we will know, this time we will know.

What happens when water meets vinyl? Do the songs dissolve into the waters like sugar? Do they float on the surface like sargasso, reaching out tendrils, reaching for unknown throats, beached on unknown shores? Certainly, the songs are insoluble. Surely, the waters do not digest them. Once at Flora's, Don Edwards spent the afternoon pestering old jazz heads about a diminished ninth chord, growing angry when they told him such a chord did not exist. Finally, Orlando, a local boy who had swelled the proud heart of the community by getting a scholarship to Berklee School of Music said it did exist, and even played it on the tinny piano inside Flora's. I couldn't understand why it was a matter of such consequence to Don, until he said, "The Lower Ninth Ward. It's a diminished ninth, but it does exist."

During his Katrina-induced exile in South Carolina, where he truly learned what it meant to miss New Orleans, Don Edwards heard snatches of what had been submerged. In a Charleston bank, waiting in line for a loan, his phone rang in his pocket and played his ring tone, Lil' Wayne's "Ride for My Niggas." The young teller, no doubt surprised and pleased that a soft-spoken elderly gentleman should have such a ring tone, decided to help a brother out, one Weezy fan to another. He let Don Edwards skip the line. When he asked Don where he was from and Don told him, he shook his head and said what a shame, what a terrible shame it was.

The diminished chord lingers.

IT WOULD SEEM THAT Hurricane Katrina was a death sentence for Black New Orleans. Not only were Black people disproportionately represented among those killed or displaced by the storm, but in the much-heralded "revitalization" of the city since 2005, New Orleans has lost almost one-third of its pre-Katrina Black population. So when the Louisiana Office of Tourism continues to feature cheerful images of all-Black brass bands on its pamphlets and billboards, when shops along Decatur Street sell postcards of mammies and Blackface voodoo dolls, when through it all Louis Armstrong's name is emblazoned on the New Orleans airport, it can feel as though a dead body is being ventriloquized by an evil marketing witchdoctor. A number of local tour companies have capitalized upon the intersection of New Orleans Blackness and sensationalist tragedy, as evidenced by the proliferation of, in addition to "voodoo" and "ghost" tours, "Hurricane Katrina Tours" for an average of $50 per person. These tours parade by bus through the Lower Ninth Ward and other neighborhoods most affected by flooding during Hurricane Katrina. Gray Line tours proudly advertises that it donates $1 per passenger to a non-profit devoted to "recovery." The Trip Advisor reviews of this service unanimously praise their guides' status as "lifelong" New Orleanians and their "first-hand experience" of the disaster.[67] The tourist industry of New Orleans continues to capitalize on the city's history of Blackness while it constantly commits acts of representational violence that obscure and displace the lived experience of Blackness in favor of a jazz-inflected spectacle of suffering. In the aftermath of Hurricane Katrina, when the levees broke, when the buses did not come, when the Superdome filled up, it would appear that the Black population of New Orleans was invisible. New Orleans historian Lynell Thomas argues in her study of post-Katrina New Orleans tourism that "New Orleans tourists . . . become acquainted with a representation of blackness that leaves actual black New Orleans invisible."[68] However, there is also a sense in which the problem is not invisibility at all, but its opposite. In the words of Claudia Rankine, "For so long you thought the ambition of racist language was to denigrate and erase you as a person. . . . You begin to understand yourself as rendered hypervisible in the face of such language acts. Language that feels hurtful is intended to exploit all the ways that you are present."[69]

The plight of New Orleans' Black population is in part due to New Orleans' highly visible status as "the ludic space, the behavioral vortex, for the rest of the nation."[70] Pat Robertson, the very same evangelical Christian who blamed the 2010 earthquake in Haiti on Haiti's "pact to the devil," also viewed Hurricane Katrina as an act of God's vengeance upon a modern-day Sodom and Gomorrah. In these narratives, New Orleans is simultaneously racialized, feminized, and demonized. Inherent even in its nickname of the Big Easy, New Orleans is represented as a languid, loose woman—desirable, but never respectable. In her study of the infamous red light district of Storyville, historian Emily Epstein Landau argues, "By the late nineteenth century, New Orleans had a reputation as the wickedest city in America. . . . It was notorious for promiscuous race mixing, interracial and illicit sex, and political corruption, as well as prostitution."[71] This nexus of images meant to convey New Orleans' supposedly carefree attitude toward perversion and corruption has become entangled with one multivalent word: Creole.[72] Even today, there are popular perceptions that the Creole (read: racially mixed) culture of the city is to blame for its carefree (read: degenerate) approach to life, given that it was conceived in sin by the unnatural mixing of races. This discourse dates back to the eighteenth century, as Doris Garraway argues in her study of the nexus of fear and desire in French colonial discourse on miscegenation, in which the blame for the fact of miscegenation was legally and ideologically attributed to mixed-race women.[73] This is also evidenced by laws that labeled concubinage as a form of prostitution, and various sumptuary laws and ordinances meant to curb the sex appeal of mixed-race women in Louisiana, Haiti, Martinique, and Guadeloupe.[74] In eighteenth-century travel writing, the mulata is represented as vain, luxurious, and sexually rapacious. According to Garraway, the fantasy of "monstrous female sexuality offered a way for colonists to resolve the paradox of transracial desire and racial paranoia into an acceptable fantasy of their own sexual slavery and submission at the hands of colored womanhood."[75] In spite of its burdened sexual history[76] and complex social implications, the term "Creole" in present-day New Orleans is primarily used by Black people to distinguish a culture of historically Francophone and/or Creolophone black people and to gesture toward an origin-point of autonomous, elite people of color.[77] Although the term describes an ethnic group of often (but not always) mixed-race people of color, many of whom under French colonization would have been called *gens de couleur libre* if they were not enslaved, its usage in contemporary New Orleans often refers less to the French colonial context and more to a history of miscegenation.

Between a caricatured Blackness and an exoticized mixed-raceness, between hypervisibility and invisibility, the Black population of New Orleans often chooses invisibility. While scholars may lament the instances of invisibility and silence in Afro-diasporic archives, invisibility can be what heals the wounds of a hypervisible Blackness in New Orleans. New Orleans might be America's most hypervisible city in the sense that its visual markers are constantly used to denigrate and invalidate its continued existence. In this context, we should take seriously the advice of one of Hurston's informants: "Sometimes you have to be able to walk invisible. Some things must be done in deep secret, so you have to walk out of the sight of man."[78] Invisibility can be a gift from the ancestors that keeps themselves and their descendants safe, but cruelly, it can also prevent us from fully accessing their knowledge.

At the time of Hurston's research in New Orleans, there were a variety of New Orleans city statutes directed against "fortune-telling," all for the purposes of stamping out the lively traffic in the supernatural.[79] However, it would be wrong to think that Black hoodoo practitioners' relative lack of visibility in the present day signals the success of these punitive laws. Hoodoo has not drowned. Rather, its subterranean existence makes itself known in strange ways and places. To miss New Orleans is to miss the space in which it is possible, at specific times, to be invisible. For instance, in the self-protective invisibility of hoodoo dance, the religious rites are both shielded and refracted by the hypervisibility of the Congo Square dances: "Now, some white people say she hold hoodoo dance on Congo Square every week. But Marie Leveau [sic] never hold no hoodoo dance. That was a pleasure dance. . . . Hoodoo is private. She give the dance the first Friday night in each month and they have crab gumbo and rice to eat and people dance. The white people come look on, and think they see all, when they only see a dance."[80] In Laveau's time, she apparently cultivated a strict delineation between public and private, between visible and invisible, and even the ostensibly visible dance maintained a hidden, private meaning for its dancers that white people could not see. As Hurston learns during her ethnographic research, by the 1920s ritual dance was actually quite rare in the context of hoodoo, only used in cases of "death to the enemy."[81] These two dances—the visible merrymaking and the invisible vengeance—are partners in the larger dance of Black representation, balancing the precarious pleasures and pains of an overdetermined Blackness without fully succumbing to either.

This interplay between visibility and invisibility does not deflect or prevent acts of racial violence, but it does allow Black people a measure of privacy. After 200 pages of detail about orgies and human sacrifices, even Robert Tallant must bow before his ultimate lack of knowledge about hoodoo. In a study that was designed to assert his mastery over the subject matter, mastery ultimately eludes him. For Tallant must admit that the scope and content of hoodoo are beyond him when, at the end of the book, a Black waiter at a restaurant confides in him, forebodingly, "I've been all over the country and I've seen signs of Voodoo almost everywhere, anywhere people of my race live. You can always find it. Of course lots of white people don't know anything about it, but we always know. Anywhere my people go they know the signs."[82]

In some sense, being Black in today's New Orleans is a matter of "knowing the signs." Fred Moten has argued that "for the fugitive, the immigrant and the new (and newly constrained) citizen to hold something in reserve, to keep a secret. The history of Afro-diasporic art, especially music, is, it seems to me, the history of the keeping of this secret even in the midst of its intensely public and highly commodified dissemination."[83] Hoodoo in New Orleans may no longer exist as a secret brotherhood (or sisterhood, for that matter) of occult practices, but it exists as a community ethos of the secret, as a part of oneself held back. The spiritual tradition that I longed to find among other Black people does not exist in the form of generations of public rituals for the *lwa*, practiced continuously since the early nineteenth century. However, there is a spiritual tradition of being Black beyond the scope of hypervisibility, outside of violently imposed forms of knowledge. This tradition has its ideological roots in hoodoo ritual, as illustrated by Hurston's narration of the ceremony of the Black Cat Bone, in which she boils a black cat alive and sucks on its bones in order to gain the power of invisibility. During the ceremony, Hurston's hard-won invisibility is accompanied by terrifying sentiments: "Great beast-like creatures thundered up to the circle from all sides. Indescribable noises, sights, feelings. Death was at hand! Seemed unavoidable! I don't know. Many times I have thought and felt, but

I always have to say the same thing. I don't know. I don't know."[84] In this ceremony, Hurston's academic certainty falls away, and she is left confused, frightened, and unable to access any knowledge or understanding of what she has witnessed. This disruption of knowledge, however, is the power of invisibility. Hurston experiences this lack of knowledge in the ceremony so that she too can have the power to disrupt the knowledge of others. The violence of the kind of knowledge exerted by Tallant and his ilk cannot stand before invisibility. Invisibility stands in defiance of false and appropriative knowledge. Invisibility is a refusal to be used.

This is perhaps what Hurston meant when she wrote to Langston Hughes during her New Orleans fieldwork: "It makes me sick to see these cheap white folks are grabbing our stuff and ruining it. I am almost sick—my one consolation being that they never do it right and so there still a chance for us."[85] The limits of appropriative knowledge and the "chance" for Black New Orleanians to safeguard their own self-representations is curiously played out in the plot and backstory of Billie Holiday's only film. The 1947 film *New Orleans*, Billie Holiday's Hollywood debut, was so traumatic that she never made another film.[86] Falling on hard times after her battle with addiction and a brief stint in a rehabilitation center, she signed the contract thinking she would be playing herself, but she realized her mistake when she saw the script: "I should have known better. . . . You just tell me one Negro girl who's made movies who didn't play a maid or a whore."[87] It was too late for her to walk out on her contract, so a drama coach was hired to "brief me on how to get the right kind of Tom feeling into this thing."[88] Most of the footage of Holiday and Louis Armstrong was not used in the final version of *New Orleans*. The released film constructs a narrative in which a maid called Endie (played by Holiday) and her boyfriend Louis (Louis Armstrong playing himself) provide the raw musical talent that the white protagonists refine and mass produce, bringing jazz to the city of Chicago and ultimately to Carnegie Hall.

During filming, Holiday was at odds with the lead white actress, Dorothy Patrick (whom Holiday calls "Blondie"), who accused Holiday of "stealing scenes from her."[89] While Holiday emphasizes her own lack of acting experience and plays off this tension as ludicrous insecurity on her colleague's part, Patrick is certainly not wrong. Indeed, Holiday's famously haunting voice upstages Patrick's rather mediocre and saccharine version of "Do You Know What It Means to Miss New Orleans?" As Patrick's maid, Holiday teaches her employer the song. But the true magic of Holiday's style is beyond melody and lyrics. The subtle and heartbreaking alchemies of tone in lines such as "Do you know what it means to miss New Orleans / When that's where you left your heart?" can be so loaded with subtext that they take the listener to the depths of despair. In this way, Holiday crafts a spirit for the song that is not replicable. The song resists Patrick's appropriation, because Holiday injects something into it that exists independently of the words. This ineffable quality is not Holiday's Blackness, but it is inextricable from it. Holiday's inflections give voice to the sad ironies of someone who has "fought [her] whole damn life to keep from being a maid," and yet "[goes] to Hollywood and ends up as a make-believe maid."[90] Holiday's voice tells an alternate but parallel story to the vague sentimentalisms of "Do You Know What It Means to Miss New Orleans": a person struggling to communicate to a listener an experience that the listener cannot know or understand. The question is rhetorical, something only Holiday's voice can answer. In the context of the film, it becomes apparent that Holiday, not Patrick, is the one who truly knows what it means to miss New Orleans.

Holiday's last appearance in the film, before Patrick's character takes her songs to Carnegie Hall, is during the closing of Storyville. The red-light district of Storyville, which operated from 1897 to 1917, served a white male clientele with, among other fetishes, an offering of "octoroons [who] bridged the antebellum past and the New South future: slavery and commercial prostitution."[91] As Joseph Roach argues, Storyville restages and replaces the spectacle of commodification of raced bodies that used to take place on the auction block.[92] In fact, Storyville's closing in 1917 marks a further solidification of Jim Crow in the city of New Orleans, following a failed attempt by the city to enforce segregation in the racially complex district.[93] Contrary to the historical reality of the white johns, racially diverse sex workers, and Black musicians who made up Storyville, the film *New Orleans* represents the closing of Storyville as an exclusively Black exodus. The scene begins in a Storyville bar, with Holiday striking up a song to comfort the soon-to-be Storyville refugees. A solemn priestess leading her enthralled congregation out of bondage, Holiday exits the film with a dignity that seems more planned than coerced, even though it is overseen by policemen idly swinging batons. The procession, complete with a lugubrious brass band, mirrors the tradition of the second line in New Orleans jazz funerals, in which a brass band accompanies the funeral procession to the site of the grave. The funeral, it would seem, is their own. This scene gives the film's finale in Carnegie Hall, meant to be a triumphant moment of jazz's incorporation into American high art, an air of tragedy. The Black characters' absence can be construed as a collective death, or perhaps a mass suicide carefully accompanied by a dirge

Looking for Marie 151

that lays the community to rest. Henceforth, there are no more appearances by Black characters in the entire film.

The collective walkout of New Orleans' Black jazz founders in the film, however, is a transition into invisibility rather than a definitive death. They are partaking in what Joseph Roach calls the "parade of circum-Atlantic identities." As in the symbolic and actual parades that characterize New Orleans life, "the participants literally succeed themselves before the eyes of the spectators. As the sound of one band dies, another arrives to lift the spirits of the audience. Generations of marchers seem to arise and pass away. Because it is an additive form, passing by a point of review in succession, its ending is always an anticlimax, a provocation, and an opening."[94] If the parade represents a uniquely New Orleans attitude toward history and inheritance, Black feminism would do well to take this model to heart. The succession of the parade does not rely upon bloodlines; it does not ask its participants to build an identity out of (or at the expense of) those who came before. This sense of an opening is not to replace or mimic one's predecessors, not to claim knowledge over them. The logic of the parade is piecemeal, connected but not always causal. The parade is unnarrativized, and as such is both resistant to oversimplifications and inviting of the wildest cognitive connections.

If the Black cast of *New Orleans* stages a walkout in 1947, Beyoncé's 2016 song "Formation" invites them back in. The song, as well as the visual album from which it comes, is saturated with New Orleans imagery and allusions to the legacy of legalized sexual subjugation of mixed-race women in Louisiana. Dressed in sumptuous but restrictive antebellum dresses, wandering through ornate Southern parlors and under oak trees wreathed in Spanish moss, Beyoncé constructs a Southern gothic backdrop for her tale of disloyalty, abandonment, and exploitation. By linking the infidelity of her husband and father to the imagery of an octoroon ball, Beyoncé simultaneously disavows the idea that there is a Creole elite exempt from Black suffering and capitalizes on its cache. In the song "Formation," Beyoncé seeks to reorder the Black social world that has been divided by narratives of Creole exceptionalism, by explicitly claiming Blackness: "I like my baby heir with baby hair and afros / I like my Negro nose with Jackson Five nostrils." In "Formation," Beyoncé calls upon a New Orleans Blackness dismembered by the displacements of Katrina and by the ideological violence of the distinction between light-skinned and dark-skinned people. It is a call to consciousness as much as it is a call to arms, as evidenced by the pun on "Okay ladies, let's get in formation": "Okay ladies, let's get information."[95] Beyoncé rallies the ladies into formation to heal not only the wounds of the interpersonal romantic violence detailed throughout the album but also the enforced fractures between Black women by encouraging coalition building among them.

As a gesture of good faith, Beyoncé features local bounce artist Big Freedia, who represents the polar opposite of the respectable and aggressively heteronormative self-construction Beyoncé has spent most of her career crafting: queer, working-class, and dark-skinned. Beyoncé must enlist Freedia's help because bounce is a genre that relies on the collective memory of New Orleans and runs on references she may not be privy to. Bounce songs are primarily composed of the repetition of a single word or catch-phrase, like Mr. Ghetto's chorus to the song "Walmart" ["Wally wally wally wally wally"] and Big Freedia's now-famous "Azz everywhere." For much of the history of bounce music before Hurricane Katrina, artists remained local and thus relied on the memorability of their catchphrases and personas to draw recurring crowds to their shows. In the wake of Hurricane Katrina, the performers and their audiences were dispersed and their shared knowledge seemingly fractured.[96] However, the knowledge rebounds in other spaces, other clubs, other states. One of Big Freedia's catchphrases is the gnomic refrain "You already know," which assumes an insider or local knowledge, to the exclusion of a voyeuristic gaze. It is a watchword, a wink, a gesture toward knowledge that, while invisible, is apparent and shared between those to whom it pertains. It is the same knowledge that compels some New Orleans residents to avoid places like Bourbon Street, which they label as "for tourists," and to direct tourists who eagerly ask for "local haunts" to places they themselves would never go, all in the effort to demarcate the invisible boundaries of a New Orleans that does not have to perform itself. So when Billie Holiday asks, "Do you know what it means to miss New Orleans," it is Big Freedia who answers across the chasm of the twentieth century, shouting over Jim Crow, over Hurricane Katrina, over the displacements and surrogacies of a rapidly gentrifying New Orleans, turning back to shout over the parade of history: "You already know!"

Conclusion
Notes on a Community Deferred

It's not easy being magic. Take it from Oda Mae Brown, Whoopi Goldberg's masterful play on the trope of the Black psychic in the 1990 film *Ghost*. The beginning of the film finds Oda Mae peering spookily into a crystal ball and guessing, unconvincingly, the name of her client's deceased husband. She is, for all intents and purposes, a fraud. Oda Mae's contact with Patrick Swayze's character (the titular ghost) is her first inkling of any supernatural gifts. Though her mother and grandmother were mediums, Oda Mae explains to the ghost, she has never before been able to communicate with the dead. Rather than celebrating the unexpected emergence of her ancestral gift, she bemoans the identity of her ghost: "A white guy? Why me?" It is almost as though she knows that throughout the film she will be commanded, cajoled, ventriloquized, and ultimately physically possessed by the spirit of this white man, to which she consents with, "You can use me. You can use my body." Even in the pivotal moment when the ghost possesses Oda Mae's body in order to embrace his girlfriend (also white), the viewer is not afforded the pleasure of seeing Whoopi Goldberg kissing Demi Moore—Goldberg's body is replaced by Swayze's, and we are left to imagine the body of the magical Black intermediary who has made this white romance possible. What is the point of being magical if we can't even use our magic for our own ends? I like to imagine a scenario in which Oda Mae Brown could have shared her magic with her sisters instead, or with her Brooklyn community, who throng her parlor when they learn that she can communicate with the dead. In the film, she dismisses them all, because she is too harried by the demands of the ghost of a white Wall Street banker. But what if, after or instead of helping this spirit of white capitalism, Oda Mae was able to funnel that magic back into herself and into her community?

Oda Mae Brown becomes magical when something slips into the sliver of flesh between fraud and authenticity. She has the gifts of her ancestors but the knowledge that these gifts can be easily faked or co-opted. In some ways, Oda Mae's journey from fake psychic, surrounded by all the accoutrement of racialized magic but possessing none of its spiritual substance, to begrudging miracle worker makes her a perfect envoy to our image-conscious age of Instagram witches and influencer priestesses. In many ways, our virtual connections have achieved the kind of Afrocentric community that Oda Mae was denied in the film. However, Oda Mae reminds us that we instrumentalize our spirituality as a personal brand, that we can conflate our spirituality with our identity, mistaking it for something we *are* rather than something we *build*. A recent surge in interest in Afro-diasporic religious and magical practice among gender-oppressed people—including Vodou and Yoruba cosmologies as well as astrology, tarot, and plant-based medicine—is not dissimilar to the earlier spiritual explorations of the Black feminists discussed throughout this book. Now, as ever before, our spiritual strivings are part of a continual pursuit for union with our estranged ancestors. Social media have made the belief systems of our ancestors more accessible than ever, but they have also made them into visual markers of Black authenticity on platforms where identity has become synonymous with advertising and where our own bodies can be used in the financial machinations of white guys just as surely as Oda Mae's was.

Such cruel surrogacies—Black women whose bodies are used by forces not our own—are a major concern in Katherine Dunham and Zora Neale Hurston's early anthropology. Both writers highlight the terrors and dangers of allowing their bodies to be used by external spiritual forces, especially in light of the historical ways Black women's bodies have been abducted, abused, and exploited. However, considering both of their works together brings us toward a framework that makes the case for the spiritual potency of (to paraphrase Fred Moten paraphrasing Edouard Glissant) "consent[ing] not to be a singular being."[1] Dunham and Hurston, while often falling short of community with one another and with their informants, make a compelling case for building spirituality as a communal practice.

Hurston narrativizes one of the first documented cases of zombification in Western anthropology in an encounter with a Haitian woman called Felicia Felix-Mentor.[2] Hurston meets Felix-Mentor in a hospital in Gonaives in 1936. She is a battered woman with "dead eyes," and she "showed every sign of fear and expectation of abuse and violence."[3] She is unable to speak. The attending doctor tells Hurston that Felix-Mentor died and was officially buried in 1907, only to appear in her hometown twenty-nine years later, naked, alone, and robbed of her mental faculties. Hurston attributes zombification not to an awakening of the dead but to a drug, "some secret probably brought from Africa and handed down from generation to generation," that "destroys the part of the brain which governs free will and action."[4] Zombies are thereby used as beasts of burden by their masters, a transformation from human to beast that Hurston describes thus:

Think of the fiendishness of the thing. It is not good for a person who has lived all his life surrounded by a degree of fastidious culture, loved to his last breath by family and friends, to contemplate the probability of his resurrected body being dragged from the vault—the best that love and means could provide, and set to toiling ceaselessly in the banana fields, working like a beast, unclothed like a beast, and like a brute crouching in some foul den in the few hours allowed for rest and food. From an educated, intelligent being to an unthinking, unknowing beast.[5]

The slippage between human and beast is pervasive across Hurston's oeuvre, shared between her reflections on gendered power dynamics, possession, and zombification. The title of *Tell My Horse* comes from the language of possession in Haitian Vodou, which refers to people who are possessed as the "horses" of the spirits. The title of *Mules and Men*, her ethnography detailing, among other things, a spiritual economy in which Black women use magical practices to right structural imbalances, can also be a commentary on the interpersonal power disparities between women and men if we consider her description of Black women as the mules of the world in *Their Eyes Were Watching God*.[6] Both titles highlight Hurston's discomfort with women's bodies robbed of agency, bodies made bestial by cruel usage. Hurston, in other words, applies the powerful metaphor of zombification, already implying conditions of enslavement and compromised agency, as an analytic of gender. Her obvious horror upon meeting Felix-Mentor—"the sight of this wreckage was too much to endure for long"—is due in large part to the fact that this is a woman who can no longer speak, cannot even narrate the damage that has been done to her.[7]

Dunham also lingers on a description of female zombification in *Island Possessed*. When she visits the home of a man called Ti Couzin, who is rumored to live with a number of women he has transformed into zombies, Dunham is morbidly fascinated with the validity of these claims. As Dunham and Hurston note, the Haitian zombie is a beast of burden, an insensible and unprotesting slave to the person who made the zombie. When the zombies become wives and constitute a kind of harem, the intersection between forced labor and sexual violence becomes pronounced. In the presence of Ti Couzin, a man whose unique combination of condescension and charisma leaves her uncharacteristically flustered, Dunham wonders "if this was the beginning of being zombi-ized."[8] Dunham is robbed of her usual articulacy and aplomb, and her fear of zombification is a recognition of her own vulnerability to the assaults to their personhood that Black women across the diaspora must face, positioned as they are under the twin yokes of patriarchy and colonial and racial violence. However, Dunham does not choose the route of martyred identification or solidarity with the zombie wives, silent and industrious women, with "faces with absolutely no expression and which might as well have been the faces of the blind or deaf."[9] Rather, she feels herself at once compelled by their plight and impotent to stop it, positioned as "a lone woman with others behind her in spectral attendance" rather than one of the specters themselves.[10] Dunham's anxiety comes from the tension between the privilege that safeguards her from the fate of zombie-wifehood and a sense of responsibility to Haitian women who do not have the freedom to travel as she does, to speak as she can, and thus stand in silent witness to all her doings. Dunham strikes a delicate balance between acknowledgment of the privilege of her position and feelings of kinship with Haitian women, without ever falling into paternalistic imperatives to "save" Haitian women.

These mutual fears of zombiehood, in other words, are Hurston's and Dunham's acknowledgment of the fragility of their own autonomy and their mobility, and their solidarity with all the Black women who never had the opportunity to be anthropologists. Their fears showcase the fickleness of their fugitivity, and an all-too-keen awareness of the possibility that their pedestals on which they have been temporarily elevated above other diasporic women might be snatched from underneath them. As, indeed, they were. Their divergent paths illustrate that very fragility. It may seem that Dunham's long and storied career as a dancer, teacher, and choreographer counters Hurston's famously impoverished and obscure death ending in an unmarked grave. However, Hurston's illustrious afterlife as a genius of the American South and Katherine Dunham's more modest legacy, which has left her out of mainstream American conceptions of Black history, call into question the permanence of their earthly success.

Due to the precarity of her success while she was alive, it is unsurprising that concerns about women's loss of agency are a constant theme throughout Hurston's work. Through her use of the trope of the beast of burden, Hurston defines possession throughout her oeuvre as a social process, as a symptom of structural violence. In *Their Eyes Were Watching God*, for instance, she represents Black laborers in Florida as physical husks prone to possession by lesser beings: "mules and other brutes occupied their skins."[11] It is not until the end of the workday that "the skins felt powerful and human."[12] I argue that this problematic in *Their Eyes Were Watching God*, which was famously written over the course of seven weeks during Hurston's time in Haiti, was crucially informed and framed by her Haitian fieldwork. When she encounters religious and supernatural forms of displaced agency, Hurston inevitably thinks of them as violent forms of social control, as social relations that mirror and reproduce the relationship between master and slave. Hurston views servitude as a crisis of consciousness, and as a result Hurston views two vastly different phenomena—spirit possession and zombification—under the same rubric of suspicion. However, contrary to Hurston's fears, this process of zombification is actually quite the opposite of the phenomenon of spirit possession. In Vodou, when a person is ridden by a spirit, the person's *gwobonanj*, the part of the soul that governs agency and which is in fact stolen during the process of zombification, is temporarily displaced to make room for the spirit. Quite the contrary to Hollywood depictions of mindless enjoyment in Vodou ritual, this can be a terrifying prospect for the person possessed, even when the person is familiar with the ritual. For Black American women like Dunham and Hurston in particular, grasping at ethnographic authority in a field that saw Black women as ethnographic raw material rather than as theorists, the loss of their hard-won self-possession was a bitter prospect (in sharp contrast, for instance, to their contemporary Maya Deren, a white anthropologist who embraced possession less ambivalently).

In Haiti, Black women's relationship with Vodou is no less fraught, though for different reasons. The spirits are demanding, their desires sometimes contradictory to one's own, and the path is never easy. What is powerful about Haitian Vodou is not just its liberatory framework, but the way in which it incorporates decidedly unliberatory feelings. Jealousy, discomfort, betrayal, selfishness—all the bad affects created by centuries of enslavement and exploitation are not spirited away by African diaspora religions. They become part of them. As Colin Dayan argues, noting at first her confusion at seeing whips and manacles as part of Vodou ceremony and iconography, Haitian Vodou was a belief system formed in the crucible of slavery and the struggle for freedom, and thus incorporates rather than neutralizes interpersonal violence.[13] In an interview, Evelyn Jean-Gilles, a contemporary *mambo* working in the north of Haiti outside Cap-Haïtien, describes in an interview the troubling influence of spirits in her life, how the spirit Ezili Freda has prevented her from having children, and how the spirits have even thrown her down the stairs and broken her bones in retaliation for her long absences from their altars. She did not even choose to serve the spirits at all, but rather was wrenched away from her life as a good Christian by the spirits and by Satan (whom she, in keeping with diasporic tradition, does not view as an evil figure).[14]

Vodou is a religion that illustrates the compromised agencies of diaspora without offering an easy way out, and in this way it elegantly validates and holds space for Dunham and Hurston's fears and desires. In the same way that Katherine Dunham and Zora Neale Hurston lived parallel struggles to bridge the enormity of their estrangement from African belief systems, so too do Haitian practitioners of Vodou depict their own estrangement from Africa with as much longing as Americans. As opposed to the practice of Yoruba-derived cosmologies in the diaspora, which make extensive use of Yoruba language and hearken back to an African past, Vodou firmly inhabits life in the break of the Middle Passage and the enormity of the cultural loss even as it stands as a monument to the resiliency of the faith of enslaved Africans. Vodou ceremonies typically begin with a prayer that expresses the sentiment of crossing the ocean and leaving Africa.[15] As anthropologist Karen McCarthy Brown translates it in her definitive ethnography, *Mama Lola, A Vodou Priestess in Brooklyn*: "The family is assembled, / Gathered in. / We are Creoles, / Who have Africa no longer."[16] And yet, in Mama Lola's version of the prayer, the congregants later sing, "My friends, everything I am doing / Is heard in Africa."[17] In Vodou both possibilities exist alongside one another: the irreparable severing, and the deep connection. If healing is ever to be found — and, I argue, it is healing Dunham and Hurston were looking for — it is only fitting to look to a religion birthed as a technology of healing, creating new rituals, new theology, and new spirits to account for our haunted lives on new continents where we never wanted to be and yet are.

Throughout this book, the exigency of life under capitalism has often relegated community to the realm of the speculative. Often, the material conditions of life in the diaspora, and the absence of funds to live in comfort or safety (let alone travel for research or leisure) often created fractures where connections should have been. These fractures are not exceptions to diasporic Blackness; they are constitutive of it. The unconsummated friendship of Zora Neale Hurston and Katherine Dunham, for instance, was not just an interpersonal dynamic but a structural one inherent to the tenuous "we" that is Black women. Considering their parallel experiences as they unknowingly crossed and uncrossed the ghosts of one another's paths in Haiti — making them speak to one another rather than alongside one another — is an exercise in funneling our magic back into our community. Here, I am taking seriously Audre Lorde's imperative in her essay "Eye to Eye": "Often we give lip service to the idea of mutual support and connection between black women because we have not yet crossed the barriers to these possibilities. . . . And to acknowledge our dreams is to sometimes

Conclusion 159

acknowledge the distance between those dreams and our present situation."[18] To speculate about a community deferred is to measure the distance we have yet to go in forging equitable connections between Black women, both across and within national affiliations. If the complementing visions of Hurston and Dunham have taught us anything, it is that anywhere we move, there is always a chorus of Black women in spectral attendance. We just have to look for them.

Notes

Abbreviations of Archival Sources

MARBL   Lucille Clifton Papers, Stuart A. Rose Manuscript, Archives, and Rare Book Library, Emory University, Atlanta, Ga.
MHS   Katherine Dunham Papers, Missouri Historical Society and Research Center, St. Louis, Mo.
SCHOM   Lorraine Hansberry Papers, Schomburg Center for Research in Black Culture, Harlem, N.Y.
SIUC   Katherine Dunham Papers, Special Collections and Research, Southern Illinois University Carbondale
SPEL   Toni Cade Bambara Collection, Spelman College Archives, Atlanta, Ga.
UF   Zora Neale Hurston Papers, Special and Area Studies Collections, George A. Smathers Libraries, University of Florida, Gainesville, Fla.

Introduction

1. For more on Haitian themes and symbology within *Their Eyes Were Watching God*, see the essays collected in Delois Jenkins, *Zora Neale Hurston*.

2. Though most scholarship on this work has recognized its paradoxes, there is not scholarly consensus regarding Hurston's level of complicity with American imperialism. In fact, sometimes different scholars will interpret the same passage from *Tell My Horse* as anti-imperialist or as culturally chauvinist. As Daphne Lamothe argues in *Inventing the New Negro*, "critics often focus their readings on that aspect of the book they consider most valuable or problematic" (149). Daphne Lamothe has argued that both viewpoints have merit and that the useful part of the text is its "narrative dissonance," which sheds light on Hurston's positionality: "The ethnographer's assumed omniscience, invisible and simultaneously all seeing, ran directly in opposition to the double-consciousness she certainly experienced as a woman of color. The narrative effect of these conflicting ways of seeing and being seen is a disorienting fragmentation of the narrative" (143). Some of the most trenchant critiques of the text's condescension toward working-class Haitians and its elision of American neocolonial violence have come from Nwankwo, "Insider and Outsider," and Carby, "Politics of Fiction," which argues that "Hurston's overtly political comments in *Tell My Horse* are usually reactionary, blindly patriotic, and, consequently, superficial" (87).

3. Hurston, *Tell My Horse*, 87.

4. For example, see Harris, "Zapping the Editor," and Raynaud, "'Rubbing a Paragraph."

5. Hurston, *Dust Tracks*, 249.

6. One of the primary proponents of anti-imperialist themes within *Tell My Horse* is Kevin Meehan in "Decolonizing Ethnography." While I agree that Hurston's "roving narrator" makes her individual stance difficult to determine, I think that Meehan's assertion that *"Tell My Horse* is adept and even radical (especially when it comes to global issues)" is an overgenerous prescription of political efficacy to a text that takes no coherent or discernable anti-imperialist stance (68). In his essay "Zora's Politics," Ernest J. Mitchell II has argued that Hurston's critique of colonialism was consistent throughout her work, but "her critiques of countries that lacked formal colonies were more ambivalent." Mitchell conducts a series of careful readings of passages of *Tell My Horse* that showed slight indications of irony within statements that, on a surface level, appear to praise the occupation. While parsing these statements may shed light on Hurston's complex personal political narrative, I argue that these critiques are so veiled as to be rendered meaningless in a public setting.

7. Hurston, *Tell My Horse*, 86.

8. Hurston, *Tell My Horse*, 81.

9. Johnson, "Truth about Haiti." This article contains much of the same information and anti-imperialist tone as Johnson's articles written for *The Nation*, but the direct address to "colored people" at the end of *The Crisis* article shows an acknowledgment of the magazine's primarily Black readership.

10. Hurston, *Tell My Horse*, 66. For more information on the Caco resistance, see Alexis, *Haiti Fights Back*.

11. Hurston, *Dust Tracks*, 254.

12. Raynaud, "Modernism."

13. *The Crisis*, *The Messenger*, and *The Negro World*—all of which published critiques by prominent Black male political figures of U.S. imperialism—were Black-run publications.

14. Hurston, "Letter to Henry Allen Moe," in *Zora Neale Hurstons*, 403. In *Wrapped in Rainbows*, Valerie Boyd argues that Hurston suspected that someone had poisoned her with the very medicinal practices she was researching in Haiti (299–300).

15. Hurston, *Dust Tracks*, 215.

16. Throughout the text, I use the term "Black American feminism" to gesture to the fact that there are distinct Black feminist traditions that have developed in other linguistic and cultural contexts outside of Anglophone North America and to signal that the Black feminists in this study are sometimes first-generation Americans and are not necessarily African Americans.

17. Brown, *Babylon Girls*, 228.

18. Davis, *Blues Legacies*, 67.

19. Higashida, *Black Internationalist Feminism*, 130. In this particular example, Higashida is referring to Terry McMillan's popular 1996 novel, *How Stella Got Her Groove Back*.

20. Gill, *Erotic Islands*, 193.

21. Williams, *Pursuit of Happiness*, 14–15 and 23.

22. Lorde, *Sister Outsider*, 36.

23. Brown, "Women's Leadership," 226.

24. Edwards, *Practice of Diaspora*, 15.

25. Nash, *Black Feminism Reimagined*, 108.

26. Lorde, *Black Unicorn*, 112.

27. Glick, *Black Radical Tragic*, 81.

28. Orisha devotion in the United States has boomed in the last sixty years due to an influx of practitioners leaving Cuba after the revolution and the subsequent cultural nationalism of African American converts, most notably by Oba Adefunmi (born Walter Eugene King). Today, devotees of the orishas far outnumber Vodou practitioners in the United States. Some reasons for this, as well as some differences between the two belief systems, will be further discussed in chapters 3 and 4.

29. Scholarship by Régine Jean-Charles, Kaiama Glover, Cae Joseph-Masséna, and Grace Sanders Johnson sheds light on the feminist import of these and other Haitian women writers. Notably, Black American writers throughout this study did engage with the writings of Haitian men like Jean Price-Mars, Arthur Holly, and Jacques Roumain. However, there is little indication that Black American women writers knew about the intellectual production of their Haitian women contemporaries, further testament to the painful disparities in power and access that plague the figures of this study.

30. Ulysse, "Vodou as Idea."

31. Hartman, *Lose Your Mother*, 75.

32. C. L. R. James, on the one hand, affords it a largely symbolic role in slave revolts, mentioning it only three times throughout all of *The Black Jacobins*. Cedric J. Robinson's *Black Marxism*, on the other hand, cites it as the framing ideology of Haitian revolt. Admittedly, these two projects were more invested in their contemporary Marxist ideological commitments than in archival engagement with materials from the Haitian Revolution. Geggus, in *Haitian Revolutionary Studies*, provides a comprehensive review of the available historiographical and archival materials on eighteenth-century Vodou and comes to the conclusion that its role in the revolution is "ancillary rather than central" (80).

33. Geggus, *Haitian Revolutionary Studies*, 81–92. As Geggus notes, the Bois-Caïman gathering may have been two separate gatherings in August of 1791, one secular and the other a religious ceremony.

34. Dubois, *Avengers*, 101.

35. Notable classic texts written about Haitian revolutionary leaders by diasporic intellectuals include C. L. R. James's *Black Jacobins*, Aimé Césaire's *La tragédie du roi Christophe*, Edouard Glissant's *Monsieur Toussaint*, Derek Walcott's *Haitian Trilogy*, Katherine Dunham's unstaged ballet *Christophe*, and Lorraine Hansberry's unfinished play *Toussaint*, among others. The focus of all of these examples on Toussaint Louverture, Jean-Jacques Dessalines, and Henri Christophe illustrates a fascination with, and in some cases a fetishization of, Black male leadership. Haitian revolutionary heroines like Sanité Bélair, Catherine Flon, and Dédée Bazile, while part of public memory in Haiti, have yet to be canonized by non-Haitians with the same enthusiasm as their male contemporaries.

36. Brown, *Mama Lola*, 221.

37. Martin, *Envisioning*, xxxvii.

38. Welele Raymond-Noël, interview with Laine-Kaplan Levinson, June 2017. Translation is my own.

39. Hurston, *Dust Tracks*, 254.

Chapter One

1. Hurston, "Thirty Days," 272.
2. Dunham, *Journey to Accompong*, 52.
3. Hurston, *Zora Neale Hurston*, 384, 399, and 403.
4. Hurston, *Zora Neale Hurston*, 385.
5. Dunham, qtd. in Boyd, *Wrapped in Rainbows*, 261.
6. Osumare, "Katherine Dunham," 612.
7. Boas, preface to Hurston, *Mules and Men*, xiii.
8. Ramsey, "Melville Herskovits," 208–9.
9. Lamothe, *Inventing the New Negro*, 15.
10. Martin, "Katherine Dunham's Notable Contribution," in *Kaiso!*, 212.
11. For a more extended analysis of the relationship of African American concert dance to the pressures of "ethnographic realism," see Manning, *Modern Dance, Negro Dance*.
12. Dunham, *Island Possessed*, 46.
13. Clifford, *Predicament of Culture*, 10.
14. Dunham, *Journey to Accompong*, 4. Emphasis mine.
15. Aikens, "On Stage with the Dunham Company," 285.
16. The term "voodoo" or "voodooism," though it has become a derisive catch-all term for any African-derived spiritual or magical practice, has its etymological provenance in the word "Vodou," which refers to an actual religion with origins in Haiti and practiced throughout the diaspora. In 2011, in the aftermath of the devastating 2010 earthquake in Haiti, a group of scholars successfully led a campaign to have the word "voodooism" changed to "Vodou" in the Library of Congress subject headings. For more on this, see Ramsey, "From 'Voodooism' to 'Vodou.'" This incident highlights the fraught cultural baggage of the word. It is a time-honored tradition for both foreigners and Haitians alike to blame Haiti's woes on a so-called pact with the devil exemplified by "voodoo," an egregious example being televangelist Pat Robertson's claim that the 2010 earthquake was caused by Haiti's "pact with the devil." Ironically, practitioners of Vodou rarely refer to themselves as practicing Vodou; in their terminology, they "serve the spirits."
17. Renda, *Taking Haiti*, 19.
18. The article goes on to describe Sam's murder: "Even then the anger of the people was not appeased. The body of the President was mutilated, and, tied to the end of a rope, it was dragged through the streets of the city." Another, more graphic description of the barbarism of Sam's murder comes from William Seabrook's *The Magic Island*, 281–82: "The mob, of course, simply tore him to pieces. Mostly they used their hands. But one woman cut off his head with a machete and marched with it. Another woman, they say, ripped out his heart and marched, tearing it to shreds with her teeth."
19. These texts are legion, but their content is predictably somewhat uniform. Orgies, drums, and a Conradian fascination with eye-rolling Black bodies are the tropes that reign supreme. Readers interested in further exploring this genre may turn to the following texts: Wirkus and Dudley, *White King of La Gonave*; Craige, *Cannibal Cous-*

ins and *Black Bagdad*; Taft, *Puritan in Voodoo-Land*; Loederer, *Voodoo Fire in Haiti*; Burks, *Black Medicine*; and Huxley, *Invisibles*. For a more detailed historical account of interwar pulp fiction and pseudo-ethnography written by interwar white visitors to Haiti, see Renda, *Taking Haiti*, 175–85 and Ramsey, *Spirits and the Law*, 118–76.

20. Seabrook, preface to Wirkus and Dudley, *White King of La Gonave*, xiv.

21. Seabrook, *Magic Island*, 42.

22. Seabrook. *Magic Island*, 42–43.

23. Craige, *Black Bagdad*, 37.

24. Craige, *Black Bagdad*, 83. For a historical account of paranoia, mental illness, and anti-Haitian violence among the occupying forces, see Renda, *Taking Haiti*, 131–39.

25. Burks, *Black Medicine*, 154; Craige, *Black Bagdad*, 37–38; Morand, *Black Magic*, 100–101.

26. Ramsey, *Spirits and the Law*, 162.

27. Indeed, these performances were such a staple of the interwar period that they later became something of a cliché in the Black arts. The musical *Stormy Weather*, starring Bill "Bojangles" Robinson, in many ways a retrospective of the Harlem Renaissance, included a parody of the genre when Robinson refuses to be taken in by the primitive spectacle of jungle imagery and feathered loincloths and begins to tap-dance on one of the tom-toms, for which he receives thunderous applause.

28. One of Dafora's most curious collaborators was the Nigerian-born actor Abdul Assen, who appeared to make a living as a professional witch-doctor impersonator. Assen began his career as a witch doctor at the 1933 Chicago Century of Progress exposition, and later appeared as a witch doctor in both *Kyunkor* in 1934 and voodoo *Macbeth* in 1936. For more on Assen, see Perpener, *African American Concert Dance*, 85. John Martin, in an enthusiastic review of *Kyunkor* from the May 9, 1934 issue of the *New York Times*, describes Assen thus: "With strange incantations chanted in falsetto, alternating with bits of tune played on a primitive pipe, with animal expletives and beatings of the breast, he works himself into a frenzy of devil-baiting" ("Native Cast Gives an African 'Opera'" 23). The fact that during the decade of the 1930s an African immigrant could make a living as a professional witch-doctor impersonator speaks volumes about the ideological climate of interwar America and its appetite for the "primitive."

29. Garcia, *Listening for Africa*, 179.

30. Hazzard-Gordon, *Jookin'*, 12.

31. Hartman, *Scenes of Subjection*, 77.

32. Hartman, *Scenes of Subjection*, 77.

33. Dunham, *Island Possessed*, 85.

34. Dunham, *Island Possessed*, 95

35. Dunham, *Island Possessed*, 99.

36. Dunham, *Island Possessed*, 143.

37. *Island Possessed* was written before the standardization of Creole orthography, so orthographic discrepancies between my analysis and Dunham's text (for example, Danbala vs. Damballa, Vodou vs. vaudun, Ginen vs. Guinée) will occur.

38. Dunham, *Island Possessed*, 32.

39. Dunham, *Island Possessed*, 40.
40. Dunham, *Island Possessed*, 206.
41. Dunham, *Island Possessed*, 210.
42. Dunham, *Island Possessed*, 79.
43. Dunham, *Island Possessed*, 59. "Prête savant" translates literally from French as "wise priest," and "Nan Guinée" refers to both Africa and the afterlife and in Vodou cosmology.
44. Dunham, *Island Possessed*, 65.
45. Deren, *Divine Horsemen*, 128. See also Katherine Dunham, "Early New York Collaborations: Excerpts from 'Minefields,'" in Clark and Johnson, *Kaiso!*, 133–34.
46. Luis-Brown, *Waves of Decolonization*, 150.
47. Hill, *Black Soundscapes, White Stages*, 97–98.
48. Edwards, "Ethnics of Surrealism," 84–135. Edwards positions Georges Bataille as one of the proponents of jazz's modernity, in opposition to Michel Leiris, who views it as indicative of ancient racial characteristics.
49. Hughes, "Negro Artist," 306. See also Helene Johnson's "Poem," in which she sings the praises of her dark-skinned lover: "Gee boy, when you sing, I can close my ears / And hear tom-toms just as plain. / Listen to me, will you, what do I know / About tom-toms? But I like the word, sort of, / Don't you? It belongs to us" (183). Like Hughes, Johnson situates the tom-toms as a symbol of some inherited vitality, as much created through music as it is inherited through blood.
50. Van Vechten, *Nigger Heaven*, 284.
51. Van Vechten, *Nigger Heaven*, 189.
52. Jean-Jacques Dessalines, the Haitian revolutionary leader, was reputed to have eradicated the French landowning population by ordering his followers, "Koupe tèt, boule kay" (Cut off heads and burn houses).
53. Hurston, "How It Feels," 154.
54. McKay, *Banjo*, 273.
55. Du Bois, *Souls of Black Folk*, 1.
56. Dunham, *Island Possessed*, 228.
57. Brown, *Mama Lola*, 6.
58. Dunham, *Island Possessed*, 228.
59. Dunham, *Island Possessed*, 127.
60. Hutchinson, *In Search of Nella Larsen*, 3.
61. Carby, *Reconstructing Womanhood*, 175.
62. Larsen, *Quicksand*, 59.
63. Larsen, *Quicksand*, 38, 54.
64. Cullen, "Heritage," 144.
65. Larsen, *Quicksand*, 59–60.
66. Larsen, *Quicksand*, 114.
67. Larsen, *Quicksand*, 113.
68. Larsen, *Quicksand*, 114.
69. Larsen, *Quicksand*, 113.
70. Larsen, *Quicksand*, 112.
71. Dunham, *Island Possessed*, 105.

72. Dunham, *Island Possessed*, 235.
73. Dunham, *Island Possessed*, 234.
74. Dunham, *Island Possessed*, 234.
75. Dunham, *Island Possessed*, 132.
76. Dunham, Rome 1954 diary, box 22, MHS.
77. Dunham, *Island Possessed*, 244.
78. Dunham, *Island Possessed*, 237.
79. Dunham, *Island Possessed*, 238.
80. Dunham, *Island Possessed*, 254.
81. Dunham, *Island Possessed*, 255.
82. In Haitian Creole: "Aprè dans, tanbou toujou lou."
83. Dunham, "Caribbean Tourist Traps," 403.
84. Dunham, *Island Possessed*, 225.
85. Stanley "Doc" Reser came to Haiti with the U.S. Navy as a pharmacist's mate during the occupation; however, he stayed in Haiti decades past the occupation, running the Pont Beudet psychiatric clinic and taking a Haitian common-law wife named Cécile, with whom Dunham was also friends. A controversial figure, Doc Reser was a Vodou practitioner and a self-professed devotee of the irreverent, foul-mouthed death spirit, Gede. A friend of Dunham's, he also makes an appearance in Hurston's ethnography, *Tell My Horse*, 245–57.
86. Dunham, *Island Possessed*, 24.
87. Haiti film, box 132, item 1, SIUC.
88. Dunham, notes on Haiti c. 1937, box 79, folder 5, SIUC. Joanna Dee Das, Dunham's biographer, notes that Dunham had several known romantic relationships with women throughout her life, despite being publicly heterosexual.
89. Dunham, "Caribbean Tourist Traps," 403.
90. Das, *Katherine Dunham*, 48.
91. Das, *Katherine Dunham*, 135.
92. Dunham, "Preface," box 51, folder 2, SIUC. My emphasis.
93. Marta Moreno Vega, "The Yoruba Orisha Tradition comes to New York City," in Clark and Johnson, *Kaiso!*, 603.
94. Though Rosita's last name is unknown, she and Dunham appeared to have a close spiritual and personal relationship for many years. Rosita even came to visit Dunham while she was in residence in Haiti in the 1970s, as evidenced by her presence in a 1973 photo album depicting Rosita and Dunham at the Kyona Beach hotel in Haiti ("Photos Haiti—Habitation Leclerc 1973," box 30, MHS).
95. Dunham, *Island Possessed*, 271.
96. Rosita to Dunham, undated letter, box 51, folder 1, SIUC. Translation is my own; the original text reads, "Todo sus asuntos estan atrasados. No le gusta oir consejos. Ud. usa su cabeza a su manera. Eso no le conviene. Hay que oir. Ud. anda como un tren sin parar. Le gusta jugar con cosas que no le convienen. . . . Ud. presume de su cabeza y su cabeza esta perdida."
97. Rosita to Dunham, undated letter, box 51, folder 1, SIUC.
98. Dunham, *Island Possessed*, 272.
99. Dunham, *Island Possessed*, 205.

100. Das, *Katherine Dunham*, 156. For a discussion of the many project phases of Habitation Leclerc after it was purchased by Dunham in 1951, see Das, 156–64 and 171–73.

101. "Photos Haiti—Habitation Leclerc 1973," box 30, MHS.

102. Das, *Katherine Dunham*, 172.

103. Rod Hafmeister, "Dunham Is Eligible for Medicare," *Belleville News-Democrat*, March 7, 1992, box 121, folder 2, SIUC.

104. Das, *Katherine Dunham*, 8.

105. Deren, *Divine Horsemen*, 36.

106. Katherine Dunham, "ABC Radio Script: Background of a Lifetime," 8, box 49, folder 8, SIUC.

107. Dunham, *Island Possessed*, 60.

108. Dunham, *Island Possessed*, 107.

109. Dunham, *Island Possessed*, 107.

110. Dunham, *Island Possessed*, 74.

111. Dunham, *Island Possessed*, 107.

112. Beauvoir, *Lapriyè Ginen*, 11–15.

Chapter Two

1. Simone, *Nina Simone Great Performances*.

2. Hansberry, *Sign in Sidney Brustein's Window*, 84.

3. Crawley, *Blackpentecostal Breath*, 29.

4. Colbert, *Radical Vision*, 10.

5. Lorraine Hansberry, *Masters of the Dew* Screenplay Third Draft pp. 1–79, 32, box 48, folder 8, SCHOM.

6. Jean-Léon Destiné first visited the United States as part of a Haitian folkloric dance troupe performing at the National Folk Festival in Washington, D.C., in 1941. In the 1940s, he performed in Katherine Dunham's Broadway show *Bal nègre* and choreographed the opera *Troubled Island* (composed by William Grant Still and written by Langston Hughes) before he began his own dance company, Destiné Afro-Haitian Dance Company. For more on Destiné, see Polyné, "'To Carry the Dance'"; Francis, "Serving the Spirit"; and Ramsey, *Spirits and the Law*.

7. For more on Roumain's ambivalence about Vodou, rooted in his desire to alleviate the suffering of rural and working-class Haitians, see Ramsey, *Spirits and the Law*, 210–18.

8. Roumain, *Masters of the Dew*, 51–52. Hansberry's annotated copy of this edition is included in her archive, SCHOM.

9. Hansberry, *Masters of the Dew* Screenplay Third Draft pp. 1–79, 33, box 48, folder 8, SCHOM.

10. In the Hughes and Cook translation, Manuel uses the word "monkeyshine" to describe ceremonies for the *lwa*, 62. Hansberry reproduces this language in *Masters of the Dew* Screenplay Third Draft pp. 1–79, 15, box 48, folder 8, SCHOM. It is a fair translation of the original French "macaqueries" in Roumain, *Gouverneurs de la rosée*, 84.

11. Simone and Cleary, *I Put a Spell on You*, 87. This is in contrast to her friendship with Miriam Makeba, with whom she shared a taste for "the same food, drinks, men, clothes"—precisely the things she had deemed, with Lorraine, as inconsequential (98). Makeba, however, shaped Simone's interest in African history and culture and is said to have inspired Hansberry's turn to Afrocentric self-presentation in the late 1960s.

12. Letter from Nemiroff to Steve (Carter?), box 42, folder 11, SCHOM. According to Nemiroff, "she was thinking of virtually all of it in essential musical terms—or as she later spoke of it as an 'opera'—with huge cast and sweeping epic larger-than-life confrontations and evocations—and the pageantry—that makes the form possible."

13. In 2013, Kevin Mumford was the first scholar to be granted access to a "restricted folder" into which Robert Nemiroff had archived all of Hansberry's queer content. His research can be found in *Not White, Not Straight*, 1–22. For more on Hansberry's queer writing, see also Perry, *Looking for Lorraine*, 79–96; Higashida, *Black Internationalist Feminism*, 59-81, and Colbert, *Radical Vision*.

14. Simone, *Amazing Nina Simone*. According to Dunham Pratt, the first thing Simone ever said to her was, "I want to meet your mother." This relationship is also perhaps a potential source of Simone's interest in Haiti.

15. Simone, *Nina Simone Great Performances*.

16. Hartman, *Lose Your Mother*, 18.

17. Lester, introduction to *Les Blancs*, 23, 24.

18. Hansberry, *Sign in Sidney Brustein's Window*, 42.

19. Hansberry, "Village Intellect Revealed."

20. Perry, *Looking for Lorraine*, 57–59.

21. Gallo, *Different Daughters*, xxvi, and Faderman, *Odd Girls*, 143.

22. Faderman, *Odd Girls*, 140.

23. Faderman, *Odd Girls*, 146–50.

24. Simone and Cleary, *I Put a Spell*, 87.

25. While her script for *The Drinking Gourd* includes two Black women characters, I would argue that their purpose is ancillary to the Black male revolutionary's development.

26. Perry, *Looking for Lorraine*, 144.

27. Hansberry, "Village Intellect Revealed."

28. Toibin, "Unsparing Confessions."

29. Higashida, *Black Internationalist Feminism*, 59.

30. Hansberry's four queer short stories were written under the pseudonym "Emily Jones," and her letters published in *The Ladder* used her initials, L.H.N.

31. Pollack-Pelzner, "Unseen Script."

32. Despite a self-avowed liking for both "Eartha Kitt" and "Eartha Kitt's looks."

33. Perry, *Looking for Lorraine*, 87–88.

34. Gallo, *Different Daughters*, xxii–xxiii.

35. Gallo, *Different Daughters*, 43.

36. L.H.N. [Lorraine Hansberry], 26.

37. L.H.N. [Lorraine Hansberry], 26.

38. L.H.N. [Lorraine Hansberry], 26.

39. Colbert, *Radical Vision*, 57.

40. Jones [Lorraine Hansberry], "Anticipation of Eve," 22.
41. Jones, "Anticipation of Eve," 28.
42. Jones, "Anticipation of Eve," 25.
43. Jones, "Anticipation of Eve," 28.
44. Perry, *Looking for Lorraine*, 86. Because of similarities in their names, Perry suggests that the interaction might be based on Hansberry's relationship with her real-life cousin Shauneille and her husband Dave.
45. Jones, "Chanson du Konallis," 22.
46. Jones, "Chanson du Konallis," 9. The names of the protagonists are drawn from the modernist poet Richard Aldington's 1926 collection, *The Love Poems of Myrrhine and Konallis*, a sapphic imagining of lesbian lovers.
47. Jones, "Chanson du Konallis," 10–20.
48. Jones, "Chanson du Konallis," 21.
49. Jones, "Chanson du Konallis," 20.
50. Jones, "Chanson du Konallis," 21.
51. Hansberry, "Toussaint," 61.
52. Moreau de Saint-Méry, *Description topographique*, 22. Translations of this text are my own.
53. Lorraine Hansberry, "Toussaint," 66. Ellipses in original.
54. Aidoo, *Slavery Unseen*, 96.
55. For more on Annie Palmer, see Donahue, "Ghost of Annie Palmer." Annie Palmer was also immortalized in Johnny Cash's song "The Ballad of Annie Palmer." For more on Delphine Lalaurie, see Long, *Madame Lalaurie*.
56. Jones-Rogers, *They Were Her Property*, 149.
57. Painter, *Sojourner Truth*, 16.
58. Aidoo, *Slavery Unseen*, 86.
59. Aidoo, *Slavery Unseen*, 90–94.
60. Aidoo, *Slavery Unseen*, 95.
61. Hansberry, "Toussaint," 66.
62. Simone and Cleary, *I Put a Spell*, 87.
63. Hansberry, "Toussaint," 63.
64. Hansberry, *Playwright at Work*.
65. Holland, *Erotic Life of Racism*, 59.
66. Qtd. in Linden, *Against Sadomasochism*, 68.
67. Hansberry, "Toussaint," 53.
68. Hansberry, "Toussaint," 65. Ellipses in original.
69. Lorraine Hansberry, *Toussaint* Drafts and Revisions with Annotations, n.d., box 42, folder 8, SCHOM.
70. Lorraine Hansberry, *Toussaint* Handwritten Scenes and Notes, box 42, folder 1, SCHOM.
71. Hansberry, "Toussaint," 67. Ellipses in original.
72. Jones, "Chanson du Konallis," 10.
73. Jones, "Chanson du Konallis," 23.
74. I conjecture that Mirine is based on the nightclub hostess and jazz singer Florence Emery Jones, who worked in Paris in the 1920s and whom Langston Hughes de-

scribes as the first person of color he ever saw being openly rude to white people. It is entirely possible that Hansberry read about Jones in Hughes's 1940 autobiography *The Big Sea* or that Hughes shared his recollections of his time in Paris with Hansberry. For more on Jones, see Magloire, "Florence's Place."

75. Jones, "Chanson du Konallis," 24.
76. Jones, "Chanson du Konallis," 26.
77. The French word *plaisir* in its most common usage is to express a feeling of contentment or agreement, although there is a less common usage that means sexual satisfaction.
78. Tinsley, *Thiefing Sugar*, 3.
79. For example, in the live version of "To Be Young, Gifted and Black" recorded for the album *Black Gold*.
80. Simone and Cleary, *I Put a Spell*, 73.
81. Simone and Cleary, *I Put a Spell*, 114.
82. Simone and Cleary, *I Put a Spell*, 131.
83. Simone and Cleary, *I Put a Spell*, 144.
84. Simone and Cleary, *I Put a Spell*, 82.
85. Simone and Cleary, *I Put a Spell*, 52.
86. Simone and Cleary, *I Put a Spell*, 91.
87. Simone and Cleary, *I Put a Spell*, 95.
88. Perry, *Looking for Lorraine*, 132, and Feldstein, *How It Feels*, 96.
89. Simone, *Amazing Nina Simone*.
90. Simone, *It Is Finished*.
91. Simone and Cleary, *I Put a Spell*, 89.
92. This is an often mistaken fact in interviews with Simone, in which the interviewers found the concept of a woman preacher so inconceivable that they would willfully mishear her and write that her father (who in fact was unemployed due to disability for much of Simone's childhood) was a preacher.
93. Simone and Cleary, *I Put a Spell*, 91.
94. Simone and Cleary, *I Put a Spell*, 94.
95. Brooks, *Searching for Sycorax*, 114.
96. Kernodle, "I Wish I Knew."
97. Feldstein, *How It Feels*, 96.
98. Keeling, *Witch's Flight*, 74.
99. Feldstein, *How It Feels*, 111.
100. Simone and Cleary, *I Put a Spell*, 16.
101. Simone and Cleary, *I Put a Spell*, 19.
102. Simone and Cleary, *I Put a Spell*, 118.
103. Exuma, *Exuma, The Obeah Man*.
104. Crawley, *Blackpentecostal Breath*, 160–61.
105. Simone, *It Is Finished*.
106. Simone and Cleary, *I Put a Spell*, 80.
107. Simone and Cleary, *I Put a Spell*, 143.
108. Simone, *Black Gold*.
109. Simone, *Black Gold*.

110. Simone, *Black Gold*.

111. Simone, *Black Gold*.

112. Lorraine Hansberry, *Toussaint* Drafts and Revisions with Annotations, n.d., box 42, folder 8, SCHOM.

113. John 19:28.

114. Simone, *It Is Finished*.

115. Simone and Cleary, *I Put a Spell*, 100.

116. Simone and Cleary, *I Put a Spell*, 27.

Chapter Three

1. As Smethurst argues in *The Black Arts Movement*, "Caricatured versions of these movements as fundamentally or unusually sexist distort them and the legacy of black women (and some men) in those movements as well as their contributions to the rise of second-wave feminism," 87. For a more comprehensive history of women's contributions to Black power ideologies, see also Farmer, *Remaking Black Power*.

2. Farmer, *Remaking Black Power*, 187.

3. Qtd. in Clarke, *After Mecca*, 59.

4. One notable exception to this is Cheryl Clarke's classic study *After Mecca: Women Poets and the Black Arts Movement*, an expansive consideration of Black women poets publishing in the late 1960s through early 1980s. In addition to considering the self-avowed poets of the movement, Clarke's work also considers those "outside the circle" who were nonetheless shaped by its ideas and responding to the same cultural context. I take Clarke's capacious scholarship as an invitation to contextualize Lorde's and Clifton's conceptions of race and gender within the central cultural and spiritual debates of their time, rather than excluding them on the basis of which literary clique they happened to frequent.

5. Smethurst, *Black Arts Movement*, 57.

6. Clarke, *After Mecca*, 93.

7. Baraka, *Kawaida Studies*, 24. Ellipses in original.

8. Farmer, *Remaking Black Power*, 99.

9. Maulana Karenga, qtd. in Farmer, *Remaking Black Power*, 99.

10. Hucks, *Yoruba Traditions*, 94. The intersection between African American and Latinx orisha worship will be discussed further in chapter 4.

11. Hucks, *Yoruba Traditions*, 95.

12. According to Hucks, Amiri Baraka asked the founder of Yoruba Temple to officiate his wedding (106), and American Yoruba lore has it that Malcolm X sent representatives to a divination session at Yoruba Temple, where he was urged to sacrifice a chicken to the spirit Oyá if he did not want to suffer dire consequences. Malcolm X ignored the prescription and died several days later (110–11).

13. This attitude appears to have been a pervasive mood throughout the 1970s, documented by Toni Cade Bambara, Akasha Gloria Hull, and Luisah Teish, whose texts will be discussed further in chapter 4. Part of their spiritual practice is indeed a feminist intervention into the masculinist argument that spirituality, like women's issues, siphons energy away from revolution.

14. From the title of her 1974 collection of poetry, *An Ordinary Woman* (included in Clifton, *Collected Poems*).
15. Lorde, *Sister Outsider*, 105.
16. De Veaux, *Warrior Poet*, 92.
17. Smethurst, *Black Arts and Movement*, 81.
18. Clarke, *After Mecca*, 132.
19. Lorde, *Black Unicorn*, 113.
20. Lorde, *Black Unicorn*, 112.
21. Lorde, *Sister Outsider*, 50.
22. Lorde, "*Sister Outsider*, 164–65.
23. Lorde, *Sister Outsider*, 44.
24. Lorde, *Sister Outsider*, 67.
25. Deren, *Divine Horsemen*, 138.
26. Lorde, *Sister Outsider*, 38.
27. Deren, *Divine Horsemen*, 137–45.
28. Deren, *Divine Horsemen*, 144.
29. Lorde, *Sister Outsider*, 165.
30. Lorde, *Sister Outsider*, 150.
31. Lorde, *Sister Outsider*, 58.
32. Lorde, *Sister Outsider*, 57.
33. Deren, *Divine Horsemen*, 144.
34. Touré, "Black Male/Female Relations," 45.
35. This reader's forum includes a variety of perspectives from the Black literati of the 1970s. Men's responses range from Kalaamu ya Salaam's earnest and clear-eyed assertion that Black men operate within a sexist society and are thus not immune to sexism, and that "as Zora Neale Hurston so eloquently addressed the issue in her book *Their Eyes Were Watching God*, it will sometimes be necessary for our women to literally, as well as ideologically, kill the men whom they love" "Revolutionary Struggle/Revolutionary Love" 22) to Askia Touré's agreement with Staples's perspective ("Black Male/Female Relations," 45–48). June Jordan's pithy response, which uses U.S. Department of Labor statistics to destroy Staples's claim that Black women make more money than Black men, is, "All I have time to say to Robert Staples is this: Are you serious?" ("Black Women Haven't 'Got It All,'" 39).
36. Staples, "Myth of Black Macho," 26.
37. Lorde, "Great American Disease," 19.
38. Staples, "Myth of Black Macho," 28.
39. Lorde, "Great American Disease," 18.
40. Lorde, *Sister Outsider*, 122.
41. Brown, *Mama Lola*, 231.
42. Lorde, *Sister Outsider*, 133.
43. Brown, *Mama Lola*, 229.
44. Brown, *Mama Lola*, 230.
45. Brown, *Mama Lola*, 233.
46. Lorde, *Sister Outsider*, 129.
47. Lorde, *Sister Outsider*, 127.

48. Lorde, *Sister Outsider*, 41.
49. Brown, *Mama Lola*, 256.
50. Brown, *Mama Lola*, 229.
51. Lorde, *Sister Outsider*, 153.
52. Clifton, *Collected Poems*, 62.
53. I am thinking, here, of her ambivalent commentary on the Black Arts movement in her interview with Charles Rowell, of her declaration "I am not a subgenre" in her interview with Susan Somers-Willet, and her similar affirmation of Black poetry as both culturally specific and universally American in her interview with Hillary Holladay in *Wild Blessings*. Taken together, these interviews demonstrate a remarkable commitment to Blackness outside of mainstream narratives of activism and resistance.
54. Clifton, "Interview with Lucille Clifton," 66.
55. Clifton, *Collected Poems*, 64.
56. Clifton, *Collected Poems*, 262.
57. Clifton, "Interview with Lucille Clifton," 57.
58. Quashie, *Sovereignty of Quiet*, 8.
59. Clifton, "Interview with Lucille Clifton," 67. Clifton goes on to quote and agree with Gwendolyn Brooks's statement: "Every time I walk out of my house, it is a political decision."
60. Clifton, *Good Woman*, 73.
61. Clifton, *Good Woman*, 66.
62. Clifton, *Good Woman*, 232.
63. Clifton, *Good Woman*, 33.
64. Morrison, "Site of Memory," 99.
65. Alexander, *Pedagogies of Crossing*, 301.
66. Clifton, *Collected Poems*, 97.
67. Clifton, "Curiosities," 10, box 29, folder 3, MARBL.
68. Clifton was incredulous at first, but over time she came to believe that it was truly the spirit of her mother: "There was no point, no single statement that said unequivocally 'this is she.' It was/is the accumulation of things, the pattern of her self. Which is how we know anyone" ("Lives/Visits/Illuminations," box 29, folders 6–8, MARBL).
69. Clifton, "Curiosities," 2, box 29, folder 3, MARBL.
70. Clifton, "Curiosities," 4, box 29, folder 3, MARBL.
71. Lucille Clifton, "Lives/Visits/Illuminations," box 29, folders 6–8, MARBL.
72. Hull, *Soul Talk*, 57.
73. To date, only two published essay make use of Clifton's archives to discuss the spirit writing: Chakraborty, "Poetics Begin after Death" and Judd, "Glossolalia." The most comprehensive published account of Clifton's practice of spirit communication can be found in Hull's *Soul Talk*, for which she conducted interviews with Clifton herself.
74. Clifton, *Collected Poems*, 625.
75. Qtd. in Hull, *Soul Talk*, 58.
76. Clifton, "Resurrections," box 29, folder 9, MARBL.
77. Qtd. in Hull, *Soul Talk*, 119.

78. Hull, *Soul Talk*, 89.
79. Hull, *Soul Talk*, 10.
80. Clifton, "Soul Signs: An Astrology for Black People," box 29, folder 10, MARBL.
81. Fred Clifton, "Writings: Meditation Journals, circa 1970s," box 80, folder 1, MARBL.
82. Qtd. in Hull, *Soul Talk*, 248.
83. Clifton, "Lives/Visits/Illuminations," box 29, folders 6–8, MARBL.
84. Clifton, "Curiosities," box 29, folder 3, MARBL.
85. The spirits listed among volunteers yet without transcribed interviews are as follows: Colette, ee cummings, Walt Disney, Marcus Garvey, Pablo Picasso, Elvis Presley, Paul Robeson, and Emmett Till ("Lives/Visits/Illuminations").
86. The drawing is included with the interview transcript.
87. Clifton, "Resurrections," box 29, folder 9, MARBL.
88. Clifton, "Lives/Visits/Illuminations."
89. Clifton, "Curiosities," box 29, folder 3, MARBL.
90. Lucille Clifton, "Gillian aka Karl," box 29, folder 13, MARBL.
91. Clifton, "Lives/Visits/Illuminations."
92. Strongman, *Queering Black Atlantic Religions*, 2.
93. Lucille Clifton, "Lives," box 29, folder 15, MARBL.
94. Indeed, the Cercle Harmonique was raided in 1858 under suspicion of practicing "voodoo," but given that its members continued to hold séances into the 1870s, it can be presumed that they were deemed by authorities to fit solidly within legal, Euro-American practices of spiritualism. See Clarke, *Luminous Brotherhood*, 26.
95. Clarke, *Luminous Brotherhood*, 11.
96. Marie Laveau rose to prominence in a milieu where the massive influx of Haitian emigrants during the revolution of 1790–1804 shaped the spiritual practices and perceptions of Black New Orleanians, adding a pantheon of spirits that spoke through the bodies of their serviteurs to the maelstrom of African-derived magical practices of healing and harming that arose among enslaved Americans. While Marie Laveau distinguished herself from later practitioners of New Orleans hoodoo by incorporating a pantheon of Haitian and African-derived spirits into her practice, it is impossible to untangle the threads of influence from a constantly shifting religious landscape. Catholicism, Spiritualism, Haitian Vodou, and hoodoo, while quite distinct and even sometimes at odds with one another, all came to be labeled by outsiders as part of the same spooky and vengeful spirituality of Black people, predicated on communicating with fretful spirits. For more on this, see Long, *New Orleans Voudou Priestess*, 102–7.
97. Clifton, "Interview with Lucille Clifton," 59.
98. Harding, "Authority," 49.
99. Alexander, *Pedagogies of Crossing*, 297.
100. Alexander, *Pedagogies of Crossing*, 329.
101. Clifton, "Lives/Visits/Illuminations."
102. Qtd. in Hull, *Soul Talk*, 234.
103. Another notable set of Clifton's poems regarding her spirit visitation is "the message from The Ones (received in the late 1970s)," found in her 2004 poetry collection *Mercy*, which is collected in *Collected Poems*, 611–33.

104. Clifton, *Two-Headed Woman*, 7.

105. Clifton, *Collected Poems*, 613.

106. As Akasha Gloria Hull argues in *Soul Talk*, "the energy that takes form in us and in everything that exists cannot be regarded as raced," yet "spiritual wisdom and timeless principles, when run through African American women, tend to emerge from a different slant" (27–28).

107. Clifton, *Collected Poems*, 427.

108. Qtd. in Hull, *Soul Talk*, 58–59.

109. Clifton, *Two-Headed Woman*, 4.

110. Qtd. in Hull, *Soul Talk*, 199.

111. Clifton, *Two-Headed Woman*, 4.

112. Clifton, *Collected Poems*, 427.

113. Clifton, *Two-Headed Woman*, 58.

114. Clifton, *Two-Headed Woman*, 41.

115. Clifton, *Two-Headed Woman*, 40.

116. Clifton, *Two-Headed Woman*, 56.

117. Qtd. in Hull, *Soul Talk*, 20.

118. Clifton received these communications through a practice of automatic writing, leaving behind hundreds of handwritten pages of continuous cursive that she had separated into individual words with backslashes. I have rendered these writings as distinct words, but because this process did not often include punctuation marks, I have not included punctuation unless included in the original.

119. Lucille Clifton, "Spirit Writing, August and September 1978," MARBL, box 31, folder 1.

120. Clifton, *Two-Headed Woman*, 20.

121. Clifton, *Collected Poems*, 35.

122. Clifton, *Collected Poems*, 632–33.

123. Adefunmi, *Tribal Origins*.

Chapter Four

1. Bambara, foreword to the first edition of Moraga and Anzaldúa, *This Bridge Called My Back*, xxix.

2. Cameron, "Gee," 45.

3. Moraga, "La Jornada," xxxix.

4. Herr, "Reclaiming Third World Feminism."

5. Farmer, *Remaking Black Power*, 172.

6. Farmer, *Remaking Black Power*, 176.

7. These included Toni Cade Bambara's *The Black Woman* (1980), Akasha Gloria Hull's *All the Women Are White, All the Blacks Are Men: But Some of Us Are Brave* (1982), Cherríe Moraga and Gloria Anzaldúa's *This Bridge Called My Back: Radical Writings by Women of Color* (1983), and Barbara Smith's *Home Girls: A Black Feminist Anthology* (1983). As Cooper argues in *Beyond Respectability*, "These works did not attempt to constitute canons of new thinkers, but rather to demonstrate the breadth of existing Black and women-of-color thinkers" (138).

8. Among them was Mary Daly, a feminist theologian whom Audre Lorde famously critiqued for her lack of attention to Afro-diasporic spirituality in her "Open Letter to Mary Daly," in Lorde, *Sister Outsider*.

9. Plaskow and Christ, preface to *Womanspirit Rising*, viii.

10. Plaskow and Christ, introduction to *Weaving the Visions*, 4.

11. Adler, *Drawing down the Moon*, 252–53. Please note that "voodoo" has negative connotations and is not used by practitioners of Vodou, and that Santería has also been rejected as a colonized term by many practitioners of Yoruba spiritualities.

12. Qtd. in Hucks, *Yoruba Traditions*, 80.

13. Hucks, *Yoruba Traditions*, 147.

14. This image is not metaphorical; Hucks describes a tense exchange between Adefunmi and a *santera* who asks him why he wears a dashiki, which leads to an argument about whether their religion came from Cuba or Africa (*Yoruba Traditions*, 142). Moreno Vega, "Yoruba Orisha Tradition," 609.

15. Hucks, *Yoruba Traditions*, 93.

16. "Dr. Marta Moreno Vega," https://martamorenovega.org/.

17. Moreno Vega, *Altar of My Soul*, 199–200.

18. Moreno Vega, *Altar of My Soul*, 206.

19. Moreno Vega, *Altar of My Soul*, 109–10.

20. Teish, *Jambalaya*, 250.

21. Starhawk, introduction to Teish, *Jambalaya*, xv.

22. Adler, *Drawing down the Moon*, 86.

23. Starhawk, introduction to Teish, *Jambalaya*, xviii.

24. Hull, *Soul Talk*, 52.

25. Hucks, *Yoruba Traditions*, 298–303.

26. Hull, *Soul Talk*, 52.

27. Bambara, *Salt Eaters*, 236.

28. Bambara, *Salt Eaters*, 193.

29. Teish, *Jambalaya*, 150.

30. Teish, *Jambalaya*, 29.

31. Teish, *Jambalaya*, 30.

32. Teish, *Jambalaya*, 29.

33. Bambara, interview by Kay Bonetti, in *Conversations*, 35. The popular maxim is paraphrased from Bambara's original formulation: "As a cultural worker who belongs to an oppressed people my job is to make revolution irresistible."

34. Bambara, *Salt Eaters*, 46.

35. Bambara, *Salt Eaters*, 134.

36. Hull, *Soul Talk*, 1.

37. Bambara, interview by Zala Chandler, in *Conversations*, 87.

38. White, *Playing the Numbers*, 87–88.

39. Putnam, *Radical Moves*, 74.

40. Wilson, "Community Well-Being," 31–34.

41. Deslippe, "Hindu in Hoodoo," 45.

42. Jessamy, "Harlem's Fakers."

43. Jessamy, "Harlem's Fakers."

44. See White, *Playing the Numbers*, 98–100.
45. Wilson, "Community Well-Being," 22.
46. For more on Madame Fu Futtam, see Harris, *Sex Workers*, 98–102.
47. Bambara, "Commitment: Toni Cade Bambara Speaks," in *Conversations*, 10.
48. Bambara, *Salt Eaters*, 86.
49. Fett, *Working Cures*, 111–41.
50. Wilson, "Community Well-Being," 26.
51. Long, *Spiritual Merchants*, 131–37. Spiritual workers in New Orleans will be further discussed in chapter 5.
52. Bambara, *Salt Eaters*, 114.
53. Bambara, *Salt Eaters*, 169.
54. Hull, *Soul Talk*, 31.
55. Bambara, *Salt Eaters*, 210.
56. Bambara, *Salt Eaters*, 245.
57. Bambara, *Salt Eaters*, 249.
58. Bambara, "Searching for the Mother Tongue," in *Conversations*, 23–24.
59. "LOA" Notebook (Notes) 1 of 4, box 5, SPEL. Many thanks to Holly Smith, Spelman archivist, for scanning and sending these materials even while the archives were closed due to the pandemic.
60. Bambara, *Conversations*, 21.
61. Bambara, *Salt Eaters*, 247.
62. Bambara, *Conversations*, 20.
63. Bambara, *Conversations*, 25.
64. My thanks to Jonathan Scott of F&F Botanica in New Orleans for this lovely way of phrasing it. Rest in power.
65. Bambara, *Salt Eaters*, 247.
66. Bambara, *Conversations*, 35.
67. Moraga and Anzaldúa, *This Bridge Called My Back*, xvi.
68. Teish, *Jambalaya*, 33.
69. Teish, *Jambalaya*, 31.
70. Moraga and Anzaldúa, *This Bridge Called My Back*, 168.
71. Teish, *Jambalaya*, x.
72. Teish, *Jambalaya*, 148.
73. Teish, *Jambalaya*, 146.
74. Teish, *Jambalaya*, 167.
75. Teish, *Jambalaya*, 151.
76. Teish, *Jambalaya*, 47.
77. Kramarae and Dale Spender, "Womanspirit." See also Diesel, "Womanspirit," 71–75.
78. Teish, *Jambalaya*, 255–57.
79. Teish, *Jambalaya*, 253.
80. Teish, *Jambalaya*, 254.
81. Teish, *Jambalaya*, xiii.
82. Teish, *Jambalaya*, 250.
83. Teish, *Jambalaya*, 181.

84. Salaam, "It's Not the Salt."
85. Major thanks to Kinitra Brooks for pointing out this reference as further proof of Bambara's investment in the New Orleans context.
86. Bambara, *Conversations*, 23.
87. Bambara, *Conversations*, 13.
88. Bambara, *Salt Eaters*, 146.
89. Hazzard-Donald, *Mojo Workin'*, 2: "Hoodoo is no longer a religion; it is the view here that Hoodoo is the reorganized remnants of what must have been, albeit short-lived, a full-blown syncretized African-based religion among African American bondsmen."
90. See Deren, *Divine Horsemen*, 77–78.
91. Bambara, *Salt Eaters*, 43.
92. Bambara, *Salt Eaters*, 145.
93. Adams and Sakakeeny, introduction to *Remaking New Orleans*, 6.
94. For a brief account of this historical trajectory, see Long, "Perceptions of New Orleans Voodoo."
95. Bambara, *Salt Eaters*, 43.
96. Bambara, *Salt Eaters*, 62.
97. Bambara, *Salt Eaters*, 238.
98. Bambara, foreword to Moraga and Anzaldúa, *This Bridge Called My Back*, xxix.
99. Bambara, *Salt Eaters*, 249.
100. Bambara, *Salt Eaters*, 222.
101. Toni Cade Bambara, interview by Claudia Tate, in Bambara, *Conversations*, 59–60.
102. Bambara, *Salt Eaters*, 167.
103. Nash, *Black Feminism Reimagined*, 83.
104. Toni Cade Bambara, Goddess Sightings (Draft), box 3, SPEL.
105. Bambara, Goddess Sightings (Draft), box 3, SPEL.
106. Qtd. in Hull, *Soul Talk*, 87–88.

Chapter Five

1. The two most comprehensive historical accounts of Marie Laveau's life are Ward, *Voodoo Queen* and Long, *New Orleans Voudou Priestess*. Most of the information for this chapter has been drawn from Long, but except for a few key differences (the identity of the second Marie Laveau, for instance), the accounts draw from the same archives and corroborate one another.
2. Long, *Spiritual Merchants*, 38.
3. Levinson, "New Orleans and Haiti." I served as the Creole translator for this project and can attest to the fact that most working-class interviewees in Port-au-Prince, Jacmel, and Cap-Haïtien had never heard of New Orleans.
4. For more on this, see Dessens, *From Saint Domingue to New Orleans*.
5. Roberts, *Voodoo and Power*, 17.
6. In a few instances in *A New Orleans Voudou Priestess*, Long cites the disparity between Tallant's representation of Laveau and the Louisiana state records and WPA interviews that (loosely) served as his source material.

7. Hurston falls squarely into this camp in *Mules and Men*. It is also important to note that contemporary popular conceptions of Marie Laveau often lean more toward this romanticization of her legacy.

8. See Tallant, *Voodoo in New Orleans*, and Castellanos, *New Orleans as It Was*.

9. On the uses of grave dust in hoodoo spells, see Hurston, "Hoodoo in America." Though hoodoo differs in important ways from the more systematized ancestor worship of African diaspora religions, it similarly centers a symbiotic relationship between ancestral spirits and human practitioners. Chireau notes in *Black Magic*, 39–40, the dichotomy between hoodoo and religion is perhaps oversimplified: "Magic is a self-serving enterprise that derives from personal, egotistical motivations; religion, a public activity, yields benefits for an entire community. And yet this delineation of private versus public interests did not apply in all cases. In many accounts of indigenous African religious life, spiritual forces were involved in rituals for personal needs as well as those affecting the larger group."

10. Gates, "Negro Way of Saying."

11. Long, *Spiritual Merchants*, 43. The title of "mother" was used by the spiritualist leaders Leafy Anderson and Catherine Seals, the latter of whom was the subject of an essay by Hurston for the WPA.

12. For instance, in the case of the nineteenth-century hoodoo leader Doctor John, he was listed in the 1860 New Orleans city directory as a physician, but the notary who transcribed it could not resist writing in parentheses "quack," as Long notes in *A New Orleans Voudou Queen*, 146. As Long notes in her study, most nineteenth-century newspaper sources speak of Marie Laveau with some degree of respect and acknowledgment of her gifts, while Dr. John is almost universally dismissed as a charlatan (137).

13. A common tenet of the Laveau Legend, according to Long in *A New Orleans Voudou Queen*, was that Marie Laveau was succeeded by one of her daughters, Marie Heloïse, but Long makes a compelling case for the falsity of this claim, given that Marie Heloïse appears to have died twenty years before her mother in 1862 (190–205).

14. Hurston, "Hoodoo in America," 320. The account of New Orleans hoodoo that appears in *Mules and Men* is a slightly abridged version of this article, which first appeared in the *Journal of American Folklore* in 1931.

15. See Trouillot, *Silencing the Past*, 26.

16. Sallie Ann Glassman, interview with the author, January 12, 2017.

17. The aphorism "If you are silent about your pain, they'll kill you and say you enjoyed it" is often attributed to Zora Neale Hurston, but I have not found the source in which she says this. It is interesting to consider which contexts push Hurston to valorize silence and which ones push her to speech.

18. Tallant, *Voodoo in New Orleans*, 8.

19. Interestingly, Tallant's accounts of spiritual and magical practices among African Americans in New Orleans are drawn almost entirely from secondhand accounts (books, newspapers, WPA interviews, hearsay) and rarely from his own observation. Unsurprisingly, no practitioners of hoodoo invited Tallant to their ceremonies.

20. Hurston, "Review," 438. The fact that Tallant's book, published ten years after *Mules and Men*, grew to become the definitive text on New Orleans hoodoo also added insult to injury for Hurston.

21. Hurston, *Mules and Men*, 2. For a discussion of this quote and its implications, see Lamothe, *Inventing the New Negro*, 3, and Ward, "Truths," 306.

22. Lamothe, *Inventing the New Negro*, 9.

23. Hurston, *Mules and Men*, 185.

24. Hurston, *Mules and Men*, 199.

25. Hurston, *Mules and Men*, 198.

26. Hurston, *Mules and Men*, 197.

27. duCille, "Occult," 601.

28. duCille, "Occult," 602. Emphasis mine.

29. Nash, *Black Feminism Reimagined*, 26–27.

30. Carby, "Politics of Fiction," 72.

31. Walker, *In Search*, 92. Emphasis in original.

32. Walker, *In Love*, 60–80.

33. Walker, *In Search*, 11.

34. Walker's search for female mentors is also a response to the masculinist bent of some of her contemporaries, whose attempts at African American literary canon formation excluded or openly denigrated the contributions of women. Take, for instance, Ishmael Reed's depiction of Marie Laveau in *The Last Days of Louisiana Red*, which represents her as a jealous and conniving woman trying to keep the hardworking Black man down—represented by Marie Laveau's contemporary, a hoodoo doctor called Doctor John. In Reed's representation, it is Marie Laveau who is responsible for the malignant, suspicious brand of sorcery known throughout the novel as Louisiana Red: "toad's eyes, putting snakes in people, excrement, hostility, evilness, attitude, negroes stabbing negroes" (140). This is in contrast, of course, to Doctor John's abiding wisdom, which was "medicine handed down through the generations and enriched by the fact that all of the African tribes merged their knowledge in the New World" (142). However, her perceived sins are ultimately dismissed by the fact that "she had fifteen children" and thus "had to hustle," and she is thus demoted to "second vice-president in charge of wit and hustle" of the American hoodoo tradition, with Doctor John installed in her place as founder. This is essentially a Fall narrative in which Black women are responsible for the original sins of the Black community.

35. Qtd. in Walker, *In Search*, 83.

36. Walker, *In Search*, 234.

37. Walker, *In Search*, 90.

38. Walker, *In Search*, 87.

39. Walker, *In Search*, 86.

40. Walker, *In Search*, 102.

41. Walker, *In Search*, 107.

42. "Successful Author Working as a Maid," box 99, folder 3, Alice Walker Papers, MARBL.

43. Hughes, *Big Sea*, 239. It is also important to note that Hughes and Hurston had a famous falling out of their coauthored play *Mule Bone*, and that in 1929 Hughes broke with their rich white patroness Charlotte Osgood-Mason over disagreements about how "primitive" his writing should be, while Hurston continued a rather taxing and complicated relationship of financial dependency with Osgood-Mason.

44. Wright, "Between Laughter and Tears."
45. Hurston, "How It Feels," 155.
46. Fannie Hurst, "Zora Neale Hurston: A Personality Sketch," *Yale University Library Gazette* 35 (July 1960): 20. Found in box 13, folder 14, UF.
47. Walker, *In Search*, 90.
48. Hartman, "Venus in Two Acts," 4.
49. Trouillot, *Silencing the Past*, 151.
50. Hurston, *Mules and Men*, 191.
51. Roberts, *Voodoo and Power*, 79.
52. Long, *Spiritual Merchants*, 123.
53. Some scholars have suggested that Hurston used pseudonyms for all of her informants and that Luke Turner was in fact a composite character based on several informants, based on the fact that the same character is called Samuel Thompson in Hurston's essay "Hoodoo in America." See also Long, *Spiritual Merchants*, 58–60.
54. Hurston, *Mules and Men*, 184.
55. Hurston, *Their Eyes Were Watching God*, 186. This quote is attributed to Janie's grandmother, whose views stand in for the hopeless utilitarianism of pre-emancipation conceptions of love.
56. Hurston, *Mules and Men*, 245.
57. Hurston, *Mules and Men*, 214.
58. Cable, *Grandissimes*, 60–61.
59. Hurston, *Mules and Men*, 193.
60. "Go to your house and build an altar. Power will come." Hurston, *Mules and Men*, 194.
61. Hurston, *Mules and Men*, 195.
62. Hurston, "Hoodoo in America," 327.
63. Hazzard-Donald, *Mojo Workin'*, 27.
64. Hurston, *Sanctified Church*, 103.
65. Hurston, *Mules and Men*, 193.
66. Hurston, *Mules and Men*, 197.
67. "Gray Line New Orleans." These tours are also described in Thomas, *Desire and Disaster*, 127–57.
68. Thomas, *Desire and Disaster*, 8.
69. Rankine, *Citizen*, 49.
70. Roach, *Cities of the Dead*, 231.
71. Landau, *Spectacular Wickedness*, 15.
72. While the word "Creole" originally referred to anyone born in the Americas (as opposed to Europe or Africa) and could thus also apply to white people, the popular usage of the word in contemporary New Orleans has come to refer to the descendants of mixed-race Francophone and/or Creolophone peoples.
73. Garraway, *Libertine Colony*, 194–239.
74. In Louisiana, the most famous of these was a 1786 ordinance by Governor Esteban Rodríguez Miró, requiring women of African descent to wear a headscarf (known in French as a *tignon*) over their hair to highlight their status as non-white and to curb their sartorial liberties. The law's fame also comes from the extravagance and beauty

of the headdresses that women of color wore to subvert it. For more on this, see Johnson, *Wicked Flesh*, 198.

75. Garraway, *Libertine Colony*, 232.

76. In Louisiana, the practice of *plaçage* is a much mythologized narrative that describes the formalized domestic and financial unions of white men and mixed-race women, who were often secondary to the men's legal white wives. Scholarship such as Aslakson, "The 'Quadroon-Plaçage' Myth of Antebellum New Orleans" argues that *plaçage* has been spectacularized by Anglo-American observers as a practice by which scheming mothers sold their innocent daughters into concubinage to depraved wealthy white men, when in reality most interracial relationships of this kind resembled common-law marriages. Either way, it stands that even long-term relationships between white men and women of color took place in spite of drastic disparities of power and legal status between the man and the woman, and as such could place the woman in a vulnerable position.

77. For more on this, see Thomas, *Desire and Disaster*, 53–91. As Thomas notes, the fantasy of New Orleans' "Creole" origins can also provide a comfortable post-racial narrative that enables white tourists to engage with a respectable multiculturalism without having to consider the troubling fact of slavery.

78. Hurston, *Mules and Men*, 220.

79. Hurston, *Mules and Men*, 192 and Long, *Spiritual Merchants*, 132.

80. Hurston, *Mules and Men*, 193.

81. Hurston, *Mules and Men*, 194.

82. Tallant, *Voodoo in New Orleans*, 247.

83. Moten, "'Words Don't Go There,'" 960.

84. Hurston, *Mules and Men*, 221.

85. Hurston, *Life In Letters*, 126. As far as "cheap white folks" go, Hurston was undoubtedly referring to the many white-owned hoodoo drugstores in New Orleans at the time, as described in colorful detail by Tallant in *Voodoo in New Orleans*, a text in which he represents gullible Black people who take the advice of white "pharmacists," who once they leave will mutter, "Hell, it doesn't hurt to help these people. . . . They are just like kids" (221). For more on white hoodoo pharmacists, see also Long, *Spiritual Merchants*, 143–50.

86. Within the three pages she devotes to the film in her autobiography, *Lady Sings the Blues*, in the poignantly titled chapter "The Same Old Story," Holiday mentions four separate times that she never made another Hollywood film.

87. Holiday, *Lady Sings the Blues*, 119.

88. Holiday, *Lady Sings the Blues*, 120.

89. Holiday, *Lady Sings the Blues*, 121.

90. Holiday, *Lady Sings the Blues*, 119.

91. Landau, *Spectacular Wickedness*, 118.

92. Roach, *Cities of the Dead*, 224–33.

93. Landau, *Spectacular Wickedness*, 154–56.

94. Roach, *Cities of the Dead*, 285.

95. Knowles-Carter, *Lemonade*.

96. New Orleans bounce is a genre of music and dance that began in the 1980s but was popularized post–Hurricane Katrina by a combination of factors: the diaspora of

displaced New Orleans residents in other parts of the country, Big Freedia's participation in the popular show *RuPaul's Drag Race*, Miley Cyrus's performance at the 2015 MTV Video Music Awards (in whose wake she was accused of appropriating Black and New Orleans culture), and its use by popular performers like Lizzo and Megan Thee Stallion. Bounce is best known as the purported provenance of twerking, a fast-paced style of dance that emphasizes rhythmic manipulation of the buttocks. For a history of bounce music, see Miller, *Bounce*.

Conclusion

1. Moten, *Black and Blur*.
2. William Seabrook also wrote about a crew of zombies working for the U.S.-run sugar company HASCO in *The Magic Island* a few years before Hurston, during the U.S. occupation of Haiti. For an excellent reading of Seabrook's anecdote, see Ramsey, *Spirits and the Law*, 172–76.
3. Hurston, *Tell My Horse*, 195.
4. Hurston, *Tell My Horse*, 196.
5. Hurston, *Tell My Horse*, 181.
6. Hurston, *Their Eyes Were Watching God*, 17.
7. Hurston, *Tell My Horse*, 195.
8. Dunham, *Island Possessed*, 200.
9. Dunham, *Island Possessed*, 199.
10. Dunham, *Island Possessed*, 200.
11. Hurston, *Their Eyes Were Watching God*, 1–2.
12. Hurston, *Their Eyes Were Watching God*, 2.
13. Dayan, *Haiti, History*, 9.
14. Evelyn Jean-Gilles, interview with Laine Kaplan Levinson, June 2017. Translation is my own.
15. At a celebration of the spirit Gede in New Orleans in November 2018, I heard it rendered as "Janbe lanmè, nou kite lafrik o" ("Crossed the ocean, we left Africa").
16. Brown, *Mama Lola*, 281.
17. Brown, *Mama Lola*, 283.
18. Lorde, *Sister Outsider*, 153.

Bibliography

Adams, Thomas Jessen, and Matthew Sakakeeny, eds. *Remaking New Orleans: Beyond Exceptionalism and Authenticity*. Durham, N.C.: Duke University Press, 2019.

Adefunmi, Oseijeman. *Tribal Origins of the African-Americans*. New York: Yoruba Temple Research Division, c. 1962.

Adler, Margot. *Drawing down the Moon: Witches, Druids, Goddess-worshippers, and Other Pagans in America Today*. [1979]. Boston: Beacon, 1986.

Aidoo, Lamonte. *Slavery Unseen: Sex, Power, and Violence in Brazilian History*. Durham, N.C.: Duke University Press, 2018.

Aikens, Vanoye. "On Stage with the Dunham Company: An Interview with Vanoye Aikens." In *Kaiso! Writings by and about Katherine Dunham*, edited by Vévé A. Clark and Sara E. Johnson, 274–87. Madison: University of Wisconsin Press, 2005.

Alexander, M. Jacqui. *Pedagogies of Crossing: Meditations on Feminism, Sexual Politics, Memory, and the Sacred*. Durham, N.C.: Duke University Press, 2006.

Alexis, Yveline. *Haiti Fights Back: The Life and Legacy of Charlemagne Péralte*. New Brunswick, N.J.: Rutgers University Press, 2021.

Aslakson, Kenneth R. *Making Race in the Courtroom: The Legal Construction of Three Races in New Orleans*. New York: New York University Press, 2014.

———. "The 'Quadroon-Plaçage' Myth of Antebellum New Orleans: Anglo-American (Mis)interpretations of a French Caribbean." *Journal of Social History* 45, no. 3 (2012): 709–34.

Baker, Houston A. *Modernism and the Harlem Renaissance*. Chicago: University of Chicago Press, 1987.

Balfour, Thelma. *Black Sun Signs: An African American Guide to the Zodiac*. New York: Atria Books, 1996.

Bambara, Toni Cade. *Conversations with Toni Cade Bambara*. Edited by Thabiti Lewis. Jackson: University of Mississippi Press, 2012.

———. *The Salt Eaters*. [1980]. New York: Vintage, 1992.

Bambara, Toni Cade, ed. *The Black Woman: An Anthology*. [1970]. New York: Washington Square Press, 2005.

Baraka, Amiri. *Kawaida Studies: The New Nationalism*. Chicago: Third World Press, 1972.

Beaubrun, Mimerose P. *Nan dòmi, recit d'une initiation Vodou*. La Roque d'Anthéron, France: Vents d'ailleurs, 2010.

Beauvoir, Max. *Lapriyè Ginen*. Port-au-Prince: Edisyon Près Nasyonal D'Ayiti, 2008.

Boyd, Valerie. *Wrapped in Rainbows: The Life of Zora Neale Hurston*. New York: Scribner, 2003.

Brooks, Kinitra D. *Searching for Sycorax: Black Women's Hauntings of Contemporary Horror*. New Brunswick, N.J.: Rutgers University Press, 2017.

Brown, Jayna. *Babylon Girls: Black Women Performers and the Shaping of the Modern*. Durham, N.C.: Duke University Press, 2008.

Brown, Karen McCarthy. *Mama Lola: A Vodou Priestess in Brooklyn*. Berkeley: University of California Press, 2001.

———. "Women's Leadership in Haitian Vodou." In *Weaving the Visions: New Patterns in Feminist Spirituality*, edited by Judith Plaskow and Carol P. Christ, 226–234. San Francisco: HarperSanFrancisco, 1989.

Burks, Arthur J. *Black Medicine*. Sauk City, Wis.: Arkham House, 1966.

Cable, George Washington. *The Grandissimes*. [1889]. New York: Scribner's Sons, 1929.

Cameron, Barbara. "Gee, You Don't Seem Like an Indian from the Reservation." In *This Bridge Called My Back: Writings by Radical Women of Color*, edited by Cherríe Moraga and Gloria Anzaldúa, 41–47. Albany: State University of New York Press, 2015.

Carby, Hazel. "The Politics of Fiction, Anthropology, and the Folk: Zora Neale Hurston." In *New Essays on Their Eyes Were Watching God*, edited by Michael Awkward, 71–93. New York: Cambridge University Press, 1990.

———. *Reconstructing Womanhood: The Emergence of the Afro-American Woman Novelist*. New York: Oxford University Press, 1987.

Castellanos, Henry C. *New Orleans as It Was: Episodes of Louisiana Life*. New Orleans: L. Graham, 1905.

Césaire, Aimé. *La tragédie du roi Christophe*. Paris: Présence Africaine, 1963.

Chakraborty, Sumita. "Poetic Networks Begin after Death." *College Literature* 47, no. 1 (2020): 230–39.

Chireau, Yvonne Patricia. *Black Magic: Religion and the African American Conjuring Tradition*. Berkeley: University of California Press, 2003.

Clark, VèVè A., and Sara E. Johnson, eds. *Kaiso! Writings by and about Katherine Dunham*. Madison: University of Wisconsin Press, 2005.

Clarke, Cheryl. *After Mecca: Women Poets and the Black Arts Movement*. New Brunswick, N.J.: Rutgers University Press, 2005.

Clarke, Emily Suzanne. *A Luminous Brotherhood: Afro-Creole Spiritualism in Nineteenth-Century New Orleans*. Chapel Hill: University of North Carolina Press, 2018.

Clifford, James. *The Predicament of Culture: Twentieth Century Ethnography, Literature, and Art*. Cambridge: Harvard University Press, 1988.

Clifton, Lucille. *The Collected Poems of Lucille Clifton 1965–2010*. Edited by Kevin Young and Michael S. Glaser. Rochester, N.Y.: BOA Editions, 2012.

———. *Good Woman: Poems and a Memoir 1969–1980*. Rochester, N.Y.: BOA Editions, 1987.

———. "An Interview with Lucille Clifton." By Charles Rowell. *Callaloo* 22, no. 1 (1999).

———. *Two-Headed Woman*. Amherst: University of Massachusetts Press, 1980.

Colbert, Soyica Diggs. *Radical Vision: A Biography of Lorraine Hansberry*. New Haven, Conn.: Yale University Press, 2021.

Cooper, Brittney C. *Beyond Respectability: The Intellectual Thought of Race Women*. Urbana: University of Illinois, 2017.

Craige, John Houston. *Black Bagdad*. New York: Minton, Balch, 1933.

———. *Cannibal Cousins*. New York: Minton, Balch, 1934.

Crawley, Ashon. *Blackpentecostal Breath: The Aesthetics of Possibility*. New York: Fordham University Press, 2017.
Cullen, Countee. "Heritage." In *Voices from the Harlem Renaissance*, edited by Nathan Irvin Huggins, 142–44. New York: Oxford University Press, 1995.
Das, Joanna Dee. *Katherine Dunham: Dance and the African Diaspora*. New York: Oxford University Press, 2017.
Davis, Angela Y. *Blues Legacies and Black Feminism: Gertrude "Ma" Rainey, Bessie Smith and Billie Holiday*. New York: Vintage, 1999.
Dayan, Colin. *Haiti, History, and the Gods*. Berkeley: University of California Press, 1995.
Delois Jenkins, La Vinia, ed. *Zora Neale Hurston, Haiti, and* Their Eyes Were Watching God. Evanston, Ill.: Northwestern University Press, 2013.
Deren, Maya. *Divine Horsemen: The Living Gods of Haiti*. New York: McPherson, 2004.
Deslippe, Philip. "The Hindu in Hoodoo: Fake Yogis, Pseudo-Swamis, and the Manufacture of African American Folk Magic." *Amerasia* 40, no. 1 (2014): 35–56.
Dessens, Nathalie. *From Saint Domingue to New Orleans: Migrations and Influences*. Gainesville: University of Florida Press, 2007.
De Veaux, Alexis. *Warrior Poet: A Biography of Audre Lorde*. New York: W. W. Norton, 2004.
Donahue, Jennifer. "The Ghost of Annie Palmer: Giving Voice to Jamaica's 'White Witch of Rose Hall.'" *Journal of Commonwealth Literature* 49, no. 2 (2014): 243–56.
Dubois, Laurent. *Avengers of the New World: The Story of the Haitian Revolution*. Cambridge, Mass.: Harvard University Press, 2004.
Du Bois, W. E. B. (William Edward Burghardt). *The Souls of Black Folk*. [1903]. New York: Oxford University Press, 2007.
duCille, Ann. "The Occult of True Black Womanhood: Critical Demeanor and Black Feminist Studies." *Signs: Journal of Women in Culture and Society* 19, no. 3 (1994): 591–629.
Dunham, Katherine. "Caribbean Tourist Traps." In *Kaiso! Writings by and about Katherine Dunham*, edited by VèVè A. Clark and Sara E. Johnson, 398–403. Madison: University of Wisconsin Press, 2005.
———. *Island Possessed*. [1969]. Chicago: University of Chicago Press, 1994.
———. *Journey to Accompong*. New York: Henry Holt, 1946.
Edwards, Brent Hayes. "The Ethnics of Surrealism." *Transition* 78 (1999): 84–135.
———. *The Practice of Diaspora: Literature, Translation, and the Rise of Black Internationalism*. Cambridge, Mass.: Harvard University Press, 2003.
Exuma. *Exuma, The Obeah Man*. [album]. Mercury Records, 1970.
Faderman, Lillian. *Odd Girls and Twilight Lovers: A History of Lesbian Life in Twentieth Century America*. New York: Columbia University Press, 1991.
Farmer, Ashley D. *Remaking Black Power: How Black Women Transformed an Era*. Chapel Hill: University of North Carolina Press, 2017.
Feldstein, Ruth. *How It Feels to Be Free: Black Women Entertainers and the Civil Rights Movement*. New York: Oxford University Press, 2013.
Fernández Olmos, Margarite, and Lizabeth Paravisini-Gebert. *Creole Religions of the Caribbean: An Introduction from* Vodou *and* Santería *to* Obeah *and* Espiritismo. New York: New York University Press, 2011.

Fett, Sharla M. *Working Cures: Healing, Health, and Power on Southern Slave Plantations*. Chapel Hill: University of North Carolina Press, 2002.
Francis, Allison E. "Serving the Spirit of the Dance: A Study of Jean-Léon Destiné, Lina Mathon Blanchet, and Haitian Folkloric Traditions." *Journal of Haitian Studies* 15, no. 1 (Spring 2009): 304–15.
Gallo, Marcia M. *Different Daughters: A History of the Daughters of Bilitis and the Rights of the Lesbian Rights Movement*. New York: Carroll & Graf, 2006.
Garcia, David F. *Listening for Africa: Freedom, Modernity, and the Logic of Black Music's African Origins*. Durham, N.C.: Duke University Press, 2017.
Garraway, Doris Lorraine. *The Libertine Colony: Creolization in the Early French Caribbean*. Durham, N.C.: Duke University Press, 2005.
Gates, Henry Louis, Jr. "A Negro Way of Saying." *New York Times*, April 21, 1985.
Geggus, David Patrick. *Haitian Revolutionary Studies*. Bloomington: Indiana University Press, 2002.
Gill, Lyndon K. *Erotic Islands: Art and Activism in the Queer Caribbean*. Durham, N.C.: Duke University Press, 2018.
Glick, Jeremy. *The Black Radical Tragic: Performance, Aesthetics, and the Unfinished Haitian Revolution*. New York: New York University Press, 2016.
Glissant, Édouard. *Monsieur Toussaint: A Play*. Translated by J. Michael Dash. Boulder, C.O.: Lynne Rienner Publishers, 2005.
———. *Poetics of Relation*. Translated by Betsy Wing. Ann Arbor: University of Michigan Press, 1997.
Goldberg, Whoopi, perf. *Ghost*. Directed by Jerry Zucker. DVD. Paramount Pictures, 1990.
"Gray Line New Orleans." Trip Advisor, accessed July 31, 2016. https://www.tripadvisor.com/Attraction_Review-g60864-d599729-Reviews-Hurricane_Katrina_Tour_America_s_Greatest_Catastrophe-New_Orleans_Louisiana.html (site discontinued).
Hansberry, Lorraine. *Les Blancs: The Collected Last Plays of Lorraine Hansberry*. New York: Random House, 1972.
———. *Playwright at Work*. By Frank Perry. National Education Television and Radio Center, December 6, 1961.
———. *The Sign in Sidney Brustein's Window*. New York: Random House, 1965.
———. *Toussaint*. In *Nine Plays by Black Women*, edited by Margaret Wilkerson, 49–67. New York: Signet, 1986.
———. "Village Intellect Revealed." *New York Times*, October 11, 1964.
Harding, Rachel Elizabeth. "Authority, History, and Everyday Mysticism in the Poetry of Lucille Clifton: A Womanist View." *Meridians: Feminism, Race, Transnationalism* 12, no. 1 (2014): 36–57.
Harris, LaShawn. *Sex Workers, Psychics, and Numbers Runners: Black Women in New York City's Underground Economy*. Urbana: University of Illinois Press, 2016.
Harris-Lopez, Trudier. "Zapping the Editor, or, How to Tell Censors to Kiss Off without Really Trying: Zora Neale Hurston's Fights with Authority Figures in *Dust Tracks on a Road*." In *South of Tradition: Essays on African American Literature*, 51–68. Athens: University of Georgia Press, 2002.

Hartman, Saidiya V. *Lose Your Mother: A Journey along the Transatlantic Slave Route*. New York: Farrar, Straus and Giroux, 2007.

———. *Scenes of Subjection: Terror, Slavery, and Self-Making in Nineteenth-Century America*. New York: Oxford University Press, 1997.

———. "Venus in Two Acts." *Small Axe: A Journal of Criticism* 12, no. 2 (2008): 1–14.

Hazzard-Donald, Katrina. *Mojo Workin': The Old African American Hoodoo System*. Urbana: University of Illinois Press, 2012.

Hazzard-Gordon, Katrina. *Jookin': The Rise of Social Dance Formations in African-American Culture*. Philadelphia: Temple University Press, 1990.

Herr, Ranjoo Seodu. "Reclaiming Third World Feminism: Or Why Transnational Feminism Needs Third World Feminism." *Meridians: Feminism, Race, Transnationalism* 12, no. 1 (2014): 1–30.

Higashida, Cheryl. *Black Internationalist Feminism: Women Writers of the Black Left, 1945–1995*. Urbana: University of Illinois, 2011.

Hill, Edwin C. *Black Soundscapes, White Stages: The Meaning of Francophone Sound in the Black Atlantic*. Baltimore: Johns Hopkins University Press, 2013.

Holiday, Billie. *Lady Sings the Blues*. New York: Avon Books, 1956.

———, perf. *New Orleans*. Directed by Arthur Lubin. DVD. Majestic Productions, 1947.

Holland, Sharon Patricia. *The Erotic Life of Racism*. Durham, N.C.: Duke University Press, 2012.

Hucks, Tracey E. *Yoruba Traditions and African American Religious Nationalism*. Albuquerque: University of New Mexico Press, 2012.

Huggins, Nathan Irvin. *Harlem Renaissance*. [1971]. New York: Oxford University Press, 2007.

Hughes, Langston. *The Big Sea: An Autobiography*. [1940]. New York: Hill and Wang, 1993.

———. "The Negro Artist and the Racial Mountain." [1926]. In *Voices from the Harlem Renaissance*, edited by Nathan Irvin Huggins, 305–9. New York: Oxford University Press, 1995.

Hull, Akasha Gloria. *Soul Talk: The New Spirituality of African American Women*. Rochester, Vt.: Inner Traditions, 2001.

Hull, Akasha Gloria, Patricia Bell-Scott, and Barbara Smith, eds. *All the Women Are Write, All the Blacks Are Men, but Some of Us Are Brave: Black Women's Studies*. [1982]. New York: Feminist Press, 2015.

Hurston, Zora Neale. *Dust Tracks on a Road*. New York: HarperPerennial, 1991.

———. "Hoodoo in America." *Journal of American Folklore* 44 (1931): 317–417.

———. "How It Feels to Be Colored Me." In *I Love Myself When I am Laughing and Then Again When I Am Looking Mean and Impressive: A Zora Neale Hurston Reader*, edited by Alice Walker, 152–55. New York: Feminist Press, 2011.

———. *Mules and Men*. [1935]. New York: Perennial Library, 1990.

———. "Review of *Voodoo in New Orleans* by Robert Tallant. "*Journal of American Folklore* 60 (1947): 438.

———. *The Sanctified Church: The Folklore Writings of Zora Neale Hurston*. Berkeley, Calif.: Turtle Island, 1981.

―――. *Tell My Horse: Voodoo and Life in Haiti and Jamaica*. [1938]. New York: Perennial Library, 1990.

―――. *Their Eyes Were Watching God*. [1937]. New York: HarperCollins, 2009.

―――. "Thirty Days among the Maroons." [1947]. In *Kaiso! Writings by and about Katherine Dunham*, edited by VèVè A. Clark and Sara E. Johnson, 272–73. Madison: University of Wisconsin Press, 2005.

―――. *Zora Neale Hurston: A Life In Letters*. Edited by Karla Caplan. New York: Doubleday, 2002.

Hutchinson, George. *In Search of Nella Larsen: A Biography of the Color Line*. Cambridge: Belknap Press, 2006.

Huxley, Francis. *The Invisibles: Voodoo Gods of Haiti*. London: Hart-Davis, 1966.

James, C. L. R. *The Black Jacobins: Toussaint Louverture and the San Domingo Revolution*. New York: Vintage, 1989.

Jessamy, Ken. "Harlem's Fakers: Streets Full of Turbaned 'Wise Men.'" *New York Amsterdam News*, August 28, 1937.

Johnson, Helene. "Poem." In *Voices from the Harlem Renaissance*, edited by Nathan Irvin Huggins, 183. New York: Oxford University Press, 1995.

Johnson, James Weldon. "The Truth about Haiti." *The Crisis* 20, no. 5 (September 1920).

Johnson, Jessica Marie. *Wicked Flesh: Black Women, Intimacy, and Freedom in the Atlantic World*. Charlottesville: University of Virginia Press, 2020.

Jones, Emily [Lorraine Hansberry]. "The Anticipation of Eve." *ONE* 5, no. 6 (1957): 21–29.

―――. "Chanson du Konallis," *The Ladder* 2, no. 12 (1958): 8–10 and 20–26.

Jones-Rogers, Stephanie E. *They Were Her Property: White Women as Slave Owners in the American South*. New Haven, Conn.: Yale University Press, 2019.

Jordan, June. "Black Women Haven't 'Got It All.'" *The Black Scholar* 10, no. 8/9 (1979): 39–40.

Judd, Bettina. "Glossolalia: Lucille Clifton's Creative Technologies of Becoming." In *Black Bodies and Transhuman Realities: Scientifically Modifying the Black Body in Posthuman Literature and Culture*, edited by Melvin G. Hill, 133–50. Lanham, Md.: Lexington Books, 2019.

Karade, Ifa. *The Handbook of Yoruba Religious Concepts*. York Beach, M.E.: S. Weiser, 1994.

Keeling, Kara. *The Witch's Flight: The Cinematic, the Black Femme, and the Image of Common Sense*. Durham, N.C.: Duke University Press, 2007.

Kernodle, Tammy L. "'I Wish I Knew How It Would Feel to Be Free': Nina Simone and the Redefining of the Freedom Song of the 1960s." *Journal of the Society for American Music* 2, no. 3 (2008): 295–317.

Knowles-Carter, Beyoncé. *Lemonade*. [album]. Columbia Records, 2016.

Kramarae, Cheris, and Dale Spender, eds. "Womanspirit." In *Routledge International Encyclopedia of Women: Global Women's Issues*, 2050. New York: Routledge, 2004.

Lamothe, Daphne. *Inventing the New Negro: Narrative, Culture, and Ethnography*. Philadelphia: University of Pennsylvania Press, 2008.

Landau, Emily Epstein. *Spectacular Wickedness: Sex, Race, and Memory in Storyville, New Orleans*. Baton Rouge: Louisiana State University Press, 2013.

Larsen, Nella. *Quicksand; And, Passing*. Edited by Deborah E. McDowell. [1928]. New Brunswick, N.J.: Rutgers University Press, 1986.

Lester, Julius. Introduction to Lorraine Hansberry, *Les Blancs: The Collected Last Plays of Lorraine Hansberry*. New York: Random House, 1972.

Levinson, Laine Kaplan. "New Orleans and Haiti: Is the Feeling Mutual?" *TriPod: New Orleans at 300*, 89.9 WWNO FM, October 27, 2017.

L.H.N. [Lorraine Hansberry]. *The Ladder* 1, no. 8 (May 1957): 26.

Linden, Robin R. *Against Sadomasochism: A Radical Feminist Analysis*. San Francisco: Frog in the Well, 1982.

Loederer, Richard A. *Voodoo Fire in Haiti*. New York: The Literary Guild, 1935.

Long, Carolyn Morrow. *Madame Lalaurie, Mistress of the Haunted House*. Gainesville: University Press of Florida, 2019.

———. *A New Orleans Voudou Priestess: The Legend and Reality of Marie Laveau*. Gainsville: University Press of Florida, 2006.

———. "Perceptions of New Orleans Voodoo: Sin, Fraud, Entertainment, and Religion." *Nova Religio: The Journal of Alternative and Emergent Religions* 6, no. 1 (2002): 86–101.

———. *Spiritual Merchants: Religion, Magic, and Commerce*. Knoxville: University of Tennessee Press, 2001.

Lorde, Audre. *The Black Unicorn*. [1978]. New York: W. W. Norton, 1995.

———. "The Great American Disease." *The Black Scholar* 10, no. 8/9 (1979): 17–20.

———. *Sister Outsider: Essays and Speeches*. Trumansburg, N.Y.: Crossing Press, 1984.

Luis-Brown, David. *Waves of Decolonization: Discourses of Race and Hemispheric Citizenship in Cuba, Mexico, and the United States*. Durham, N.C.: Duke University Press, 2008.

McKay, Claude. *Banjo; A Story Without a Plot*. [1929]. New York: Harcourt, Brace, Jovanovich, 1970.

Magloire, Marina. "Florence's Place: Hostessing Revolution in Interwar Paris." *Palimpsest: A Journal on Women, Gender, and the Black International* 10, no. 1 (2021): 23–42.

Manning, Susan. *Modern Dance, Negro Dance: Race in Motion*. Minneapolis: University of Minnesota Press, 2004.

Martin, John. "Katherine Dunham's Notable Contribution." In *Kaiso! Writings by and about Katherine Dunham*, edited by VèVè A. Clark and Sara E. Johnson, 211–13. Madison: University of Wisconsin Press, 2005.

Martin, Kameelah. *Envisioning Black Feminist Voodoo Aesthetics: African Spirituality in American Cinema*. Lanham, Md.: Lexington, 2016.

Meehan, Kevin. "Decolonizing Ethnography: Spirit Possession and Resistance in 'Tell My Horse.'" *Obsidian* 9, no. 1 (2008): 59–73.

Miller, Matt. *Bounce: Rap Music and Local Identity in New Orleans*. Amherst: University of Massachusetts Press, 2012.

Mitchell, Ernest J., II. "Zora's Politics." *Journal of Transnational American Studies* 5, no. 1 (2013).

Moraga, Cherríe. "La Jornada." In *This Bridge Called My Back: Writings by Radical Women of Color*, edited by Cherríe Moraga and Gloria Anzaldúa, xxxv–xli. Albany: State University of New York Press, 2015.

Moraga, Cherríe, and Gloria Anzaldúa, eds. *This Bridge Called My Back: Writings by Radical Women of Color*. [1983]. 4th ed. Albany: State University of New York Press, 2015.

Morand, Paul. *Black Magic*. Translated by Hamish Miles. New York: Viking, 1929.

Moreau de Saint-Méry, Médéric Louis Elie. *Description topographique, physique, civile, politique et historique de la partie francaise de l'isle Saint-Domingue: Avec des observations générales sur la population, sur le caractère & les moeurs de ses divers habitans; sur son climat, sa culture, ses productions, son administration, &c. &c. Accompagnées des détails les plus propres à faire connâitre l'état de cette colonie à l'époque du 18 octobre 1789; et d'une nouvelle carte de la totalité de l'isle*. Vo1. 1. Philadelphia: Pauteur, 1797.

Moreno Vega, Marta. *The Altar of My Soul: The Living Traditions of Santería*. New York: Ballantine, 2000.

———. "The Yoruba Orisha Tradition Comes to New York City." In *Kaiso! Writings by and about Katherine Dunham*, edited by VèVè A. Clark and Sara E. Johnson, 603–11. Madison: University of Wisconsin Press, 2005.

Morrison, Toni. "The Site of Memory." In *Inventing the Truth: The Art and Craft of Memoir*, edited by William Zinsser, 83–102. New York: Houghton Mifflin, 1995.

Moten, Fred. *Black and Blur*. Durham, N.C.: Duke University Press, 2017.

———. "'Words Don't Go There': An Interview with Fred Moten." By Charles Rowell. *Callaloo* 27, no. 4 (2004): 955–66.

Mumford, Kevin. *Not White, Not Straight: Black Gay Men from the March on Washington to the AIDS Crisis*. Chapel Hill: University of North Carolina Press, 2016.

Nash, Jennifer. *Black Feminism Reimagined: After Intersectionality*. Durham, N.C.: Duke University Press, 2018.

Nwankwo, Ifeoma C. K. "Insider and Outsider, Black and American: Rethinking Zora Neale Hurston's Caribbean Ethnography." *Radical History Review* 87 (2003): 49–77.

Osumare, Halifu. "Katherine Dunham, a Pioneer of Postmodern Anthropology." In *Kaiso! Writings by and about Katherine Dunham*, edited by VèVè A. Clark and Sara E. Johnson, 612–23. Madison: University of Wisconsin Press, 2005.

Painter, Nell Irvin. *Sojourner Truth: A Life, a Symbol*. New York: W. W. Norton, 1996.

Palmié, Stephan. *Wizards and Scientists: Explorations in Afro-Cuban Modernity and Tradition*. Durham, N.C.: Duke University Press, 2002.

Perpener, John O. *African-American Concert Dance: The Harlem Renaissance and Beyond*. Urbana: University of Illinois Press, 2001.

Perry, Imani. *Looking for Lorraine: The Radiant and Radical Life of Lorraine Hansberry*. Boston: Beacon, 2018.

Pettinger, Alasdair. "'Eh! Eh! Bomba, hen! Hen!': Making Sense of a Vodou Chant." In *Obeah and Other Powers: The Politics of Caribbean Religion and Healing*, 80–102. Durham, N.C.: Duke University Press, 2012.

Plaskow, Judith, and Carol P. Christ, eds. *Weaving the Visions: New Patterns in Feminist Spirituality*. San Francisco: HarperSanFrancisco, 1989.

———. *Womanspirit Rising: A Feminist Reader in Religion*. [1979]. San Francisco: HarperSanFrancisco, 1992.

Pollack-Pelzner, Daniel. "Unseen Script Offers New Evidence of a Radical Lorraine Hansberry." *New York Times*, June 3, 2020.

Polyné, Millery. "'To Carry the Dance of the People Beyond': Jean Léon Destiné, Lavinia Williams and 'Danse Folklorique Haïtienne.'" *Journal of Haitian Studies* 10, no. 2 (2004): 33–51.

Putnam, Lara. *Radical Moves: Caribbean Migration and the Politics of Race in the Jazz Age*. Chapel Hill: University of North Carolina Press, 2013.

Quashie, Kevin E. *The Sovereignty of Quiet: Beyond Resistance in Black Culture*. New Brunswick, N.J.: Rutgers University Press, 2012.

Ramsey, Kate. "From 'Voodooism' to 'Vodou': Changing a US Library of Congress Subject Heading." *Journal of Haitian Studies* 18, no. 2 (2012): 14–25.

———. "Melville Herskovits, Katherine Dunham, and the Politics of African Diasporic Dance Anthropology." In *Dancing Bodies, Living Histories*, edited by Lisa Doolittle and Anne Flynn, 205–12. Banff, Alberta: Banff Centre Press, 2002.

———. *The Spirits and the Law: Vodou and Power in Haiti*. Chicago: University of Chicago Press, 2011.

Rankine, Claudia. *Citizen: An American Lyric*. Minneapolis: Graywolf, 2014.

Raynaud, Claudine. "Modernism, Anthropology, Africanism and the Self: Hurston and Herskovits on/in Haiti." In *Afromodernisms: Paris, Harlem and the Avant-Garde*, edited by Fionnghuala Sweeney and Kate Marsh, 103–25. Edinburgh: Edinburgh University Press, 2013.

———. "'Rubbing a Paragraph with a Soft Cloth?': Muted Voices and Editorial Constraints in Zora Neale Hurston's *Dust Tracks on a Road*." In *De/Colonizing the Subject: The Politics of Gender in Women's Autobiography*, edited by Sidonie Smith and Julia Watson, 34–64. Minneapolis: University of Minnesota Press, 1992.

Reed, Ishmael. *The Last Days of Louisiana Red*. New York: Random House, 1974.

———. *Mumbo Jumbo*. Garden City, N.Y.: Doubleday, 1972.

Renda, Mary A. *Taking Haiti: Military Occupation and the Culture of U.S. Imperialism, 1915–1940*. Chapel Hill: University of North Carolina Press, 2001.

Roach, Joseph R. *Cities of the Dead: Circum-Atlantic Performance*. New York: Columbia University Press, 1996.

Roberts, Kodi A. *Voodoo and Power: The Politics of Religion in New Orleans, 1881–1940*. Baton Rouge: Louisiana State University Press, 2015.

Robinson, Cedric J. *Black Marxism: The Making of the Black Radical Tradition*. Chapel Hill: University of North Carolina Press, 2000.

Roumain, Jacques. *Gouverneurs de la rosée*. [1944]. Paris: Zulma, 2013.

———. *Masters of the Dew*. Translated by Langston Hughes and Mercer Cook. New York: Reynal and Hitchcock, 1947.

Salaam, Kalamu ya. "It's Not the Salt; It's the Sugar That Will Kill You." The Feminist Wire, November 20, 2014. https://thefeministwire.com/2014/11/anti-sexism-work/.

———. "Revolutionary Struggle/Revolutionary Love." *The Black Scholar* 10, no. 8/9 (1979): 20–24.
Seabrook, William. *The Magic Island*. New York: Literary Guild of America, 1929.
Shakur, Assata. *Assata: An Autobiography*. Chicago: Lawrence Hill Books, 2001.
Simone, Nina. *The Amazing Nina Simone*. Directed by Jeff L. Lieberman. Re-Emerging Films, 2015.
———. *Black Gold*. [album]. RCA, 1970.
———. *It Is Finished*. [album]. RCA, 1974.
———. *Nina Simone Great Performances: College Concerts and Interviews*. Directed by Andy Stroud. Andy Stroud, Inc., 2009.
Simone, Nina, and Stephen Cleary. *I Put a Spell on You: The Autobiography of Nina Simone*. New York: Pantheon, 1991.
Smethurst, James. *The Black Arts Movement: Literary Nationalism in the 1960s and 1970s*. Chapel Hill: University of North Carolina Press, 2005.
Smith, Barbara, ed. *Home Girls: A Black Feminist Anthology*. New York: Kitchen Table Women of Color Press, 1983.
Staples, Robert. "The Myth of Black Macho: A Response to Angry Black Feminists." *The Black Scholar* 10, no. 6/7 (1979): 24–33.
Strongman, Roberto. *Queering Black Atlantic Religions: Transcorporeality in Candomblé, Santería, and Vodou*. Durham, N.C.: Duke University Press, 2019.
Taft, Edna. *A Puritan in Voodoo-Land*. New York: The Literary Guild, 1935.
Tallant, Robert. *Voodoo in New Orleans*. [1946]. New York: Pelican, 1984.
Teish, Luisah. *Jambalaya: The Natural Woman's Book*. New York: HarperCollins, 1988.
Thomas, Lynell L. *Desire and Disaster in New Orleans: Tourism, Race, and Historical Memory*. Durham, N.C.: Duke University Press, 2014.
Tinsley, Omise'eke Natasha. *Ezili's Mirrors: Imagining Black Queer Genders*. Durham, N.C.: Duke University Press, 2018.
———. *Thiefing Sugar: Eroticism between Women in Caribbean Literature*. Durham, N.C.: Duke University Press, 2010.
Toibin, Colm. "The Unsparing Confessions of Giovanni's Room." *New Yorker*, February 26, 2016.
Touré, Askia M. "Black Male/Female Relations: A Political Overview of the 1970s." *The Black Scholar* 10, no. 8/9 (1979): 45–48.
Trouillot, Michel-Rolph. *Silencing the Past: Power and the Production of History*. Boston: Beacon, 1995.
Ulysse, Gina Athena. "Vodou as Idea: On Omise'eke Natasha Tinsley's 'Ezili's Mirrors.'" *Los Angeles Review of Books*, September 28, 2018. https://lareviewofbooks.org/article/vodou-as-idea-on-omiseeke-natasha-tinsleys-ezilis-mirrors.
Van Vechten, Carl. *Nigger Heaven*. New York: Knopf, 1926.
Walcott, Derek. *The Haitian Trilogy*. New York: Farrar, Straus and Giroux, 2002.
Walker, Alice. *In Love and in Trouble: Stories of Black Women*. San Diego: Harcourt Brace Jovanovich, 1973.
———. *In Search of Our Mothers Gardens: Womanist Prose*. San Diego, Calif.: Harcourt Brace Jovanovich, 1983.

Ward, Cynthia. "Truths, Lies, Mules and Men: Through the 'Spyglass of Anthropology' and What Zora Saw There." *Western Journal of Black Studies* 36, no. 4 (2012): 301–13.

Ward, Martha. *Voodoo Queen: The Spirited Lives of Marie Laveau*. Jackson: University Press of Mississippi, 2004.

White, Shane. *Playing the Numbers: Gambling in Harlem between the Wars*. Cambridge, Mass.: Harvard University Press, 2010.

Williams, Bianca C. *The Pursuit of Happiness: Black Women, Diasporic Dreams, and the Politics of Emotional Transnationalism*. Durham, N.C.: Duke University Press, 2018.

Wilson, Jamie. "Community Well-Being and the Criminalization of Magico-Religious Workers in Harlem, New York, during the 1920s." *International Social Science Review* 82, nos. 1&2 (2007): 20–38.

Wirkus, Faustin, and Taney Dudley. *The White King of La Gonave*. Garden City, N.Y.: Doubleday, 1931.

Wright, Richard. "Between Laughter and Tears." *New Masses*, October 5, 1937.

Index

Abby (film), 9
Adefunmi, Oseijeman, 71, 99, 103, 105, 177n14
Adler, Margot, 102
"africa" (Clifton), 84–85
Afrocentrism, 12, 70–71, 72, 86–87, 99
Afro-diasporic spiritualities, 7–8, 65–67. *See also* Haitian Vodou; New Orleans hoodoo; spiritualities
Afrofuturism, 98–99
Against Sadomasochism (Linden), 55–56
Agwe, 5
Aidoo, Lamonte, 54, 55
AIDS crisis, 38
Alexander, M. Jacqui, 86, 93
The Amazing Nina Simone (documentary), 43
anger, 78–81
angry Black woman trope, 78–81
anthropology, 14–16. *See also* Dunham, Katherine; Hurston, Zora Neale
"The Anticipation of Eve" (Hansberry), 49–50, 51
anti-imperialism, 161n2, 162n6, 162n9
Anzaldúa, Gloria, 102, 114
"Apples of Autumn" (Hansberry), 47
archives and archival research, 5; ancestors in, 130, 141; of Bambara, 111, 112; of Clifton, 88, 92; of Dunham, 36; of Hansberry, 41; of Hurston, 139; of Laveau, 129, 140; silences of, 53, 131, 138, 148; of Simone, 43
Armstrong, Louis, 146, 150
Assen, Abdul, 165n28
astrology, 89, 105, 155
authenticity politics, 11, 14–15, 70, 102, 115, 154–55

Baldwin, James, 47, 62
Balfour, Thelma, 105
Ballet Nègre, 21
Bambara, Toni Cade, 5, 124; *The Salt Eaters*, 12, 87, 100, 105–14, 117–25; on *This Bridge Called My Back*, 100
Baraka, Amiri, 70–71, 72, 172n12
Barbados, 60, 64
Barrow, Clyde, 90
Barrow, Errol, 60
Bassa Moona (Dafora), 20
Beaubrun, Mimerose, 7, 8
Beethoven, Ludwig von, 90–91
belief, 40–41
"La Belle Zoa" (Pratt), 10
Benin, 5
"Between Ourselves" (Lorde), 74
Beyoncé, 152–53
Big Freedia, 153, 184n96
The Big Sea (Hughes), 171n74
Black American feminism, 3–10, 162n16. *See also* Third World feminism; Vodou feminism
Black Arts Movement, 69, 70, 172n1, 172n4, 174n53
Black Cat Bone ceremony, 149
Black dance, 16
Black Dionysiac, 18–19
Black Feminism Reimagined (Nash), 6, 123–24
Black Gold (Simone), 66
Black liberation, 69–70, 156–57. *See also* Clifton, Lucille; Lorde, Audre
Black nationalism, 69, 83
Black Panthers, 63, 82, 113
Blackpentacostal Breath (Crawley), 41, 65
The Black Radical Tragic (Glick), 7
The Black Scholar (publication), 78, 79

Black spiritualities, 102–9. *See also* Haitian Vodou; New Orleans hoodoo; spiritualities
Black Sun Signs (Balfour), 105
Black Tao, 117
The Black Unicorn (Lorde), 11, 73
Black women in anthropology, 14–16. *See also* Dunham, Katherine; Hurston, Zora Neale
Black Women's Alliance, 100–101
Les Blancs (Hansberry), 47
blaxploitation films, 9
blues music, 3, 17
Boas, Franz, 15
Bois-Caïman ceremony, 8, 163n33
The Book of Night Women (James), 53–54
both/and, 93
Boukman, 8
bounce music, 153, 183n96
Brooks, Gwendolyn, 70, 174n59
Brooks, Kinitra, 62
Brown, Adrienne Marie, 98
Brown, Karen McCarthy, 8–9, 28, 76, 80, 159
Bunche, Ralph, 49
Bush, George H. W., 38
Butler, Octavia, 98

Cable, George Washington, 9
Cacos, 2, 19
cafuné, 54–55
"ca'line's prayer" (Clifton), 85
Cameron, Barbara, 100
Carby, Hazel, 29, 54, 136
Caribbean Cultural Center African Diaspora Institute (CCCADI), 103
Caribbean musical practice, 17
Cassidy, Jack, 91
Castro, Fidel, 45
Cercle Harmonique, 92, 175n94
"Chanson du Konallis" (Hansberry), 50–51, 57–59
Chauvet, Marie Vieux, 7
choreography, 21
civil rights movement, 60–64, 106

clairvoyance. *See* spirit possession and communication
Clark, Emily Suzanne, 92
Clarke, Cheryl, 46, 70, 73, 172n4
Clifford, James, 17
Clifton, Lucille, 5, 11–12, 69–70; "the 1970s," 83; "africa," 84–85; "ca'line's prayer," 85; "jonah," 86; spirit possession and communication by, 87–99, 174n68, 174n73; spirit writing by, 88–89; *Two-Headed Woman*, 86–87, 93–96, 98; "why some people be mad at me sometimes," 83–84
COINTELPRO, 78
Colbert, Soyica Diggs, 41, 43, 49
The Color Purple (Walker), 87
Comhaire-Sylvain, Suzanne, 7
Communist Party and McCarthyism, 44, 45–46
Congo, 5
Cook, Mercer, 42
Cortez, Jayne, 69, 70
Courlander, Harold, 73
Craige, John H., 19
Crawley, Ashon, 41, 65
Creole, as term, 147–48, 182n72
The Crisis (publication), 2, 162n9
Cuba, 36, 45, 103–4, 113, 163n28
Cuban Revolution, 45
Cullen, Countee, 30
cultural chauvinism, 1, 161n2

Dafora, Asadata, 20, 165n28
Daily Picayune (publication), 142
Daly, Mary, 75, 177n8
"Dambala" (song by Simone), 61–62, 64
Damballah/Danbala, 12, 32, 106–14, 165n37
dance: companies of, 21; of Danbala, 114; Dunham and, 16, 32–33; Hansberry and, 41–42; ritual, 16–17, 32–34, 149; by Simone, 40, 43–44
Dantò, Ezili, 75, 80–82, 96
Das, Joanna Dee, 36, 37, 38, 167n88
Daughters of Bilitis, 48–49

Davis, Angela, 3
Dayan, Colin, 76
décalage, 6
"Depi nan Ginen, nèg rayi nèg" (proverb), 74
Deren, Maya, 8, 25, 76
Deslippe, Philip, 108
Dessalines, Ezméry, 22
Dessalines, Jean-Jacques, 166n52
Destiné, Jean-Léon, 42, 168n6
devas, 112
diasporic communities, 21–23, 34–35
Dickinson, Emily, 91
disaster tourism, 146–47
Divine Horsemen (Deren), 76
djinns, 112
dreams, 107
The Drinking Gourd (Hansberry), 169n14
Dr. John, 180n12, 181n34
drumming, 19–20. *See also* tom-toms
Dubois, Laurent, 8
Du Bois, W. E. B., 27–28, 45
DuCille, Ann, 135–36
Dumont, Sally, 54
Duncan, Isadora, 91
Dunham, Katherine: *Bal nègre* by, 168n6; description of, 14; ethnographic work by, 8, 10–11, 15–18; Habitation Leclerc of, 33–34, 37–38; Hurston and, 14–15; *Island Possessed*, 10, 16–17, 25, 34–35, 36–37, 39, 156; *Journey to Accompong*, 14, 17; primitivism and, 10, 17, 21–27, 41, 165nn27–28, 181n43; Rosita and, 36–37, 167n94; use of choreography by, 21, 114; on Vodou and belonging, 28, 32–39; zombification and, 156–57
Dust Tracks on a Road (Hurston), 1
Duvalier, François "Papa Doc," 35

Earth (Basshe), 20
Edwards, Brent Hayes, 6
either/or, 93
The Emperor Jones (O'Neil), 20
enslavement: dancing and, 21, 25; Haitian Revolution against, 8; liberation from, 4; in literature, 52–54; Lorde on, 74; New Orleans and, 147–48, 151, 183n77; Starhawk on witch trials vs., 104; Vodou and, 5, 158. *See also* Middle Passage; servitude
Envisioning Black Feminist Voodoo Aesthetics (Martin), 7
eroticism, 30, 53, 55, 59, 71, 77–78
essentialism: Bambara and, 111, 114, 120, 122; Blackness and, 4, 16–17, 30–32; by Dunham, 17–18; Lorde on, 6, 12; in music, 17, 169n12; in New Orleans hoodoo, 129; spiritualities and, 12, 72–73; in Third World feminism, 101, 122, 124
Estrada, La Rosa, 36
exceptionalism, 4, 15, 89, 120, 128, 152
exorcism, 34, 37–38
Exuma, 64
"Eye to Eye" (Lorde), 74–75, 76–77, 159–60
Ezili Dantó, 5, 75, 80–81, 96
Ezili Freda, 5, 75, 76, 96
Ezili's Mirrors (Tinsley), 7, 75

Farmer, Ashley D., 69, 71, 101
Fatiman, Cécile, 8
FBI surveillance, 44, 45–46
Feldstein, Ruth, 61, 63
femininity: Anzaldúa on, 114; Deren and, 76; Dunham and, 24; essentialism in, 12, 72; Hansberry and, 48, 56, 57, 59; Lorde and, 75, 79
feminisms: Black American women, 3–10, 162n16; Third World, 4, 12, 100–102, 105, 107, 113–14, 122–24; Vodou, 6–10, 158–59
feminist spiritualities, 101–6. *See also* spiritualities
fetishization, 8, 27, 56, 72–73, 127, 151, 163n35. *See also* primitivism
First International Conference of Orisha Tradition and Culture, 103
"Flowers for the General" (Hansberry), 47

Index 199

folk healing, 109-10. *See also* plant-based medicine
"Formation" (Beyoncé), 152-53
fraud, 107, 108, 154
Freud, Sigmund, 107
Futtam, Madame Fu, 108-9
futurity, 40-41, 98-99

Garcia, David F., 21
Garraway, Doris, 147
Gates, Henry Louis, Jr., 130
gay rights movement, 48-49
Gede, 167n85, 184n15
gender roles, 69, 108
Ghana, 7-8
Ghost (film), 87, 154
Gill, Lyndon K., 4
Ginen, as term, 39
Giovanni, Nikki, 70
Giovanni's Room (Baldwin), 47
Glassman, Sallie Ann, 131-32
Glick, Jeremy, 6-7
Glissant, Edouard, 155
global salvation, 97-99
goddesses, in literary works, 70-82, 106, 112, 116
Goddess movement, 116-17
going native, 14
"Go Limp" (Simone), 63
The Grandissimes (Cable), 9
Guggenheim Foundation, 15
Gumbs, Alexis Pauline, 98
gwobonanj, 158
Gyn/Ecology (Daly), 75

Habitation Leclerc, 33-34, 37-38
Haiti: 2010 earthquake, 147; Dunham and, 4; Hurston on, 1-3, 4; New Orleans and, 10, 128-29, 179n3; U.S. imperialism in, 1-3, 18, 37-38; violence in, 18, 22-23
Haitian Revolution, 7, 8, 124, 163n32
Haitian Vodou: Bambara and, 110-11; on conflict, 5; Dunham and, 22-26, 157-59; feminist geography of, 6-10, 158-59; Haitian Revolution and, 163n32; Lorde and, 75; origins of, 5; Seabrook on, 18-19. *See also* New Orleans hoodoo
Hansberry, Lorraine: "The Anticipation of Eve," 49-50, 51; "Apples of Autumn," 47; on belief and movement, 40-41; *Les Blancs*, 47; "Chanson du Konallis," 50-51, 57-59; "Flowers for the General," 47; *The Marrow of Tradition*, 47; queerness and, 44-59, 169n13, 169n30; *A Raisin in the Sun*, 47; *The Sign in Sidney Brustein's Window*, 44-45, 47; Simone's friendship with, 40, 42-44, 59, 60, 169n14; *Toussaint*, 11, 43, 47-48, 52-53, 56-57, 61, 67; unpublished works of, 41, 43; *What Use Are Flowers?*, 44
Harding, Rachel Elizabeth, 92
Harlem, New York, 107-8
Harlem Renaissance, 10, 165n27
Harlem Yoruba Temple, 72, 103, 172n12
Harris, LaShawn, 107
Hartman, Saidiya, 7-8, 22, 44, 130, 140
Hazzard-Donald, Katrina, 119
Hazzard-Gordon, Katrina, 21
Hearn, Lafcadio, 129
Hemenway, Robert, 137
Henry, Velma, 110
"Heritage" (Cullen), 30
Herskovits, Melville, 15, 73
Higashida, Cheryl, 47, 162n19
Hindu traditions, 112
Holiday, Billie, 90, 91, 150
Holland, Sharon, 56
homophobia, 41, 46, 50, 69. *See also* sexism
hoodoo. *See* New Orleans hoodoo
hoodoo women, 87
"How It Feels to Be Colored Me" (Hurston), 27, 139
Hughes, Langston, 20, 26, 42, 97, 139, 170n74, 181n43

Hull, Akasha Gloria, 88–89, 107, 125, 175n106
hunger strike, 38
Hurricane Katrina (2005), 146, 153
Hurston, Zora Neale: on belonging, 13; description of, 14; Dunham and, 14–15; *Dust Tracks on a Road*, 1; ethnographic work by, 8, 148–51; father of, 62; on Haiti, 1–3; "How It Feels to Be Colored Me," 27, 139; on Laveau, 140–45; *Mule Bone*, 181n43; *Mules and Men*, 1, 12, 15, 119, 131, 142, 143, 156; on New Orleans hoodoo, 130; on proverb, 74; "Seeing the World as It Is," 2; *Tell My Horse*, 1, 156, 162n6; *Their Eyes Were Watching God*, 1, 139, 142, 156, 157–58; Walker's search for grave of, 12, 135, 136–38; zombification and, 155–56
Hutchinson, George, 29

"if something should happen" (Clifton), 98
imagined community, 10–11
In Concert (Simone), 63
initiation ceremony, 24–25
interracial coalitions, 100–103
invisibility, 12, 57, 119, 147–50, 152, 153, 161n2
Islamic traditions, 112
Island Possessed (Dunham), 10, 16–17, 25, 34–35, 36–37, 39, 156
It is Finished (Simone), 11, 64, 68

Jamaica, 4, 14, 17
Jambalaya (Teish), 12, 104, 116, 117
jazz, 17, 25–27, 50, 61, 150–52, 166n48. *See also* New Orleans
Jean-Gilles, Evelyn, 158
Jessamy, Ken, 108
Johnson, James Weldon, 1–2, 3
"jonah" (Clifton), 86
Jones, Florence Emery, 170n74
Jones-Rogers, Stephanie E., 54
Journal of American Folklore (publication), 132

Journey to Accompong (Dunham), 14, 17
jungle trope, 27–34, 165n27. *See also* primitivism; tom-toms

Karenga, Maulana, 71
Katherine Dunham's Performing Arts Training Center (PATC), 114
Kawaidaism, 70–71
Keeling, Kara, 63
Kwanzaa, 70–71
Kyunkor (Dafora), 20, 165n28

The Ladder (publication), 46, 48
Lamothe, Daphne, 15–16, 132, 161n2
Landau, Emily Epstein, 147
Larsen, Nella, 3, 28–32
The Last Days of Louisiana Red (Reed), 181n34
Laveau, Marie, 10, 12, 92, 119, 126–33, 140–45, 175n96, 181n34
lesbianism, 44–59. *See also* queerness
Lester, Julius, 44
liberation, 3–5, 8
Liberia, 65–66
The Life and Works of Marie Laveau (pamphlet), 141, 144
literary criticism, 135
Long, Carolyn Morrow, 179n1
Looking for Lorraine (Perry), 47
"Looking for Zora" (Walker), 137
Lorde, Audre: "Between Ourselves," 74; *The Black Unicorn*, 11, 73; "Eye to Eye," 74–75, 76–77, 159–60; "Open Letter to Mary Daly," 75, 177n8; "Poetry Is Not a Luxury," 4, 76; on sadomasochism, 55, 56; *Sister Outsider*, 11; spiritual geographies of, 69–82
Lose Your Mother (Hartman), 7–8
Louisiana laws and practices, 110, 182n74, 183n76. *See also* New Orleans
Louisiana Red, 181n34
Louverture, Toussaint, 163n35. *See also Toussaint* (Hansberry)
Luis-Brown, David, 25
lwa, 5, 42, 111, 119, 149, 168n10

Index 201

Macbeth (production by Welles), 20, 165n28
The Magic Island (Seabrook), 18, 164n18, 184n2
Makeba, Miriam, 169n11
Malcolm X, 72, 172n12
Mama Day (Naylor), 87
Mama Lola (Brown), 8, 80, 159
mambo, 8, 9, 34, 127, 158
Mardi Gras celebrations, 35, 117–18
Maroon communities, 17
The Marrow of Tradition (Hansberry), 47
Martin, John, 16
Martin, Kameelah, 7, 9
Marxism, 42, 163n32
Mary, 96–97
masculinity: essentialism in, 12; Hansberry and, 47, 56, 59; Simone and, 59; Teish on, 106; in Vodou, 8. *See also* misogyny
Masters of the Dew (Hansberry), 41
Matthews, Dorothy, 108–9
McCarthyism, 44, 45–46
McKay, Claude, 27, 30
Medical Practice Bill (1922), 109–10
Mendoza, Julio, 36
Middle Passage, 10, 21, 25, 39, 86, 111, 159. *See also* enslavement
Mina, Ma, 103–4
misogyny, 69, 106, 137, 139
"Mississippi Goddam" (Simone), 60, 62, 63, 68
Moraga, Cherríe, 100, 114
Morrison, Toni, 85–86, 117–18
Morrow, Carolyn, 129
Moten, Fred, 149, 155
Moynihan Report *(The Negro Family)*, 78
Mule Bone (Hughes and Hurston), 181n43
Mules and Men (Hurston), 1, 12, 15, 119, 131, 142, 143, 156
Mumford, Kevin, 43
"The Myth of the Black Macho" (Staples), 78

NAACP (National Association for the Advancement of Colored People), 1–2
Nan dòmi (Beaubrun), 8
Nash, Jennifer, 6, 123–24
The Nation (publication), 2, 162n9
"The Negro Artist and the Racial Mountain" (Hughes), 26
Nemiroff, Robert, 47
neo-paganism, 104, 116
New Age spiritualities, 88–89, 102, 104–5, 116. *See also* spiritualities
New Orleans, 115–25, 146–49; bounce music of, 153, 183n96; Haiti and, 10, 128–29, 179n3; laws in, 110; as site of Black American feminism, 9–10. *See also* jazz; Laveau, Marie; New Orleans hoodoo
New Orleans (film), 150, 151, 152
New Orleans hoodoo, 1, 115, 118–21, 126–33, 137, 140–49, 175n96, 179n89, 180n9, 180n12. *See also* Haitian Vodou; Laveau, Marie
New Orleans Jazz Fest, 10
New York Amsterdam News (publication), 108
Nigeria, 5, 65, 103
Nigger Heaven (Van Vechten), 26
nonessentialism. *See* essentialism

Obatalá, 71–72
obeah woman, 67
"Obeah Woman" (Simone), 64, 65
Ochún, 71, 79
Oda Mae Brown (character), 87, 154–55
Oliana, Christopher, 103
ONE (publication), 46, 49–50
The Ones, 97–98
"Open Letter to Mary Daly" (Lorde), 75, 177n8
orgies, 18–19, 142
orisha worship, 7, 36, 37, 71, 103–4, 105, 115, 120, 163n28. *See also* Yoruba spirituality
Osgood-Mason, Charlotte, 181n43
Osumare, Halifu, 15

202   Index

Ouanga! (White), 20
Ouija board, 87
Oyá, 71, 79, 104, 172n12

paganism, 104, 116
Painter, Nell Irvin, 54
Pan-Africanism, 7, 11, 16, 18, 21, 25, 34–35
Passing (Larsen), 3
Patrick, Dorothy, 150–51
Perry, Imani, 43, 47, 61
"Pirate Jenny" (Simone), 61, 63
plaçage, 183n76
plant-based medicine, 155. *See also* folk healing
Plessy v. Ferguson, 129
"Poem" (Johnson), 166n49
poetry, 4, 11
"Poetry Is Not a Luxury" (Lorde), 4, 76
poto mitan, 38
The Practice of Diaspora (Edwards), 6
Pratt, Frances Hammond, 10
Pratt, Marie-Christine Dunham, 43
primitivism, 10, 17–18, 21, 24–27, 41, 165nn27–28. *See also* jungle trope; tom-toms
Property (Martin), 53–54
purposeful travel, 3, 23, 34

Quashie, Kevin, 6, 84
queerness, 11, 43, 44–59, 90–91
Quicksand (Larsen), 3, 28–32

"Race" (Cortez), 69
racial capitalism, 98, 159–60
Rainey, Ma, 3
A Raisin in the Sun (Hansberry), 47
Ramsey, Kate, 15, 19
Ransom, Minnie, 119
Raymond-Noël, Welele, 10
Reckless Eyeballing (Reed), 78
Reed, Ishmael, 70, 78, 181n34
reincarnation, 87, 89, 91, 98, 99. *See also* spirit possession and communication

Remaking New Orleans (eds. Adams and Sakakeeny), 120
Reser, Stanley "Doc," 35, 167n85
respectability politics, 48–49
"The Revenge of Hannah Kemhuff" (Walker), 137
revolutionary art, 44–45, 60–61, 177n33
Rich, Adrienne, 72
ritual dance, 16–17, 32–34, 149
Roach, Joseph, 151, 152
Roberts, Kodi A., 129
Robertson, Pat, 147, 164n16
Robeson, Paul, 45, 175n85
Robinson, Bill "Bojangles," 165n27
rootworkers, 87
Rosenwald Foundation, 14–15, 21
Rosita, 36–37, 167n94
Roumain, Jacques, 42

sadomasochism, 55–56
Saint-Domingue, 5
Salaam, Kalamu ya, 113, 117, 173n35
The Salt Eaters (Bambara), 12, 87, 100, 105–14, 117–25
Sam, Vilbrun Guillaume, 18, 164n18
Sanchez, Sonia, 70
Santería, 102, 103, 177n11
Seabrook, William, 18–19, 27, 164n18, 184n2
"Seeing the World as It Is" (Hurston), 2
self-love, 78–79
servitude, 156–58. *See also* enslavement
"the 70s" (Clifton), 83
sexism, 70, 78, 79, 173n35. *See also* homophobia; misogyny
sexual violence, 54–55, 91, 156–57
Shange, Ntozake, 78–79
Shango (spirit), 103
Shango Temple, 103
The Sign in Sidney Brustein's Window (Hansberry), 44–45, 47
silence, 12, 131–33, 180n17
Simone, Nina: *Black Gold*, 66; *In Concert* (album), 63; "Dambala," 61–62, 64;

Simone, Nina (cont.)
  dancing by, 40, 43–44; early name of, 64–65; "Go Limp," 63; Hansberry's friendship with, 40, 42–44, 59, 60, 169n14; *It is Finished*, 11, 64, 68; "Mississippi Goddam," 60, 62, 63, 68; "Obeah Woman," 64, 65; parents of, 62, 171n92; "Pirate Jenny," 61, 63; "Sinnerman," 62; spiritual geographies of, 59–68; Stroud's relationship with, 59–60; "Take Me to the Water," 40, 62; "To Be Young, Gifted and Black,," 40, 66; "Westwind," 66–67
"Sinnerman" (Simone), 62
Sister Outsider (Lorde), 11, 79
Smethurst, James, 70
Smith, Barbara, 46
Smith, Bessie, 3, 90
Soul Talk (Hull), 88, 176n106
The Sovereignty of Quiet (Quashie), 6
spirit possession and communication, 18–19, 28, 44, 87–98, 154. See also *names of specific spirits*
spiritual geographies, 59–68
Spiritualism, 92
spiritualities, 4–6, 40–41, 65–67, 101–9. See also Haitian Vodou; Yoruba spirituality
spirit writing, 88
Staples, Robert, 78–79, 173n35
Starhawk, 104
Stormy Weather (film), 165n27
Strongman, Roberto, 91
Stroud, Andrew, 59–60
Student Nonviolent Coordinating Committee (SNCC), 101

"Take Me to the Water" (Simone), 40, 62
Tallant, Robert, 129, 132, 149, 180nn19–20
tarot, 155
Teish, Luisah, 7, 106, 115–17; *Jambalaya*, 12, 104, 116, 117
Tell My Horse (Hurston), 1, 156, 162n6

Their Eyes Were Watching God (Hurston), 1, 139, 142, 156, 157–58
Thiefing Sugar (Tinsley), 59
Third World feminism, 4, 12, 100–102, 105, 107, 113–14, 122–24. See also Black American feminism
Third World Women's Alliance, 100–101
This Bridge Called My Back (ed. Moraga), 100, 102, 114, 121
Tinsley, Omise'eke Natasha, 7, 59, 75
Tobago, 4
"To Be Young, Gifted and Black" (Simone), 40, 66
Tom-Tom (Du Bois), 20
tom-toms, 20, 25–27, 165n27, 166n49. See also drumming; primitivism
Toure, Askia, 78
Toussaint (Hansberry), 11, 43, 47–48, 52–53, 56–57, 61, 67
transnational feminism, as term, 100. See also Third World feminism
transnationalism, 4, 123–24
travel, 3–4, 23, 34
Travel Magazine (publication), 34
Trinidad, 103–4
Troubled Island (Still), 20, 168n6
Trouillot, Michel-Rolph, 140
Truth, Sojourner, 54
twerking, 184n96
Two-Headed Woman (Clifton), 86–87, 93–96, 98
two-headed women, 87

Ulysse, Gina Athena, 7
United States: imperialism in Haiti by, 1–3, 18, 37–38; McCarthyism in, 44, 45–46. See also Black American feminism; Louisiana laws and practices; New Orleans

Van Vechten, Carl, 26, 27
Vega, Marta Moreno, 36, 103
Vietnam, 113
Vodou. See Haitian Vodou

Vodou feminism, 6–10, 158–59. *See also* Black American feminism
Voodoo (Freeman), 20
Voodoo in New Orleans (Tallant), 132
"voodoo" plays, 20
"voodoo" pulp fiction, 18, 164n19
"voodoo queen" trope, 9, 10
voodoo *vs.* Vodou, as term, 164n16, 177n11

Walker, Alice: clairvoyance of, 88; *The Color Purple*, 87; Hurston's grave and, 12, 130, 135, 136–38, 144; Reed on, 78; representation of Hurston by, 140; "The Revenge of Hannah Kemhuff," 137; on sadomasochism, 55–56; in *Weaving the Vision*, 102
Wallace, Michele, 78
Ward, Cynthia, 132
water, 85–86
Waymon, Eunice. *See* Simone, Nina
Waymon, Sam, 43
Weaving the Vision (eds. Plaskow and Christ), 101–2
Welles, Orson, 20
"Westwind" (Simone), 66–67
What Use Are Flowers? (Hansberry), 44
Wherry, Kenneth, 46
White, Shane, 107

white hoodoo pharmacies, 183n85
"why some people be mad at me sometimes" (Clifton), 83–84
Williams, Bianca C., 4
witch-doctor trope, 165n28
The Witch's Flight (Keeling), 63
witch trials, 104
womanspirit movement, 115–16
Womanspirit Rising (eds. Plaskow and Christ), 101–2
women's rights, 182n74, 183n76
World's Fair (1984), 115
Wright, Richard, 139

yanvalou, 114
Yemayá, 71, 79
Yoruba spirituality: Dunham and, 36; language and African tradition in, 159; orisha worship in, 7, 36, 37, 71, 103–4, 105, 115, 120, 163n28; recent interest in, 155; Santería and, 102, 103, 177n11; spirits of, 71–72, 120, 124. *See also* spiritualities
Yoruba Temple of Harlem, 72, 103, 172n12
Young Lords, 113

zombification, 155–57, 158, 184n2
"Zora's Politics" (Mitchell), 162n6

www.ingramcontent.com/pod-product-compliance
Lightning Source LLC
Chambersburg PA
CBHW032024230426
43671CB00005B/194